W9-AJN-834

DISPERSING POPULATION

JAMES L. SUNDQUIST

DISPERSING POPULATION
What America Can Learn from Europe

THE BROOKINGS INSTITUTION
Washington, D.C.

Copyright © 1975 by
THE BROOKINGS INSTITUTION
1775 Massachusetts Avenue, N.W., Washington, D.C. 20036

Library of Congress Cataloging in Publication Data:

Sundquist, James L
  Dispersing population.
  Includes bibliographical references and index.
  1. Migration, Internal—United States. 2. Migration, Internal—Europe. 3. Europe—Population policy. 4. United States—Population policy.
I. Title.
HB1951.S85   301.32'6'094   75-5942
ISBN 0-8157-8214-4
ISBN 0-8157-8213-6 pbk.

9 8 7 6 5 4 3 2 1

Board of Trustees

Douglas Dillon
Chairman
Louis W. Cabot
Chairman, Executive Committee
Vincent M. Barnett, Jr.
Lucy Wilson Benson
Edward W. Carter
William T. Coleman, Jr.
George M. Elsey
John Fischer
Kermit Gordon
Gordon Gray
Huntington Harris
Roger W. Heyns
Luther G. Holbrook
William McC. Martin, Jr.
Robert S. McNamara
Arjay Miller
Barbara W. Newell
Herbert P. Patterson
J. Woodward Redmond
H. Chapman Rose
Warren M. Shapleigh
Gerard C. Smith
J. Harvie Wilkinson, Jr.

Honorary Trustees

Arthur Stanton Adams
Eugene R. Black
Robert D. Calkins
Colgate W. Darden, Jr.
Marion B. Folsom
John E. Lockwood
John Lee Pratt
Robert Brookings Smith
Sydney Stein, Jr.

THE BROOKINGS INSTITUTION is an independent organization devoted to nonpartisan research, education, and publication in economics, government, foreign policy, and the social sciences generally. Its principal purposes are to aid in the development of sound public policies and to promote public understanding of issues of national importance.

The Institution was founded on December 8, 1927, to merge the activities of the Institute for Government Research, founded in 1916, the Institute of Economics, founded in 1922, and the Robert Brookings Graduate School of Economics and Government, founded in 1924.

The Board of Trustees is responsible for the general administration of the Institution, while the immediate direction of the policies, program, and staff is vested in the President, assisted by an advisory committee of the officers and staff. The by-laws of the Institution state, "It is the function of the Trustees to make possible the conduct of scientific research, and publication, under the most favorable conditions, and to safeguard the independence of the research staff in the pursuit of their studies and in the publication of the results of such studies. It is not a part of their function to determine, control, or influence the conduct of particular investigations or the conclusions reached."

The President bears final responsibility for the decision to publish a manuscript as a Brookings book or staff paper. In reaching his judgment on the competence, accuracy, and objectivity of each study, the President is advised by the director of the appropriate research program and weighs the views of a panel of expert outside readers who report to him in confidence on the quality of the work. Publication of a work signifies that it is deemed to be a competent treatment worthy of public consideration; such publication does not imply endorsement of conclusions or recommendations contained in the study.

The Institution maintains its position of neutrality on issues of public policy in order to safeguard the intellectual freedom of the staff. Hence interpretations or conclusions in Brookings publications should be understood to be solely those of the author or authors and should not be attributed to the Institution, to its trustees, officers, or other staff members, or to the organizations that support its research.

Foreword

SINCE THE DISAPPEARANCE of the American frontier nearly a century ago, almost all growth of population in the United States has been concentrated in its cities. In the last three decades the country's largest metropolitan areas have spread and merged to form great urban regions along the Atlantic seaboard, around the southern shores of the Great Lakes, and in California. Three-fourths of the American people now live in urban agglomerations of a million people or more. The rural areas and small towns outside the commuting range of these densely populated areas have, in these years, stagnated or declined.

By the end of the 1960s and the beginning of the 1970s, a political consensus had been reached that the trend toward population concentration should be checked. The President, the Congress, both major political parties, and national organizations of governors and mayors had all declared that the continuing concentration was undesirable for communities at both ends of the migration stream—the overcongested metropolitan areas at one end, and the depleted rural areas at the other. But while population dispersion was accepted as a policy objective—and written into law—implementing policies were not adopted. The President made no recommendations and Congress enacted no new measures for the purpose. No government agency had the task of planning a population distribution scheme for the United States. Indeed, the basic concepts that would underlie a population policy had not been refined enough to permit planning even to begin.

This study seeks to help bridge the gap between objective and implementation by reviewing the experience of five countries—Great Britain, France, Italy, the Netherlands, and Sweden—that had faced the problem of population concentration, had concluded that the growth of their largest cities should be checked, and then had enacted ambitious and comprehensive programs to achieve that end. The author, James L. Sundquist, a senior fellow in the Brookings Governmental Studies program, reports on what each country set out to do, what it has accomplished, the status of its program, and what—in the view of politicians, administrators, and independent observers—are the current problems and future directions of its effort. In assessing the implications of the European experience for the United States, Mr. Sundquist comments on new trends in the United States that are altering somewhat the character of the problem here.

The Brookings Institution and Mr. Sundquist join in expressing their gratitude to all the organizations and persons in the five countries whose cooperation made the study possible. In particular, they are grateful to the Department of Social and Economic Research of the University of Glasgow, Scotland, which appointed Mr. Sundquist a research fellow in 1972–73. Director L. C. Hunter, his assistant Betty Patterson, and an efficient secretarial staff facilitated the study in every way; Gordon C. Cameron, sponsor of the project, arranged for most of the interviews in Britain and provided wise counsel throughout; Kevin J. Allen made the basic arrangements for the author's visit to Italy and reviewed the chapter on that country; and Malcolm C. MacLennan arranged introductions to leading French scholars in the field.

Mr. Sundquist extends thanks to those in the other countries who provided office space and secretarial and interpreter service, and arranged and set up interview schedules. These included Kenneth Orski, Lindsay McFarlane, and Errol Ezra of the Organisation for Economic Co-operation and Development, Paris; Paul Brace of the U.S. Embassy, Paris; Joseph Lajugie of l'Université de Bordeaux; Paolo Baratta and Gustav Schachter of the Associazione per lo Sviluppo del Mezzogiorno (SVIMEZ), Rome; Silvana Prisinzano of La Cassa per il Mezzogiorno, Rome; A. J. Hendriks of the Nederlands Economisch Institut, Rotterdam; and Sture Persson of Civildepartmentet and Sture Öberg of Inrikesdepartmentet, Stockholm. He is indebted, also, to scholars and officials in those countries who carefully reviewed individual chapters of the manuscript, including Jean-Pierre Falque and Michel Vaquin, France; Augusto Graziani, Italy; Dr. Hendriks, W. A. J. Kerpel, Jan H. Toby, and J. G. A. M. Hafkemeijer, the Netherlands; and Mr. Öberg and Sven Rune Frid, Sweden.

Finally, he expresses his appreciation to those in the United States who were especially helpful—to Niles M. Hansen, Ralph R. Widner, Lowdon Wingo, Jerome P. Pickard, Calvin L. Beale, James J. Zuiches, and Jerry B. Waters.

The study was planned with the help of Gilbert Y. Steiner, director of Governmental Studies at Brookings. Gloria M. Jimenez patiently and cheerfully typed the manuscript in its several stages and provided secretarial services. Alice M. Carroll edited the manuscript, and the index was prepared by Florence Robinson.

The conclusions are those of the author and do not necessarily reflect the views of the persons or organizations whose assistance is acknowledged above, or of the trustees, officers, or other staff members of the Brookings Institution.

KERMIT GORDON
President

January 1975
Washington, D.C.

Contents

Tables

Figures

CHAPTER ONE

Population Concentration as an
American Policy Issue

For the past 30 years our population has . . . been growing and shifting. The result is exemplified in the vast areas of rural America emptying out of people and of promise. . . . The violent and decayed central cities of our great metropolitan complexes are the most conspicuous area of failure in American life today.

I propose that before these problems become insoluble, the Nation develop a national growth policy. . . . We must create a new rural environment which will not only stem the migration to urban centers, but reverse it. If we seize our growth as a challenge, we can make the 1970s an historic period when by conscious choice we transformed our land into what we want it to become.

—President Richard M. Nixon, 1970[1]

IN RHETORIC—though not action—the United States in the late 1960s and early 1970s reached a political consensus that a new issue of public policy must be confronted. That was the issue of the increasing concentration—already an overconcentration, some argued—of the country's population in its major metropolitan complexes. Another hundred million people, it was then estimated, would be added to the population by the end of the century. Where would they live?

More important, where should they live? If current trends continued, almost all of the additional hundred million would be crowded into the metropolitan areas where most Americans already lived. Was this wise? Was it desirable? As the questions became more insistent, the country's political institutions began to express a common response: further concentration was not wise, it was not desirable, and something should be done about it.

As late as the early 1960s, population concentration had been on few lists of major public issues. But a decade later it had been acknowledged as an important question by all of the country's authoritative political

1. State of the Union Message, January 22, 1970, *Public Papers of the Presidents: Richard M. Nixon, 1970*, p. 14.

institutions—the President, the Congress, both major political parties, the nation's governors, and many others—in solemn, official pronouncements. All called for measures to stem the growth of big cities, to check and reverse the decades-old trend of migration from rural areas to the cities and from smaller cities to larger ones.

Emergence of a Public Problem

What accounts for the sudden emergence of a public problem? Cities had been building and rural areas emptying for a long time, in the United States as in every other advanced country. Mechanization of agriculture had released manpower from the land. Most rural counties had reached their population peaks decades ago, as early as 1850 in some cases and commonly before the end of the century. Nearly half the counties of the nation—almost all of them rural—lost population in the 1940s and about the same number (although not necessarily the same counties) in the 1950s, and the trend had continued in the 1960s. The country's major metropolitan concentrations, fed by a rural migrant stream and by immigration from abroad, had grown steadily and, since the Second World War, explosively. As they grew in population, the metropolitan areas expanded at an even faster rate geographically and merged into one another to form huge urban regions. In 1940, ten urban regions of over a million persons each could be defined, including 54 million persons and covering 95,000 square miles; by 1960, sixteen such regions included 101 million persons and spread over 197,000 square miles—nearly 60 percent of the people living on less than 6 percent of the land.[2]

All this had happened without the expression of much public concern. True, the plight of areas with a declining economic base had attracted some sympathy, and in 1961 the Area Redevelopment Act was passed to assist depressed areas, both urban and rural, to create new jobs. But that

2. Jerome P. Pickard, "U.S. Metropolitan Growth and Expansion, 1970–2000, with Population Projections," in Sara Mills Mazie, ed., *Population Distribution and Policy*, vol. 5 of research reports prepared for the U.S. Commission on Population Growth and the American Future (1972), pp. 142–45. Pickard defines an urban region as "a coterminous area within which urban population predominates," with a population of at least one million. It is composed of one or more contiguous metropolitan areas and adjacent or intervening counties with relatively high population density or with a major transportation corridor that links two or more metropolitan areas.

act, and subsequent measures for regional development, or rural development, were passed not as population distribution measures but simply as relief measures for unemployed and low-income families. While any governmental action that succeeded in reviving the economies of the stricken areas would have the effect of slowing out-migration from those areas and hence of retarding the growth of the major metropolitan centers, the latter was never an expressed objective. The legislation was not seen as a means of executing anybody's conception of a national population dispersal policy—or "balanced growth" or "national growth" policy, in the terms that were later commonly adopted. As late as the mid-1960s, such phrases were not even in the political lexicon.

The turning point can perhaps be identified in a single word—Watts. After the Watts riots in Los Angeles in 1965, and those that followed in other major cities in the next three summers, the people of the cities saw their own problems in a harsh new light. The social and economic soundness, the livability, even the governability, of great population concentrations came into question. For the first time, the declining rural areas that had pressed their pleas for help in the face of urban indifference—if not hostility—found allies in the cities. The population flow that had resulted from rural stagnation and decline might not, it turned out, have been the cities' boon. Cities and countryside alike might have been ill served by the forces that had made for population concentration. In a newly discovered mutual interest, then, lay the basis for political coalition. So the phraseology shifted. Politicians continued to speak of a rural development policy or an urban growth policy or an area redevelopment policy, but more and more they came to talk of a *national* growth policy as the context in which all of the more limited policies would be rationalized.

President Nixon's language in his State of the Union Message of 1970 clearly reflected the dual urban-rural motivation. On the one hand he spoke of the "emptying out" of rural America, on the other of the problems of the "violent" cities. These two themes he interwove repeatedly in speeches and messages. "Just pouring more and more people into already overcrowded cities isn't the way to build a better country. . . . So our goal is a balanced growth for America, and the key to that is a program to revitalize the American countryside."[3] Of the prospective

3. Remarks at the dedication of a dam near Centerville, Iowa, July 31, 1971, *Public Papers, 1971*, p. 843.

100 million additional Americans, he asked: "Where are those 100 million going to be? You can't pour them into New York, into Los Angeles, into Chicago and the rest and choke those cities to death with smog and crime and all of the rest that comes with over population."[4] "Many of the small towns which dot the countryside have to struggle for existence," he observed, while "many of our cities have . . . become inefficient and less and less governable" with "at times . . . near-paralysis of public services in our largest cities."[5] Rural regions "can become a new magnet for people seeking the good life, so that we can begin to see a reversal of the decades-long migration trend from rural America to urban America —a trend which has too often acted to deplete the countryside and overburden the cities, to weaken the heart of America and to add to the fat which saps our strength."[6] So he brought the two themes together: "This is one Nation, and for the good of all Americans we need one national policy of balanced growth."[7]

In the same year, 1970, that a president for the first time advocated a national growth policy in a message to the Congress, that body committed itself to the desirability of such a policy. It made the commitment not once but twice, and significantly the two actions reflected the dual motivation. One declaration, "The Congress is . . . committed to a sound balance between rural and urban America," came in an agricultural act that urged "the highest priority" for "the revitalization and development of rural areas."[8] The other came in the Urban Growth and New Community Development Act of 1970, originated by congressional committees concerned primarily with urban problems. It declared that "the Federal Government must assume responsibility for the development of a national urban growth policy" that would, among other things, "help reverse trends of migration and physical growth which reinforce disparities among States, regions, and cities." The policy would "serve as a

---

4. Address to American Farm Bureau Federation, Dec. 8, 1969, *Public Papers, 1969*, p. 1002.

5. Special Message to the Congress on Special Revenue Sharing for Rural Community Development, March 10, 1971, *Public Papers, 1971*, pp. 409–10.

6. Remarks at dedication of a navigation system at Catoosa, Okla., June 5, 1971, ibid., p. 717.

7. Special Message on Rural Community Development, p. 410.

8. Agricultural Act of 1970, P.L. 91-524, sec. 901 (a). In 1967 and 1969 the Senate had passed resolutions sponsored by Karl E. Mundt, Republican of South Dakota, to create a commission on balanced economic development to conduct a study and develop recommendations for policy at all governmental levels, but both measures died in the House.

guide in making specific decisions at the national level . . . and . . . provide a framework for development of interstate, state, and local growth and stabilization policy."[9] Neither act set forth the rationale of the Congress. But the Senate had included in its version of the agricultural act a paragraph of findings, deleted in the House-Senate conference, that read in part:

The devastating consequences of the population shift are evident everywhere—in both urban and rural America. Countless rural communities, once thriving and prosperous, are facing social and economic bankruptcy because too few residents remain to support essential public services and civic institutions. On the other hand, our large cities are facing gradual strangulation. Our giant cities are finding themselves increasingly unable to deal with the large influx of uneducated rural migrants who are ill-prepared for urban living. The congested traffic arteries, the pollution of the water and the air, the soaring crime rates, the housing blight, and the simple lack of adequate elbow room are rapidly making our larger cities unlivable as well as ungovernable.[10]

Earlier, the objective of population dispersal had been discovered by both major political parties at their national conventions. In 1968, for the first time, both parties recognized the problem and made promises—and the dual source of motivation is reflected in the contrasting contexts. The Republican declaration came under the heading "Crisis of the Cities": "Success with urban problems in fact requires acceleration of rural development in order to stem the flow of people from the countryside to the city." The Democratic pledges, on the other hand, were under the heading "Rural Development": "Balanced growth is essential for America. . . . To achieve that balanced growth, we must greatly increase the growth of the rural non-farm economy."

Meanwhile, other official groups had spoken. The National Governors' Conference in 1968 found that "population imbalance is at the core of nearly every major social problem facing our Nation today" and urged policies to bring about "a more even distribution of population" among the states.[11] In the next year, the National League of Cities called for "a specific policy for the settlement of people throughout the nation to balance the concentration of population among and within metropolitan and non-metropolitan areas while providing social and economic

9. P.L. 91-609, sec. 702.
10. *Congressional Record*, vol. 116 (Sept. 14, 1970), p. 31607.
11. *Proceedings of the National Governors' Conference, Annual Meeting* (1968), pp. 135-37.

opportunity for all persons."[12] The National Association of Counties and the United States Conference of Mayors likewise advocated a national urban growth policy. The Advisory Commission on Intergovernmental Relations found in 1968 "a specific need for immediate establishment of a national policy for guiding the location and character of future urbanization . . . so as to achieve generally a greater degree of population decentralization throughout the country."[13] And still another commission created by statute, the Commission on Population Growth and the American Future, recommended in 1972 that the federal government develop "a set of national population distribution guidelines."[14]

But Rhetoric Is Not a Program

In advocating their common objective, various groups used different terms. These differences are important because they reflect differences in concern and emphasis that have to some extent stood in the way of arriving at a common program. To begin with, the concept of population distribution or of growth has two components, usually separable and often distinct. One is the distribution of population and of growth *among* regions and larger or smaller urban complexes—that is, concentration or dispersal on a national scale. The other is the distribution *within* metropolitan areas, particularly the larger ones—the division between central cities and their suburbs and between old and new communities, and the choices between centralized and decentralized settlement patterns on a local scale. For convenience, the one may be referred to as the *macro* aspect of population distribution, and the other as the *micro* aspect.

One of the two blocs into which the advocates of a national dispersal policy divide themselves is concerned—as is this study—only with the macro component of the question, the issue of national population dispersal. That is the rural-centered bloc whose interest arose out of a concern for economic decline and community decay in rural areas—represented by spokesmen such as former Governor William L. Guy of North Dakota, who was the moving spirit in getting the Governors'

---

12. Quoted in White House, National Goals Research Staff, *Toward Balanced Growth: Quantity with Quality* (July 1970), p. 45.

13. *Urban and Rural America: Policies for Future Growth* (1968), pp. 129–30.

14. U.S. Commission on Population Growth and the American Future, *Population and the American Future* (1972), p. 120.

Conference on record in favor of dispersal policies. Originally they spoke of "rural development" or "area development" or "regional development," but as the concept broadened, the term "balanced national growth" or simply "national growth policy" came into use. The other bloc, the metropolitan-centered one that arrived at an advocacy of population dispersal out of concern for the problems of the major cities, has an interest in both the macro and the micro aspects of population distribution policy, but usually more in the micro. Its spokesmen have preferred to speak of a national "urban" policy or "national urban growth policy," as it was called in the Urban Growth and New Community Development Act of 1970, which clearly defined the policy to include both the micro and the macro components. But sometimes the urbanists drop the word *urban*, too, and speak simply of "national growth policy," particularly when they want to emphasize the macro component. The national growth policy that an urban planner advocates may therefore have a different, and broader, range of content than the one being sought by a spokesman for rural interests. In this study the term *national population dispersal policy* refers to macro policy only; the terms *national growth policy* and *population distribution policy* include both the micro and the macro components.

Regardless of whether they were concerned about both or only one of the components of a national growth policy, however, as of the early 1970s the President and the Congress, the Republicans and the Democrats, the governors and the mayors were all on record in support of policies for dispersing the American population.

Given such unanimity of opinion, one might expect that a national growth policy would by now have been defined and programs to effectuate it would be, if not enacted, at least on the drawing boards. But such is not the case. The country is no nearer to the definition of a policy now than it was in 1968 and 1970, when the declarations of principle were made. Indeed, it has not even established a process for the formulation of a policy.

President Nixon did include "the movement of people" between urban, rural, and suburban areas among matters to be considered by the Urban Affairs Council, which he created at the outset of his first administration in 1969, and the council in turn established a subcommittee on internal migration, which initiated a series of studies. After the Domestic Council was created in July 1970 to supersede the Urban Affairs Council, it created a Committee on National Growth, headed by Secretary of Housing and Urban Development George M. Romney, with the mission of converting the President's State of the Union commitment to a national growth policy into a legislative program that could be presented to the Congress in 1971. But despite a diligent effort throughout the summer and fall, nothing came of the committee's work. "The whole thing was impossible to get hold of," said a close observer of the committee's efforts. "First of all, the technical information base simply wasn't there. Comprehensive data and economic and sociological models needed to evaluate alternative policies were lacking. Secondly, there had simply not been enough national political dialogue. There was little clear understanding of what was politically acceptable and what was not. The Council had been given a mandate, yet in trying to fulfill it, it found itself operating largely in a vacuum."[15]

By early 1970 leading Democrats in the Congress had become convinced that no coherent national growth policy was likely to be developed unless a specialized agency with recognized stature were created to develop it. In the Senate, John J. Sparkman of Alabama and Edmund S. Muskie of Maine and in the House, Thomas L. Ashley of Ohio and others proposed a council on urban growth in the Executive Office of the President, patterned after the Council of Economic Advisers and the Council on Environmental Quality. The new council would advise and assist the President in developing a national urban growth policy and assist him in the preparation of a biennial report to the Congress on progress of federal efforts to carry out the policy. The administration protested against a further proliferation of special-purpose councils, contending that the new general-purpose Domestic Council was fully able to do the job and "that the Congress should not attempt to organize the President's household."[16] The Democrats retreated most of the way. The Urban Growth and New Community Development Act of 1970 retained the requirement for the report on urban growth, to be delivered in February of each even-numbered year, but the President was required only to utilize "an identified unit of the Domestic Council" and to see that his office was

15. Jerry B. Waters, "Scope and National Concerns Underlying the Increased Emphasis on Rural Development" (paper presented to a conference of the North Central Regional Center for Rural Development, Chicago, May 9, 1972; processed), pp. 7–8.

16. *Congressional Record*, vol. 116 (Dec. 2, 1970), p. 39456.

"adequately organized and staffed for the purpose." The Romney Committee on National Growth presumably met that requirement.

But the committee proved no more able to develop a national urban growth policy in 1971 than it had been in 1970. The first biennial report, delivered to the Congress in February 1972, offered little beyond a review of the growth trends and problems that had already been well defined. The report was entitled *Report on National Growth* rather than *Report on Urban Growth* because, it was explained in the introduction, "rural and urban community development are inseparably linked." The country needs "a new general strategy for national development . . . a clear and coherent approach," but "developing a single comprehensive strategy—a national growth policy—. . . is an extremely difficult undertaking." It "requires a searching consideration of our national objectives and priorities." While "in the abstract, the concept of growth policy commands nearly universal support," individuals disagree about the particulars—about "which problems in the growth area are most pressing" and even about "whether a particular consequence of growth is indeed a problem at all." Decisions as to where people should live or businesses locate "cannot be dictated." Moreover, the United States is "a vast country," with a federal system of government, and hence "it is not feasible for the highest level of government to design policies for development that can operate successfully in all parts of the Nation."[17] So the report's analysis of trends in population distribution and the problems those trends portended gave rise to no proposals at all for a national growth policy. The President used the document merely as a vehicle for advocating major items contained in the legislative program he had already submitted to the Congress.

"It clearly falls short of the mark and the expectations of the Congress," Congressman Ashley said of the report as he opened hearings on national growth policy in June 1972. "The President's . . . ringing words [in his 1970 State of the Union Message] certainly do not appear in this report."[18] Witnesses at the hearings had few kinds words for the report and many caustic ones. From the American Institute of Planners: "It

17. *Report on National Growth 1972*, pp. ix, 28–31.
18. *National Growth Policy*, Hearings before the Subcommittee on Housing of the House Committee on Banking and Currency, 92 Cong. 2 sess. (1972), pp. 97 and 511.

avoided the hard questions and . . . fails to show leadership by the executive branch in defining a comprehensive policy."[19] From the National Association of Home Builders: "Despite [the] clear direction provided by Congress and despite the vast resources of the Federal Government . . . this report falls far short of our expectations. . . . It, unfortunately, contributes little to the body of knowledge necessary."[20] From the National Association of Housing and Redevelopment Officials: "This report has abdicated its responsibility."[21] From the American Institute of Architects: "In essence the report calls for a 'no policy' policy and this is unacceptable."[22] From the National Association of Counties: "We are disappointed in the coverage of the report. The apparent deemphasis of the role of the planning process to guide community growth is deplorable."[23] From the Conservation Foundation: "It fails almost entirely to confront the issues."[24] From a geographer: "In this Nation today there exists neither the ideological base, nor the desire, nor the will to develop affirmative national growth policies."[25] From two Urban Institute staff members: "The result is not a very useful policy statement, and helps relatively little in developing one."[26] From a sociologist: "This Report . . . can be faulted for failing to face up to the need for evaluating national priorities, setting broad national goals. . . . Implicit throughout the report is the Administration's conviction that a strong central government is in itself an evil."[27] And from a planner: "The President's first report abandons the notion that there should or could be major national policies on urban growth. . . . [It is] indeed a sorry reflection upon the United States of America and its national leadership . . . an apparent confession of intellectual bankruptcy."[28]

None of which, of course, meant that the critics were prepared to agree on a policy. The President's report was assuredly correct in noting that once the advocates of a national growth policy get beyond endors-

19. Alan Rabinowitz of the University of Washington, ibid., p. 376.
20. Stanley Waranch of Norfolk, Va., president of NAHB, ibid., p. 398.
21. Albert A. Walsh of New York City, president of NAHRO, ibid., p. 419.
22. Archibald C. Rogers, vice president of AIA, ibid., p. 487.
23. Thomas H. Haga of Genesee County, Mich., ibid., p. 520.
24. Arthur A. Davis, vice president of the foundation, ibid., p. 93.
25. Brian J. L. Berry of the University of Chicago, ibid., p. 633.
26. Richard P. Burton and Harvey A. Garn, ibid., p. 652.
27. Philip M. Hauser of the University of Chicago, ibid., pp. 737 and 739.
28. William L. C. Wheaton of the University of California, Berkeley, ibid., pp. 889–90.

ing the abstract idea that a policy should be developed, they fall into disagreement about its content. The urban and rural blocs arrived at their interest in growth policy from different starting points and by different routes. To the rural groups the question of interregional migration is paramount; to the urban bloc it is likely to be peripheral. The urgent and immediate preoccupations of the urban group are more likely to be the solution of urban-suburban and racial conflicts, the economic development of declining central cities, and the checking of urban sprawl through orderly development of suburbs, including new communities. Indeed, before Watts the question of national action to check urban and metropolitan growth was rarely even raised by urban planners or writers on urban topics. Further growth was treated as inexorable, or even as desirable: the "booster" spirit, after all, extends into even the largest metropolitan centers. And once the violence in the black ghettos subsided, the cry for relief from further migration began to fall again. Agitation for growth policies began to develop then in another quarter—among environmentalists, mainly in the suburbs—but only in a few places, so far, have they been able to attain a political influence that offsets the combined weight of the builders, property owners, lenders, merchants, and all the others who have a direct financial stake in urban and metropolitan growth. Meanwhile, the ghettos, with their high unemployment, are likely to look with suspicion on any proposal to channel economic growth toward rural areas.

So to many in the cities a national growth policy to stem migration is seen as antiurban in its inspiration and inimical to their pecuniary interests. A national growth policy that treats rural and urban development as "inseparably linked," as the President put it, must reconcile the views of two groups who do not arrive naturally at a common view of what is the country's ideal population pattern, who—even when they agree in principle on the need for a national policy—regard each other with a mixture of indifference, rivalry, suspicion, and even hostility. Yet the advocates of a national growth policy, from both sides, could properly complain that the President was in the best position to propose a basis for reconciliation and that he should undertake leadership in the matter, for it was hardly likely anybody else would.

The Congress had shown neither the capacity nor the disposition to take the lead. The structure of its committees was conducive not to reconciling the conflict between the rural and the urban points of view, but rather to institutionalizing and rigidifying it. It was symbolic, indeed, that its call for a national growth policy in 1970 had been expressed in two acts—one originated by the agriculture committees, the other by housing subcommittees concerned with urban development. Meanwhile, some of the most important programs aimed at developing rural regions and hence checking migration flow—particularly the Appalachian regional development program and the assistance to nonmetropolitan communities authorized by the Public Works and Economic Development Act of 1965—were under the jurisdiction of still another pair of committees, the public works committees of the two houses. A national growth policy obviously could not be written in the Congress without the creation of a special committee with a broader jurisdiction than any of the standing groups. And, given the natural resistance of all congressional committees to invasions of their jurisdictions, special committees are created only in circumstances of the most compelling necessity. National growth policy, it was clear, had not yet achieved that degree of urgency.

A Senate Program: Tax Incentives

Even in the absence of a settled national policy, the advocates of population dispersal had managed to enact some measures that served their ends, and others had come close to passage. The laws enacted primarily authorized public works to help communities in depressed or rural areas create the infrastructure necessary for industrial development, and credit programs to assist enterprises locating in those communities.

In presenting these measures, to be sure, their supporters had not emphasized population distribution policy as such. Their plea was simpler: communities were in distress—communities of low income or high unemployment or economic decline, or all three—and deserved assistance. The context was one of relief, of welfare. Yet population dispersal was in the context, too, for the most visible symptoms of decline were out-migration and population loss, and the sponsors of relief measures cited repeatedly in congressional debate the hardships visited on families who were forced to migrate—the separation of parents from children, the losses suffered by families that had to "pull up roots" and move to distant cities unprepared for new occupations and for big city life. The argument was for help that would enable families to remain in their home communities and permit young people entering careers to live and work there, too, if they chose. To check the trend toward population concentration would be the consequence, if not always explicitly the purpose.

The key to population distribution is, of course, job availability. A few persons—retirees notably, and some independent professionals such as artists, writers, and inventors—may be free to live in any locality they choose but, for the rest, people are compelled to distribute themselves in whatever pattern is dictated by the distribution of employment opportunities. Some investors may locate their investment in areas of surplus labor voluntarily, and so check the migration flow, and others may be induced by government assistance to do so. But if neither of these happens—if the jobs do not go to where the workers are—the workers must go to the jobs, if they are not to accept welfare as a way of life. When population distribution is an end, then, job distribution is inevitably the means.

Even as the early acts were being placed on the statute books, a consensus was developing among advocates of regional development that public works measures, even if supplemented by loans, cannot influence sufficiently the distribution of employment. Development of an industrial infrastructure gives no assurance, either to the local community that creates it or to the national government that helps finance it, that industry will come. Sometimes it comes; sometimes it does not. In the latter case, when the infrastructure is not utilized, the public expenditures are largely wasted. To make sure that the purpose is accomplished, industry has to be given a stronger incentive than just the availability of public facilities and credit. The investor needs, in short, a cash subsidy, paid to him either directly or indirectly.

The mechanism commonly proposed in the United States has been tax incentives. The Democratic platform of 1968 was specific in its pledge to use "tax and other incentives" for creating jobs "in small towns and rural areas." The Republican platform of that year was not specific, but a party task force in 1967 had proposed tax incentives for locating factories in rural areas.[29] In 1970 a task force appointed by President Nixon recommended that accelerated tax depreciation or investment tax credit

29. Republican National Committee, Task Force on Job Opportunities and Welfare, *Revitalizing our Rural Areas* (July 1967).

for companies located in designated rural development areas should be "explored."[30] The Advisory Commission on Intergovernmental Relations in its 1968 report recommended that financial incentives, including not only tax subsidies and loans but direct payments, be considered.[31] The National Governors' Conference suggested tax incentives as one means of achieving its goal of "a more even distribution of population."[32] President Johnson's National Advisory Commission on Rural Poverty, reporting in 1967, endorsed tax incentives.[33] So did the National Advisory Commission on Civil Disorders in 1968.[34] Various of these groups proposed other measures, particularly new credit institutions to serve rural enterprises and preferential treatment for depressed or rural areas in government procurement and location of facilities, but the major support went to tax subsidies as the most effective program measure that might prove to be politically feasible.

As early as 1967, twenty-four senators of both parties, led by James B. Pearson, Republican of Kansas, joined in sponsoring a bill for tax credits for investment in rural areas, and a similar measure in 1969—this time with thirty-nine cosponsors—reached the stage of hearings before the Senate Finance Committee. The committee shelved the idea, but an opportunity to press for its enactment came that year when President Nixon as part of a general tax reform measure proposed to eliminate the 7 percent tax credit on manufacturing investment that was then in effect nationwide. When the bill reached the Senate floor, Ted Stevens, Alaska Republican, proposed that when the credit was eliminated for the rest of the country, it be retained for areas in which farm employment had declined substantially and which therefore had experienced "substantial out-migration" and either suffered "substantial and persistent unemployment or underemployment" or were causing such consequences in other areas.[35] The amendment, offered with little advance publicity and without the support of any organized activity by pressure groups, was accepted by the Senate, 35 to 33. But not having been considered by the

30. Task Force on Rural Development, *A New Life for the Country*, Report to the President (March 1970), p. 22.

31. *Urban and Rural America*, p. 137.

32. *Proceedings* (1968), p. 136.

33. *The People Left Behind* (1967), p. 115.

34. *Report of the National Advisory Commission on Civil Disorders* (Bantam Books, 1968), pp. 423–24; the commission recommended that the benefits be available to both urban and rural poverty areas.

35. *Congressional Record*, vol. 115 (Dec. 6, 1969), pp. 37509–10.

House, it was rejected by the House members of the House-Senate conference committee.

Two years later, an opportunity was again presented when President Nixon proposed the restoration of the investment tax credit that had been repealed in 1969. This time, Senator Pearson proposed an amendment based on the bill he had regularly introduced—and which in 1971 had acquired fifty-two cosponsors—to offer tax credits to rural industry. The amendment proposed a differential tax credit for most rural areas amounting in the final version of the amendment to 3 percentage points —10 percent compared to 7 percent for the rest of the country. The amendment was estimated to cost $250 million a year. In offering his amendment, Pearson used the familiar dual argument: on the one hand, the "crisis of the cities . . . many of which show disturbing signs of becoming economically inefficient, socially destructive, and politically unmanageable" demonstrated that "the process of massive, unguided urbanization has gone awry"; on the other hand, "underdeveloped rural communities" were "declining and threatened with extinction."[36] Senator Mark Hatfield, Oregon Republican, contended that increased population density brought not only the "normal problems of . . . pollution, transportation, waste disposal, police protection, housing, energy supply, and so forth" but "also a deeper social and psychological effect—the erosion of trust between people and increasing impersonality."[37]

But Senator Abraham A. Ribicoff, Connecticut Democrat, upset the Pearson strategy by demanding equal treatment for the central cities. Their social and economic problems, he argued, were as severe as those of the rural areas, and that argument Pearson—given his own description of the cities—could hardly deny. Recognizing that without urban support his plan was beaten, he agreed to the Ribicoff amendment—which would extend the differential tax credit to all central cities with unemployment over 6 percent—and it was approved, 56 to 24. But that was too much for Chairman Russell B. Long, Democrat of Louisiana, and other senior members of the Finance Committee. They opposed the combined Pearson-Ribicoff amendment on the ground that the cost to the treasury

36. Ibid., vol. 117 (Oct. 9, 1971), p. 36658. Pearson defined rural areas as areas lying outside the standard metropolitan statistical areas (SMSAs), but he proposed to exclude from benefits any rural area that had grown in population at a rate faster than the national average during the 1960s or any part of which lay within 25 miles of an SMSA with a population of 250,000 or more.

37. Ibid. (Nov. 16, 1971), p. 41502.

would be as much as $750 million a year and, since they were the Senate members of the House-Senate conference committee, the amendment was once more deleted there.

The Paucity of Data

Insofar as a political consensus had been reached on the desirability of a more dispersed population distribution pattern for the nation, it was the product of political sensitivity and intuition—the politicians' own "gut feelings" about big cities and small towns and their response to pressures from their constituencies. The debates cited no systematic analysis of the social and economic consequences of population concentration based on objective, quantified data. Indeed, not much data has been assembled, and what has been brought together is inconclusive.[38]

ECONOMIC PRODUCTIVITY

The principal argument advanced in favor of the concentration of population in large aggregations relates to economic productivity. As cities grow, employers are able to tap larger and more diversified labor markets, obtain better access to credit, to advanced technology, and to the varied business services they may require, shorten the distance to suppliers, and sell to large and concentrated markets. The result is a rising productivity, which is reflected in the higher wages and higher living standards of urban societies.

Productivity rises at different rates for different industries, however, and some find that the higher costs of labor, land, local transportation, and other services in the larger urban agglomerations are not offset by increases in output per worker. They find it advantageous to exchange their big city locations for sites with inferior services but lower costs. Manufacturing, in particular, has been moving from larger to smaller communities; in the 1960s, total manufacturing employment grew at a

---

38. An excellent compilation of available data bearing on the question of the desirability or undesirability of population concentration, entitled *City Size and the Quality of Life*, was published in July 1974 by the Center for the Study of Social Policy of the Stanford Research Institute. Prepared for the National Science Foundation, the report covers the economic, social, environmental, and governmental consequences of concentration, as well as public attitudes toward city size.

faster rate in the country's nonmetropolitan areas as a whole than in its metropolitan areas. Nevertheless, studies by William Alonso and others suggest that for the entire economy of metropolitan areas, productivity continues to rise with increasing size at least to the three-to-five-million population level, and possibly even beyond that.[39]

Free market economists sometimes contend that any generalization about the economies and diseconomies of city size is irrelevant, for the judgment as to location is one that each individual employer should make, based on his own cost calculations, and the sum of the individual judgments will produce the greatest aggregate efficiency. Many employers do make careful cost calculations as the basis for locational decisions—although others do not. But to rely wholly on the employer's profit motive leaves out of the calculation the costs that may be imposed on the public at large and on employees as a group by the combined decisions of many thousands of employers. Corporate economies of scale, and economies of agglomeration, in other words, may be achieved only through public and individual diseconomies. These costs need to be considered with production costs, therefore, in the same computation.

PUBLIC SERVICE COSTS

The costs of concentration imposed on the national and local public treasuries might appear to be one of the most easily measured of all the factors bearing on the question, for public expenditure figures are readily available. Yet, even here, conclusive analyses have not been made. "The most heavily urban areas have grown far past the size range in which a community can function most economically," President Nixon told the Congress in 1971. "It often costs far more per capita to provide essential services, such as police protection, sanitation collection, and public transportation in our dense urban areas. . . . Many of our cities have, in short, become inefficient."[40] The President may have felt that his basic thesis was self-evident: highways obviously cost more to build in densely settled areas, smaller cities have no need for such expensive public works as subways, water has to be brought longer distances in large metropolitan

39. William Alonso, "The Economics of Urban Size," in *Regional Science Association Papers*, vol. 26 (1971), pp. 67–83. His findings and others are brought together in Tom Thomas, "The Economics of City Size," in Stanford Research Institute, *City Size and the Quality of Life*, app. F.

40. Special Message on Rural Community Development, pp. 409–10.

areas (but perhaps at the same, or less, cost per gallon), refuse has to be hauled farther, expenditures necessary to meet air quality standards are higher, and so on. But precisely what the diseconomies of scale in public services amount to, and the point in the range of city size at which they begin to appear, are not known. The Advisory Commission on Inter-governmental Relations (ACIR) did find a limited amount of data indicating diseconomies of scale in the larger cities, but it had to label its findings "tentative." The data revealed that "for most functional categories, the larger municipalities spent or employed more per capita," but the commission qualified its conclusion because only a few large cities were included in its comparisons and because other possible explanatory factors—particularly the quality of the services rendered—could not be taken into account. Input comparisons alone are obviously an inadequate measure of relative efficiency. Moreover, the study covered only three states, analyzed only cities rather than metropolitan complexes, disregarded the distribution of state and federal expenditures for services to urban populations, and included no city over a million population.[41] So whether the New York, Chicago, and Los Angeles metropolitan areas as a whole, for instance, have grown beyond efficient size as measured in the cost of public services is a question that still lies wholly within the realm of speculation and common-sense judgment. At the opposite end of the size range, it seems clear that the cost per capita of public services has to be relatively high—assuming equal quality—in very small rural communities. But here again, data are lacking as to the population levels at which the diseconomies begin.[42]

COSTS (AND BENEFITS) TO INDIVIDUALS AND FAMILIES

A balance sheet of the costs and benefits to individuals and families resulting from population concentration would be exceedingly complex, even if all the factors could be identified and measured.

41. *Urban and Rural America*, p. 50. The report, pp. 45–50, compared costs among cities in three states—New Jersey, Ohio, and Texas.
42. Niles M. Hansen, "A Preliminary Overview," in Niles M. Hansen, ed., *Public Policy and Regional Economic Development: The Experience of Nine Western Countries* (Ballinger, forthcoming). He summarizes findings from studies in other countries that attempt to calculate the economies and diseconomies of scale, either for the public sector alone or for both the public and private sectors; generally they favor the intermediate-sized city, with the lower limit somewhere between 30,000 and 200,000 and upper limit between 250,000 and 1 million.

In a simple income-expenditure calculation, some of the entries can be calculated readily enough. Earnings vary directly with the size of the urban community; in 1969, among male nonagricultural workers, median earnings were 21 percent higher in metropolitan areas than in nonmetropolitan areas, and among female workers 23 percent higher.[43] This is explained in part by the richer occupational mix in the metropolitan areas and the higher educational and occupational qualifications of the metropolitan population, but in part it is the result of higher pay for comparable work—made possible, presumably, by the greater productive efficiency of the larger aggregations. On the other side of the balance sheet are the higher living costs in the metropolitan areas—calculated by the Labor Department at 9–19 percent.[44] As among metropolitan areas, both living costs and earnings are progressively higher in the larger areas. Taking both the higher earnings and higher living costs into account, the lifetime real earnings gain to various categories of rural-urban and South-North migrants are in most cases substantial.[45] Yet many cost factors need to be considered that do not enter into the cost-of-living index. The index reflects the higher tax costs of local public services in urban areas but not the higher quality of the services. No figure has been placed on one of the most important costs of concentration—the time lost by millions of workers in their daily commutation journeys, which also varies progressively with size of place. For migrant families, the cost of moves from smaller to larger places—never measured in any study—must itself be entered into the calculation. And there are miscellaneous items: for instance, a study of air pollution costs in the Washington metropolitan area found that an average family would save $335 a year if the national capital's air were as pure as that of rural areas.[46] Could all these items be

43. U.S. Bureau of the Census, "Social and Economic Characteristics of the Population in Metropolitan and Nonmetropolitan Areas: 1970 and 1960," *Current Population Reports*, Series P-23, No. 37 (June 24, 1971), Table 17, p. 66.

44. Bureau of Labor Statistics news release, June 16, 1974, based on autumn 1973 figures. The metropolitan-nonmetropolitan differential was 9 percent for the lowest of three hypothetical family budgets, 14 percent for the intermediate, and 19 percent for the highest.

45. Richard F. Wertheimer II, *The Monetary Rewards of Migration within the U.S.* (Washington: Urban Institute, 1970). Migration out of the South yields an earnings difference of about $800 a year for most migrants, rural-urban movement a differential of $600 to $1,100 a year; ibid., p. 57.

46. The study, conducted by a private contractor for the Public Health Service, was based on 6,500 questionnaires; it covered extra costs for cleaning, painting, et cetera. *Washington Post*, Dec. 14, 1967.

quantified and totaled, the advantage would probably still be on the side of metropolitan areas, but the difference might not be great. Whether large metropolitan areas would have any significant advantage over smaller ones is not clear, because detailed comparisons have not been made.

The noneconomic factors may well be more important, in any case. Advocates of population concentration commonly point to the improved access that residents of larger communities have to educational, cultural, and recreational opportunities and to public and private services of various kinds. But here the calculation is complicated by many factors that almost defy quantification—the quality of services, and the value that various individuals assign to different kinds of opportunity. Only the largest communities, it is true, have fine museums, a wide range of theatrical productions and musical events, and major league athletic teams. The larger the community the more diverse and stimulating the intellectual life. But the smaller communities have easier access to the open countryside and opportunities for outdoor recreation, and less air and noise pollution. Larger metropolitan areas offer a greater range of higher educational facilities than smaller places, but their public school systems are not necessarily superior. Larger centers usually offer better specialized medical facilities, but their general hospitals may be no better. For many of the routine public services, the quality of service may follow the same U-shaped curve as per capita cost, since higher costs tend to depress the level of service that a community can finance; consequently, the advantage here may lie with the middle-sized communities. Certainly, problems of organizing and administering local public services are greatest in the large metropolitan concentrations, where many jurisdictions, often located in more than one state, have to be organized in cooperative arrangements; but leadership and administrative talent are probably greatest in the metropolitan centers too.

The social and psychological consequences of population concentration have to be considered even if they too, for the most part, defy measurement. One social evil that is clearly correlated positively with city size is violent crime. Federal Bureau of Investigation statistics show that cities over 250,000 population have consistently suffered a crime rate 1.5 to 2.5 times as great as have cities in the 100,000–250,000 population bracket and five to nine times as high as that of cities under 10,000.[47] Since

47. Executive Office of the President, Office of Management and Budget, *Social Indicators, 1973*, Chart 2/3, p. 45.

these figures are for cities rather than urban agglomerations, part of the difference reflects the higher crime rates of large poverty-ridden central cities compared to their more affluent suburbs that fall in the smaller size categories. The differences are so great, however, that it seems unlikely they could be explained entirely by differences between central cities and suburbs or by differing employment, income, educational, or other characteristics of the populations of communities in the several categories.

Very few studies have even tried to relate other types of social pathology to city size. The National Advisory Commission on Civil Disorders did not identify urban concentration as such as a cause of disorder, beyond observing that the "chronic unemployment problems in the central city" were "aggravated by the constant arrival of new unemployed migrants."[48] The ACIR report cited the opinions of some sociologists, psychologists, political scientists, and planners that population concentration may be inimical to mental health, sense of community, and civic participation and morale, and may contribute to juvenile delinquency, family breakdown, and other social ills. But these were opinions only, lacking in documentation.[49] And some, at least, of the social and psychological evils that are found to a higher degree in cities may be related simply to the density of the population concentrations in slum areas and the overcrowding of living quarters, which would be remedied merely by achieving a more dispersed pattern of settlement within the large agglomerations. Senator Hatfield, in speaking of the "deeper social and psychological effect—the erosion of trust between people" that results from population density—could do no better than cite a study showing that "individuals needing help were between 2 and 5 times more likely to be let into the home of a stranger in a smaller town than in New York City."[50] If there is indeed a correlation between city size and the incidence of social pathology and the correlation is not attributable to other causes such as differences in population composition, that could well be the decisive factor in the formulation of a national growth policy. Yet beyond the crime statistics, which have not been adequately analyzed, and the occasional and severely limited survey of the kind cited by Senator Hatfield, social science offers no clue as to whether a correlation does exist.

48. *Report*, p. 258.
49. *Urban and Rural America*, pp. 55–56.
50. *Congressional Record*, vol. 117 (Nov. 15, 1971), p. 41502.

Finally, one of the social consequences of population concentration is the hardship and psychological strain imposed on the families and individuals who find themselves pushed unwillingly into the migrant stream by the forces of population concentration. The rural development and depressed areas legislation arose largely out of compassion for families whose source of livelihood had disappeared and who were consequently forced to leave the homes and communities to which they had become attached, or for old folks who had to watch their sons and daughters go. For whole communities in decline, as in Appalachia or the rural South, the consequence can be a widespread social malaise that is more than a strictly economic loss—another cost of concentration that cannot be neatly reckoned.

COSTS IN UNEMPLOYMENT AND INFLATION

Finally, the macroeconomic consequences of the processes by which the population of an advanced nation concentrates have been scarcely remarked on in the United States, much less measured. Assuming that conditions approaching full employment are maintained, a concentration of investment in metropolitan areas—and disproportionately among them—results in labor shortages in the growing areas and labor surpluses in others. To the extent the geographical mismatch between investment and labor supply continues, it will eventually be eased (at the same time that other mismatches develop) through migration of workers, at costs to individuals, families, and communities. But migration always lags to some extent, because settled families submit to some degree of unemployment or underemployment before making the decision to uproot themselves and relocate. When concentration processes are at work, therefore, regional and national unemployment and underemployment rates are higher than they would be if the distribution of jobs conformed more closely to the more dispersed distribution of available labor, and the gross national product is lower. Meanwhile, in the congested centers the labor shortages create inflationary pressures that tend to be generalized over a wider geographical area through collective bargaining processes, and these can be damped only at the cost of allowing the general unemployment level to rise.

Concentration apparently gives rise also to a second type of structural unemployment that can be solved only with the greatest difficulty, and at considerable public expense, if at all. Industrial investment has been concentrated not only in certain metropolitan areas but also at certain places within those areas, specifically on the suburban fringe, and another geographic mismatch has been created—this time between the poverty areas of the central cities, particularly the black ghettos, and the suburbs—that impairs the generally superior efficiency of the larger labor markets. About three-fourths of all employment gains in metropolitan areas are in the suburbs, out of reach of the central-city poor, and new jobs in central cities are suited to the skill levels of suburbanites, not to those of ghetto residents. Relocation of the potential workers is prevented both by the cost of housing and by discrimination practices, and the organization of daily commutation travel has often proved impossible—prohibitively expensive in terms of a public mass transportation solution and administratively insuperable in terms of any other. In smaller population clusters, in contrast, movement of workers to jobs is easier and transportation difficulties are of lesser importance as a cause of joblessness. Concentration has thus contributed to the high rates of unemployment and underemployment that are characteristic of the black ghettos of the major cities.[51]

In sum, to plot the balance of advantages and disadvantages of urban concentration involves an equation of enormous complexity, few of whose factors can now be quantified in any but the most preliminary way. For a long time to come, American policymakers will have to make their judgments on the basis of their own and their constituents' intuition, not on the basis of hard, provable facts. In the meantime, at least a word of caution is in order: policymakers should look with skepticism on any summing up of the "objective" case for or against population concentration that gives exclusive or preponderant weight to any single factor or set of factors in the long list of items that need to be considered in any true cost-benefit balance sheet—whether that factor be the supposed superior economic efficiency of large metropolitan areas, the supposed social evils that arise from population concentration, or any other.

51. See, for instance, the comments of the National Advisory Commission on Civil Disorders, *Report*, pp. 251–65 and 392–93. This problem is discussed at length in Neil N. Gold, "The Mismatch of Jobs and Low-Income People in Metropolitan Areas and Its Implications for the Central-City Poor," in Mazie, ed., *Population Distribution and Policy*, pp. 441–86. Bennett Harrison, *Urban Economic Development: Suburbanization, Minority Opportunity, and the Condition of the Central City* (Washington: Urban Institute, 1974), suggests that the mismatch is less severe than has been commonly assumed; see particularly chap. 3.

What Do People Want?

If the objective data do not yield a clear answer as to what pattern of population distribution is best for the country in economic and social terms, policymakers can turn to the subjective data: What do people want? Yet the subjective judgment of the people is itself objective, in a sense, for it reflects the people's own totaling and balancing of at least some of the objective costs and benefits of population concentration— those that apply to individuals and families. If the people feel better off in big concentrations, then in their view the benefits—economic, social, cultural, aesthetic, recreational—outweigh the costs. Or vice versa. And assuming that sound measures can be devised to influence the distribution of jobs to conform more nearly to the popular preference, without imposing excessive offsetting social and economic costs that appear elsewhere on the balance sheet, then in a democratic society that could appropriately become the overriding consideration.

Considerable evidence has been gathered on what the people want, through public opinion polls. Unfortunately, those data are not conclusive either. Many attitude surveys have produced a substantial body of evidence suggesting that the American people dislike large cities and would prefer a less concentrated settlement pattern than now exists. A major study undertaken for the Commission on Population Growth and the American Future in 1971, for instance, found that more than half the respondents would have preferred to live in a rural or small town setting; another third preferred a small urban place, and only 13 percent a large city or its suburbs. This compared to their actual place of residence, by percent of the total sample, as follows: [52]

	Large urban center	*Small urban center*	*Rural or small town*
Preferred residence	13	33	53
Actual residence	28	41	32
Difference	−15	−8	21

52. Survey by Opinion Research Corp. of 1,700 adults, who were asked: "Where would you prefer to live? On a farm, open country (not on a farm), in a small town, in a small city, in a medium-sized city, in a large city, in a suburb of a medium-sized city, in a suburb of a large city?" Responses to the first three of these categories are grouped under "rural or small town," to the small city, medium-sized city, and suburb of a medium-sized city categories under "small urban center," and to the

Table 1-1 reveals how dissatisfaction with size of community increases as size itself increases. Only one in eight of the people interviewed in rural communities or small towns would prefer to live in a larger place. Almost half of those in small and medium-sized cities and their suburbs were dissatisfied, and a large majority of them preferred a smaller community. In the large cities and their suburbs, fewer than two in five were content; 60 percent would prefer living in a smaller community, and more than half of those specified the open country or a small town.

Table 1-1. *Preferred and Actual Places of Residence, by Community Size, U.S. National Survey, 1971*

Percent of respondents

	Preferred place of residence			
Actual place of residence	*Large urban center*	*Small urban center*	*Rural or small town*	*Total*
Large urban center[a]	39	26	34	99[b]
Small urban center	6	55	39	100
Rural or small town	2	10	88	100

Source: Sara Mills Mazie and Steve Rawlings, "Public Attitude Toward Population Distribution Issues," in Sara Mills Mazie, ed., *Population Distribution and Policy*, vol. 5 of research reports prepared for U.S. Commission on Population Growth and the American Future (1972), p. 605. See footnote 52, above, for identification and explanation of survey.

a. Two percent had no opinion.
b. Does not add to 100 because of rounding.

These findings confirm those of other surveys. A Harris poll in 1970 found 48 percent of respondents would prefer to live in a city or suburb, while 47 percent favored either a small town away from a city or a farm.[53] A series of Gallup surveys between 1966 and 1972, summarized in Table 1-2, showed preferences falling in the same general range. The

large city and suburb of a large city categories under "large urban center." One percent of the respondents expressed no preference. Percentages may not add to 100 because of rounding. Results of the survey are reported in Robert Parke, Jr., and Charles F. Westoff, eds., *Aspects of Population Growth Policy*, vol. 6 of research reports prepared for U.S. Commission on Population Growth and the American Future (1972), app. A, pp. 498–509, and analyzed by Sara Mills Mazie and Steve Rawlings, "Public Attitude Toward Population Distribution Issues," in Mazie, ed., *Population Distribution and Policy*, pp. 603–15.

53. Survey by Louis Harris and Associates, reported in Mazie and Rawlings, "Public Attitude," p. 604. The question was: "If you could find just what you wanted in the way of a place to live and didn't have to worry about where you worked, would you want to live in a city, a suburb, a small town away from a city, on a farm, or where?"

Table 1-2. *Preferred Place of Residence, by Community Size,*
U.S. National Surveys, 1966–72

Percent of respondents

		Preferred place of residence			
Year	City	Suburban area	Small town	Farm	No opinion
1966	22	28	31	18	1
1968	18	25	29	27	1
1970	18	26	31	24	1
1972	13	31	32	23	1

Source: James J. Zuiches, "Residential Preferences and Population Mobility" (report to Center for the Study of Metropolitan Problems, National Institute of Mental Health, November 1974; processed). The surveys are by the American Institute of Public Opinion (Gallup poll). The question was: "If you could live anywhere in the United States that you wanted to, would you prefer a city, a suburban area, a small town, or farm?"

series also showed a shift in preference from the cities to rural areas between 1966 and 1968—at the time of the urban riots—that was sustained in the later surveys.

Americans express opposition, too, to further population concentration. When asked in the population commission's survey, "Do you think the Federal government should discourage or should not discourage further growth of large metropolitan areas?" 52 percent thought it should and 33 percent that it should not (15 percent had no opinion). Significantly, the residents of the large metropolitan areas themselves were only slightly more favorable to the large cities than the national average, splitting 51–36 in favor of curtailing metropolitan growth. To a question, "Do you feel the Federal government should or should not try to encourage people and industry to move to smaller cities and towns?" the national sample replied 58 percent to 33 percent in the affirmative. Again the residents of large urban areas departed only slightly from the general view, breaking 56 to 37 in favor of small town development.[54]

54. Opinion Research Corp. survey, reported in Mazie and Rawlings, "Public Attitude," p. 614. A 1972 survey conducted for Glenn V. Fuguitt and James J. Zuiches by National Opinion Research Corp. confirmed the finding of popular support for federal programs to assist rural regions; reported in James J. Zuiches, "Residential Preferences and Population Mobility" (report to Center for the Study of Metropolitan Problems, National Institute of Mental Health, November 1974; processed). The sample was favorable by a 63–33 margin in response to the question: "How about the idea of government programs to encourage people to stay, or move to the more rural regions of the country?" But in response to the question, "How do you feel about the idea of government programs to slow down the flow

The Commission on Population Growth and the American Future was cautious in drawing conclusions from the survey data gathered for it, saying only that "Americans express dissatisfaction with the city and think something should be done" and that "many people evidently dislike the trend" toward urbanization.[55] What troubled the commission were data on an additional facet of the public attitude gathered in another survey. Respondents to that survey who preferred to live in a small community were further asked whether they would like that community to be within thirty miles of a city over 50,000. The answers were 70 percent affirmative.[56] But in Wisconsin, where the survey was made, only 54 percent of the population lived at that time within 30 miles of a metropolitan city. "If the results of the Wisconsin survey reflect national attitudes," observed the commission, "it means people want the best of both worlds —the serene and clean environment of rural areas and the opportunity and excitement of the metropolis."[57]

When the Wisconsin survey was extended to a national sample, the results were the same. As shown in Table 1-3, if people had their wishes, fewer than half as many as now live in cities over 500,000 would live there and only two-thirds as many would live in cities between 50,000 and 500,000. But the gains would be in smaller communities within commuting range of cities over 50,000. The more remote areas would be approximately stable. This is "not too different from the redistribution now taking place."[58]

In 1974 the 52 percent who wished to be within commuting range of a city over 50,000 were further asked whether they preferred that the city be under or over 500,000 in population; they broke 40 to 9 (3 were

---

of population into large urban areas?" the vote was 46 percent in favor to 47 percent against. The wording of this question may have carried an overtone of interfering with freedom of movement that the impersonal tone of the population commission's question about discouraging the growth of metropolitan areas did not have.

55. *Population and the American Future*, p. 34.

56. James J. Zuiches and Glenn V. Fuguitt, "Residential Preferences: Implications for Population Redistribution in Nonmetropolitan Areas," in Mazie, ed., *Population Distribution and Policy*, pp. 617–30. The initial question was: "If you could live in any size community you wanted to, would you prefer to live in a large city of 50,000 or over, in a suburb next to a large city, in a medium-size city, in a small city or town, or in a rural area?" Those favoring the medium-size city, small city or town, or rural area were asked: "Would you prefer to live within commuting distance—say within 30 miles—of a large city, or be further away from a large city?"

57. *Population and the American Future*, p. 34.

58. Zuiches, "Residential Preferences and Population Mobility."

Table 1-3. *Preferred and Actual Places of Residence, by Community Size and Proximity to a Metropolitan Center, U.S. National Surveys, 1972 and 1974*[a]

Percent of respondents

	Size of community			
			Smaller community	
Preferred or actual residence	City over 500,000	City of 50,000– 500,000	Within 30 miles of city over 50,000	More than 30 miles from city over 50,000
1972				
Preferred residence	9	16	55	19
Actual residence	20	24	34	21
Difference between preferred and actual	−11	−8	21	−2
1974				
Preferred residence	9	13	52	26
Actual residence	20	22	37	21
Difference between preferred and actual	−11	−9	15	5

Source: Zuiches, "Residential Preferences and Population Mobility."

a. In 1972, all respondents were asked: "First, we are interested in the kind of community you would prefer to live in now, if you had your choice. In terms of size, if you could live in any size community you wanted, which of these would you like best? A large metropolitan city (over 500,000 in population). A medium-sized city (50,000 to 500,000 in population). A smaller city (10,000 to 50,000 in population). A town or village (under 10,000 in population). In the country, outside of any city or village. Don't know." (The preference of 1 percent of the respondents was not ascertained.) Those respondents preferring a community under 50,000 were asked: "In terms of location, would you like that place to be within 30 miles of a large or medium-sized city, or would you rather be farther away from such a city?" The 1974 questions were identical in import though different in wording. The "smaller city" and "town or village" categories were combined into one category of "smaller city or village."

undecided) in favor of the smaller. These findings, then, like those of the other polls, indicate a strong preference for a more dispersed pattern of settlement than now exists.[59]

Uncertainties inevitably arise about the value of simple responses to one or a very few questions used to measure what may be a complex and perhaps ambivalent set of attitudes. The residents of big cities who express a preference for small town or rural life, for instance, may have a

59. Polls taken in the state of Washington in 1971 and 1973 and in Arizona in 1973 confirm that people prefer to be in or near small metropolitan areas rather than larger ones. Respondents were asked to indicate their preference as among nonmetropolitan areas and metropolitan areas of various sizes, without distinguishing

romantic, nostalgic notion of what that life is like. They may presuppose the existence there of better-paid jobs than could in fact, under any set of policies, be established in small places, and they may underestimate the gap between the services offered in a big city and those available in a small town. On the other hand, rural or small town people who express a preference for city life may be discounting entirely the prospect that economic opportunities and public services can be improved in their communities. For example, over 60 percent of the persons who preferred city living in one of the surveys cited better jobs and higher wages as among their reasons.[60] Presumably, any national growth policy favoring a more dispersed settlement pattern would have to use as its means the improvement of job and income opportunities in smaller places, as well as the upgrading of various facilities and services. To the extent that opportunity and service gaps can be narrowed, and the improvements become known, the already strong preference for smaller places that appears throughout the polling data will be strengthened.[61]

---

between central city and suburbs within those areas. Only a minority in each case—48 percent in the Arizona study, 39 percent and 28 percent in the two Washington surveys—wanted to live in a metropolitan area of any size. And the antipathy toward large metropolitan areas was clear. Only 3 percent or 4 percent of the sample chose the metropolitan area over 500,000 (Seattle and Phoenix, respectively), compared to from 24 percent to 45 percent who preferred a metropolitan area in the 50,000–500,000 range. Two of the surveys which provided an option between metropolitan areas of 50,000–150,000 and 150,000–500,000 showed a three-to-two preference for the former. Sixty percent of the respondents in the Seattle metropolitan area preferred a smaller metropolitan region, only 7 percent a region of Seattle's size. And Seattle ranks only seventeenth among the country's metropolitan areas. The studies "suggest a desired redistribution [of population] to fairly small (but not the smallest) cities." All "show a lack of interest in living in extremely small, remote places." Don A. Dillman, "Population Distribution Policy and People's Attitudes: Current Knowledge and Needed Research" (paper prepared for the Urban Land Institute, Washington, Oct. 15, 1973; processed), pp. 28–42. The study includes an analysis and tabulation of all available state and national polls on residential preferences by city size.

60. Zuiches, "Residential Preferences and Population Mobility."

61. The crucial role of job opportunities is indicated in a poll, cited by President Nixon, of graduates of the University of South Dakota, 85 percent of whom had left the state; asked if they would return if there were job opportunities in South Dakota, 50 percent said yes. *Public Papers, 1970*, pp. 622–23. The very strong preference of young people to remain at home in nonmetropolitan areas rather than go to the city, if wages were equal, is clearly shown also in polls of young persons, mostly high school seniors, in Eastern Kentucky (two surveys), South Texas (Mexican Americans), the Southwest (Indians), and Southwest Mississippi; except for the sample of southwestern Indians, the proportion preferring not to migrate was in the 64–75 percent range. Niles M. Hansen, "The Case of Government-Assisted Migra-

Accordingly, any national policy that sought to conform the geographical distribution of jobs more closely to the preferred settlement
pattern of the people would need more sophisticated data than now exist
to measure the public preference. But this, at least, is well within the
present capacity of social science.

The Prospect of Further Concentration

If the net disadvantages that the political leadership of the early 1970s
saw in population concentration did in fact exist, they appeared certain to
get worse as the total population of the United States increased. For the
prospect ahead—in the absence of a national growth policy that would
reverse the trend of the postwar period—was that five-sixths of the entire
net growth of the United States during the coming decades would be
concentrated in metropolitan population clusters of more than a million
persons. Assuming a birth rate at only the replacement level, the population of the United States would reach 265.5 million in the year 2000,
compared to 203.2 million in 1970. Of the 62.3 million increase, 53.0 million—or 85 percent—would be added to the population of just forty-
four metropolitan areas that, at the end of the period, would have reached
the 1-million population level, according to projections of postwar trends
prepared for the Commission on Population Growth and the American
Future.[62]

---

tion," in Mazie, ed., *Population Distribution and Policy*, pp. 686–87. A survey of a
recent graduating class of the Fort Scott, Kans., high school similarly revealed that
a majority of those who had left the state had tried unsuccessfully to find suitable
jobs in Kansas and would have preferred to remain there. "Are Young Kansans
Staying in Kansas," *Kansas Government Journal*, March 1974, pp. 124–25.

62. Projections of Pickard, "U.S. Metropolitan Growth and Expansion," Table 4,
p. 135. The projections of metropolitan growth cited here are based on the Census
Bureau's Series E projection of total population growth, which assumes an average
of 2.1 children per woman in the population, which is the rate at which a parental
generation exactly replaces itself. This figure would result in a rate of population
increase of 1.0 percent annually until near the end of the 1970–2000 period. That is
less than experienced in the United States in the decades prior to 1970 but more
than the 0.7 percent increase registered in 1973. The sharp drop in the rate of increase since 1970 suggests that even the Series E projections may turn out to be
high. Pickard also gives higher metropolitan growth projections based on the Census
Bureau's Series B population projections, which assumes 3 children per woman.
Since 1970, the urbanization trends of the 1940–70 period that formed the basis of
Pickard's projections have changed significantly. The rural-urban flow that has
characterized U.S. internal migration since the country's beginning gave way in

Figure 1-1. *Projected Urban Regions, Containing Five-sixths of the American People, as of the Year 2000*[a]

Source: Jerome P. Pickard, "Urbanization and Economic Change in North American Regions" (1973; processed).

a. Based on two-child family projection. Alaska, not shown on the map, has no urban region. In Hawaii, also not shown, the city-county of Honolulu is an urban region.

Moreover, the forty-four metropolitan areas could be expected to merge, by the year 2000, into twenty-five "urban regions," as shown on Figure 1-1. Each of these regions would have a population of more than 1 million, and most of them would consist of two or more metropolitan areas that would have grown together along major transportation corridors. In these regions would live 220 million people, or 83 percent of the country's population. About half of these would reside in two vast concentrations that by the end of the century would have become connected —the Atlantic Seaboard region extending from Maine to Virginia, and the Lower Great Lakes region reaching from Utica, New York, and cen-

---

1970–73 to a reverse movement from metropolitan to nonmetropolitan areas. The new trends, which have not yet been fully analyzed and interpreted, are discussed in chapter 7. Pickard's projections are used here because they were accepted in the late 1960s and early 1970s, when the political consensus on the need for dispersal measures was reached, as the most authoritative available description of the population distribution outlook.

tral Pennsylvania to Green Bay, Wisconsin, and spreading southward to Cincinnati and northward through the southern half of Michigan. Another 35 million would live in one consolidated urban region in California extending from Sacramento to the Mexican border, and 13 million in a single urban complex covering most of the Florida peninsula. In all, five-sixths of the population would live in regions comprising one-sixth of the land area, while most other communities in the country barely maintained themselves or declined.[63]

Contemplating this prospect, the commission concluded that "the losses resulting from a continuation of current trends in population distribution are sufficiently serious that we should attempt to moderate them." It recommended—reinforcing the political consensus reached earlier by the Congress, the President, the political parties, the governors, and the mayors—that the federal government develop "a set of national population distribution guidelines." The guidelines should incorporate a "growth center strategy" for the revival of declining areas; certain expanding cities in the 25,000–350,000 population range that have the capacity to reach 50,000–500,000 should be selected for encouragement to grow toward those limits (or perhaps somewhat higher ones). But as to what form the encouragement should take, the commission was hesitant. Efforts of the Economic Development Administration, the Appalachian Regional Commission, and other regional commissions had met with "only limited success." "Substantial increases in funding" and "better focusing of investment" would be necessary, it suggested, but many questions concerning the selection of growth centers and the most efficient means of stimulating their growth "are yet to be answered." The commission cautioned against wasting subsidies on places that would grow without further stimulus, against catering to limited rather than regionwide interests, against "simply relocating industries from one area to another" that would aggravate the problems of the former, and against producing "overurbanization" inadvertently. Implementing the strategy "will not be easy," the group concluded, and it recommended more research. To take the lead in developing the objectives and criteria for national population distribution policies, as well as those relating to population growth policies, it recommended the creation of an Office of Population Growth and Distribution within the Executive Office of the President.[64]

63. The regions are defined in ibid., pp. 142, 147, and 158.
64. *Population and the American Future*, pp. 120, 125–26, and 138–39.

Relevance of the European Experience

As the United States gropes its way toward a national growth policy, one ready source of useful data is the experience of the other advanced industrial countries of the world. Without exception, they all have adopted policies for dispersing population. To the American mind, unaccustomed to social and economic planning by government, some of those policies are surprisingly explicit. They have evolved through trial and error over periods as long as forty years, and while they are still evolving, the principles now seem firmly established. The policies, and the programs to effectuate them, are supported by a political consensus in each country that is also surprising—given the interregional tensions that population distribution policies would be expected to arouse.

Great Britain, France, Italy, the Netherlands, and Sweden are among the democratic, industrialized countries that have had long experience in attempting to influence and control their internal settlement patterns. As a group these five have the oldest, broadest, most vigorous, and most innovative programs in Western Europe, and probably in the world. How their national population distribution policies came into being, what they consist of, how they were justified and defended in the political arena, how they are carried out, what has been accomplished, and what are seen by officials and observers in those countries as the principal current policy issues and administrative problems are therefore instructive for Americans.

The setting is different, of course: The European countries are much smaller in area and population and far more homogeneous than the United States; they are unitary rather than federal (now excepting Italy), and they have a tradition and acceptance of national governmental planning and leadership that has never existed here. Each has its own unique migration and concentration patterns, which may differ markedly from American patterns. The European policies and programs represent a degree of public intervention in the locational decisions of private firms beyond anything seriously suggested in the United States. Nevertheless, when and if the United States—and the fifty states as well—grapple with the development of national and state policy for dispersing population, there is clearly much in the European experience that is applicable.

The five countries, profiting from one another's experience over the years, have evolved policies and programs having fundamental similari-

ties. All embody a philosophy of dispersal; they are aimed at damming
at least some of the streams of internal migration, particularly those leading to the major population centers—London, Paris, Milan, Amsterdam,
Stockholm, and so on. The objective, like that proclaimed for the United
States by President Nixon in 1970, is to reverse the migration flow if possible but in any case to stem it. And all five countries have employed for
that purpose, with varying degrees of emphasis, four approaches—
infrastructure measures to prepare areas of out-migration for industrial
growth, *incentive measures* to induce private investors to go to those
areas, *controls and persuasion* to discourage investment in the major
metropolitan areas, and *direct action* by the government in locating
its own activities, including the expansion projects of state-controlled
industries.

In each country the original political force giving rise to action was
concern for the plight of economically depressed areas (always identified eventually in European countries, as in the United States, by a euphe-
mism such as "development areas"). These were regions where a weak
or declining economic base was proving inadequate to support the natural increase in population, and which therefore suffered disproportionate
unemployment, underemployment, and out-migration. These might be
old mining and industrial areas, such as South Wales and the Glasgow
and Newcastle areas in Britain or the coal, steel, and textile provinces of
northern and eastern France. Or they might be underdeveloped rural
areas with a problem of surplus agricultural labor, like southern and
western France, the southern half of Italy, and the northern counties of
Sweden. In either case, the politicians responded to appeals for help—
much as politicians in the United States responded to the pleas of Appalachia and other depressed regions. As in this country, the program measures were initiated on a limited and experimental scale, but they were
invariably broadened and made more generous in the European countries
as the tenacity of the structural unemployment problem became more
clearly understood.

Again as in the United States, the concern for the depressed areas
came sooner or later to merge with another stream of motivation—a
reaction to what was seen as the overcongestion of the major metropolitan centers. As soon as the purpose of restraining growth in the expanding areas was added to that of stimulating growth in the lagging
ones, the concept of the national policy broadened. The nations moved

from "depressed areas" and "rural development" policies to "population distribution" and "balanced growth" policies. In countries with a tradition and acceptance of governmental planning, the objective of balanced growth might come to be expressed in quantitative targets. France, with its elaborate process of national "indicative" economic planning, has developed procedures for preparing regional plans articulated with the national plan. Sweden undertook a few years ago to set a population target not only for every county but for every commune.

Meanwhile, in each country, land-use planning for the purpose of controlling and channeling growth within urban or urbanizing areas has been progressing on its own momentum, and the scale of the plans has been expanding steadily to embrace metropolitan and regional as well as local objectives. In the development areas, regional land-use planning has come naturally to embrace, and emphasize, planning for regional industrial infrastructure to guide and stimulate development. All of the countries have adopted, in one form or another, the "growth center strategy" advocated in the United States by the Commission on Population Growth and others, and through the regional planning process the growth centers have been identified and investment concentrated. In the smallest of the five countries, the Netherlands, the techniques of regional planning could be applied on a national scale, and that country's national land-use plan has become the central instrument of national population distribution planning.

In most of the European countries, as in the United States, the appropriate division of responsibility for programs relating to population distribution between the national government and lower levels of government—regions, provinces, or counties—is an unsettled and in some cases an urgent question. The long-established units of local government, designed for the delivery of a limited range of public services in a simpler age, have proved inadequate to the tasks of designing and carrying out broad economic development strategies. So France has improvised a new regional level of government between the national capital and the traditional departments. Britain is experimenting with regional planning bodies, and Sweden has created new mechanisms at the county level to undertake new responsibilities. Italy, in the most drastic transition of all, has become a federal state with the creation of a system of regional governments; mandated by the postwar Italian constitution for reasons quite apart from population distribution and economic development planning, the new governments will have a major—if not yet fully determined—role in those processes.

So, among the issues relating to national growth policy that now confront and perplex American policymakers, there is none that has not been met, and dealt with in one fashion or another, by these five European countries. Ascertaining what each country's policies were intended to accomplish has, of course, proved easier than finding out what they have actually achieved. The policy objectives are defined in readily available, official documents. But the results, which often are reached only over a long period, may not have been compiled and reported at all by the government agencies, or at least not in summary form in documents easily accessible. The same may be true of costs. Where the official data are available, they may not have been subjected to authoritative independent analysis; only in Britain and the Netherlands, apparently, have thorough-going attempts been made to quantify the consequences of specific governmental programs. Perhaps, however, absence of independent evaluation is itself a reflection of the absence of controversy—and that may be, at least, a measure of the political success of the European policies.

CHAPTER TWO

Great Britain: Stemming the Drift to the South

In the last analysis, the need for regional policy is not simply a regrettable aspect of a temporary economic sickness. . . . It is a normal part of the life of any economic community that likes (or even tolerates) change, but has the humanity to recognize that the economy was made for man and not man for the economy.—Professor A. J. Brown, 1972[1]

THE COMPLEX and comprehensive set of population distribution policies now being pursued in Great Britain has evolved over the course of more than four decades—since the discovery, in the late 1920s, of what were then called "depressed areas." Those were the areas of the country that had failed to recover from the severe postwar depression that reached its climax in 1921. In the coal regions, reduced demand and increased productivity had created a surplus of at least 200,000 miners untrained for other work and highly concentrated in a few regions, notably South Wales, the Durham-Northumberland region of North East England, and the area of Scotland centered on Glasgow. In the latter two areas, the coal depression was compounded by the decline in a second basic industry—shipbuilding.

The initial response of the Conservative government then in power was simple and logical enough: retrain the surplus workers and help them move to other areas, both within Britain and overseas. The Ministry of Labour in proposing that solution admitted that it would encounter obstacles.[2] There was the psychological factor—"ties of home and locality." There was the fact that every other area of Britain had some unemployment too, and the receiving areas might not be cooperative. But, rea-

---

1. A. J. Brown, *The Framework of Regional Economics in the United Kingdom*, National Institute of Economic and Social Research, Economic and Social Studies 27 (Cambridge, England.: Cambridge University Press, 1972), p. 347.
2. *Report of the Industrial Transference Board*, presented by the Minister of Labour to Parliament, Cmd. 3156 (His Majesty's Stationery Office [HMSO], 1928).

soned the government, if the county of Glamorgan in Wales had an unemployment rate of 24 percent, with individual communities up to 62 percent, while South East England and the Midlands enjoyed rates of 5–10 percent, it made better sense to let the Welsh miners compete for jobs elsewhere—if they could be retrained—than to encourage them to stay where they were in the vain hope that the pits would reemploy them.

The miners' union endorsed the policy of "industrial transference." And while the opposition Labour party might ridicule the proposal as inadequate, it could hardly object to the principle. So industrial transference went into effect in 1928. Training programs were established in the mining areas and workers were offered relocation grants "to encourage the will to move." But the program was scarcely under way when the worldwide Great Depression struck. Then unemployment rose and remained so high in every area that any program for moving the jobless from place to place would be largely futile.

By that time, however, many Britishers were convinced that the transference of workers was the wrong approach in any event. While transference could be useful in individual cases, it clearly could not solve the whole problem of depressed areas.[3] In 1934 the program in West Cumberland was branded by a review team as a failure. In North East England investigators found that it had been "very difficult" to transfer men over thirty-five years old, especially those with families. In South Wales there was "resentment" that the young and able-bodied should be forced to leave home, in Scotland "lack of enthusiasm." Two of four regional reports on the program observed that a large proportion—one said "the vast majority"—of the transferred workers had eventually come home, in some cases even though they had to return on foot.[4]

3. In the first nine years of the program 150,000 men and 40,000 women were transferred; 50,000 of the men and 5,600 of the women had returned home by 1937, according to official figures of that year. Brown, in *Framework of Regional Economics*, p. 281, estimates that by 1938, 150,000 relocated workers had remained in their new locations, the equivalent of nearly one-third of the "excess of unemployment rates" in the depressed areas compared to the more prosperous regions. Altogether, net migration from the less prosperous regions during the period, Brown figures, was about 500,000.

4. *Reports of Investigations into the Industrial Conditions in Certain Depressed Areas*, Cmd. 4728 (HMSO, 1934).

Development Incentives for the Depressed Areas (*1936–45*)

So the policy was reversed. Relocation grants remained available and workers continued to be encouraged to move from areas of heavy unemployment,[5] but emphasis shifted from transferring workers to dispersing jobs. "Bring the work to the workers" was the slogan. By the time the Second World War began, "industrial transference" had all but vanished from the vocabulary in which the problem of heavy localized unemployment was discussed.

Bringing the work to the workers began on a modest and experimental scale. The coalition government headed by Ramsay MacDonald appointed two commissioners—one for England and Wales and one for Scotland—with broad and general powers to assist the depressed areas (now called "special areas") but only $10 million for the first year. The commissioners used their funds primarily for public works, such as water and sewer systems, that were basic prerequisites if the depressed areas were ever to attract new industry. Beyond that, they intervened with government purchasing officials to try to steer contracts into the depressed regions. They managed to obtain a proviso, when the government extended credit to the railroads, that railroad procurement would give preference to the special areas, "other things being equal." Eventually, this became the rule in all government contracts. The commissioners also gave financial assistance to nonprofit companies in three areas to build "advance factories" (built speculatively in advance of finding a tenant) to rent to private firms. Most of all, the commissioners recommended new programs and greater expenditure.

Three new programs were enacted by the Conservative government of Neville Chamberlain in 1936 and 1937.[6] The commissioners' power to

5. In 1972–73 the program assisted 6,000 workers. *Regional Development Incentives*, Second Report from the Expenditure Committee, House of Commons, Session 1973–74, par. 90.

6. Details of British program development during this and later periods are given in Gavin McCrone, *Regional Policy in Britain*, University of Glasgow Social and Economic Studies (London: George Allen and Unwin, 1969), pp. 91–148; Alan J. Odber, "Regional Policy in Great Britain," in U.S. Department of Commerce, Area Redevelopment Administration, *Area Redevelopment Policies in Britain and the Countries of the Common Market* (1965), pp. 327–427; Geoffrey Denton, Murray Forsyth, and Malcolm MacLennan, *Economic Planning and Policies in Britain,*

finance construction of *state-owned factories* was confirmed and broadened. Private firms were offered *financial assistance* through government-guaranteed loans up to $50,000 for capital investment, direct loans, and grants to help the firms pay rent. The commissioners were also authorized to contribute to local and national *tax relief* for firms in the special areas, and the firms were exempted when a new tax was imposed for national defense.

When the outbreak of war brought the programs abruptly to a halt, publicly built factories employing some 12,000 workers were coming into production. The government lending agencies had disbursed less than $10 million.[7] Contributions toward taxes and rents totaled only $250,000. Given the massive unemployment in the depressed areas, the programs were little more than a token effort; nevertheless, the proportion of the national total of new factories located in the special areas rose to 17 percent in 1938 (although most of those in the special areas were small) from less than 3 percent in each of the years between 1932 and 1936.[8] Most important, the techniques and methods of developing the areas had been tested, they had been proven effective at least to some degree, and a body of experience had been built.

During the war, for strategic as well as economic reasons, the depressed areas received more than their share of munitions factories. But the Ministry of Reconstruction, assigned to look beyond the wartime boom to the shape of postwar Britain, saw no reason to believe that depressed areas would not reappear even in a generally prosperous economy, just as they had done in the decade after the First World War. Therefore, the government concluded, a permanent depressed areas program was essential, with flexible arrangements for adding new areas and dropping old ones.

France and Germany (London: George Allen and Unwin, 1968), pp. 299–313; James Douglas McCallum in "A Review History of British Regional Policy" (paper prepared for a conference in 1971 sponsored by Resources for the Future, Inc., Washington, and the University of Glasgow; processed); and Peter J. Randall, "The History of British Regional Policy," in Graham Hallett, Peter Randall, and E. G. West, *Regional Policy For Ever* (London: Institute of Economic Affairs, 1973). Brown, *Framework of Regional Economics*, chap. 11, appraises the effects of the successive policies, from the earliest to 1969.

7. *Distribution of Industry*, Cmd. 7540 (HMSO, 1948), pars. 19–21. The Nuffield Trust provided an additional $11 million for loans and equity capital in the special areas.

8. Brown, *Framework of Regional Economics*, p. 285.

The postwar planners put their proposals in a new and sophisticated economic context, as part of a policy for full employment. A "high and stable level of employment" was, by universal agreement, to be a primary economic goal. To that end, policies for the "general maintenance of purchasing power" would be pursued. But a high level of purchasing power nationally would not be enough in itself to solve programs of disproportionately high unemployment in particular industrial regions unless, through a long-drawn-out process, the depressed industrial regions were partially depopulated. But "much social capital is already invested there in the form of houses, shops, public services, etc. Neither this social capital nor the corporate life of these communities can be sacrificed." A few small and isolated mining villages might have to be abandoned but large industrial populations would neither be compelled to move nor left to "prolonged unemployment and demoralisation." Besides, wartime experience had shown that production could be just as efficient in the depressed areas as elsewhere.[9]

The depressed areas program the ministry proposed was a codification and extension of the approaches used in the prewar period, with one exception—the tax incentives were discarded. The Distribution of Industry Act, enacted in early 1945, empowered the Board of Trade to build advance factories in the depressed areas for lease or sale. It authorized grants and loans to firms locating there. It authorized special grants and loans for basic services—transportation, power, housing, health facilities, community services of all kinds. And it added a new authority for the Board of Trade to acquire and clear "derelict lands" in mining and industrial areas or make grants to local authorities to do so.

The act also broadened the concept of special areas—or, as the act once more renamed them, development areas. Whereas in the prewar period eligibility for assistance had been restricted to the individual communities, usually small ones, that were experiencing heavy unemployment, it was now extended to include major cities to which the smaller communities were tributary. Thus, Glasgow was included with the depressed mining towns that surrounded it. And the South Wales development area was extended from the mining valleys to include the coastal cities of Cardiff, Newport, and Swansea. Newcastle was added to the North East England area. Assistance, then, could go to the whole of a region that was a single labor market and an economic unit. The popula-

---

9. *Employment Policy*, Cmd. 6527 (HMSO, 1944), pars. 1, 24, and 29.

tion in the eligible areas was increased from less than 4 million to about 6.5 million—one-seventh of the country's population.[10]

Disincentives for the Growth of London   *(1936–47)*

Struggling to revive the depressed mining regions of England and Wales in the 1930s with his limited powers and funds, the commissioner for the special areas, Sir Malcolm Stewart, observed with increasing chagrin that the factories he wanted for his jobless miners were being located for the most part in the area of Greater London (that is, the entire London conurbation). In 1935, only two new factories had been built in the two English special areas that made up his domain (the Durham-Northumberland area and West Cumberland), and none at all in South Wales. But no fewer than 213 factories had been built in Greater London. That was 40 percent of new factory construction in the whole of Britain.

It was an "outburst" of Sir Malcolm "in a moment of disappointment" that started the second strand of policy that has been woven into the British population distribution fabric.[11] If the rest of the country was ever going to be revived, Sir Malcolm wrote in his 1936 report, the government had to stop the indiscriminate growth of London. Sir Malcolm was against the Labourite notion of "compulsory location of industry," he made clear, but enough compulsion to keep industry out of London was a national necessity.[12] The growth of London was destroying open space needed for recreation in the metropolis, as well as some of the country's best agricultural land. Transportation could not keep up with need; commuters were spending as much as 20 percent of their income on transportation, riding for one-half to three-quarters of an hour and often standing all the way. The number of private cars in Greater London had doubled in eight years. The new industries were locating to the north and northwest of London, while the workers were on the other side, to

10. Northern Ireland, the most depressed region of Great Britain, is not included in these figures or covered elsewhere in this chapter; as a semiautonomous region it administers its own incentives programs (which generally parallel those of the rest of Britain).

11. According to Hugh Dalton, president of the Board of Trade in 1945; *Parliamentary Debates (Hansard)*, March 21, 1945, vol. 409, col. 844.

12. *Report of the Commissioner for Special Areas, England and Wales, for the year ended 30th September 1937*, Cmd. 5595 (HMSO, 1937).

the east and southeast. And, perhaps most urgent, such concentration of industry was a strategic danger; close to half the country's aircraft plants, for example, were located there. Already the world's largest conurbation, with 8 million people, Greater London would reach 9 million by 1941 and 10 million shortly afterward. And this growth would be at the expense of the rest of the country, which would be paying the cost of educating London's workers, "a subsidy to London industry borne very largely by the rest of the country."

Sir Malcolm's outburst led, in the British manner, to appointment of a royal commission, headed by a former Conservative minister of labour, Sir Montague Barlow, and named, significantly, the Royal Commission on the Distribution of the Industrial Population. When it finished its two-year study, just before the outbreak of war in 1939, it had come to agree completely with Sir Malcolm. Its report, the seminal document in British population distribution policy,[13] guided directly the actions of both Labour and Conservative governments in the early postwar periods, and the objectives it set forth are still the central goals of British policy.

The Barlow commission noted that London and the seven "home counties" that made up its metropolitan region,[14] which comprise 7 percent of the country's area, had grown from 18 percent of the total population in 1801 to 20 percent in 1861, 23.5 percent in 1921, and 25.7 percent in 1937. Between 1921 and 1937 the region had enjoyed 55 percent of the country's total growth, gaining at a rate two and a half times that of the country as a whole. London was not only a great port and a national capital but a large factory center—clothing, milling, drugs, paper, chemicals, iron and steel finishing, motor vehicles, other metal goods, and aircraft. Especially were the expanding light industries concentrating in Greater London; between 1932 and 1937, three of every seven new factories built in Britain (1,400 of 3,220) were inside the conurbation.[15] But since other regional economies rested on declining industries, the disparity in terms of net increase was even more startling: Greater London had a net increase of 532 factories, the rest of the country, 112.

Why was this? The mere size of the London market, first of all. Not

13. *Report of the Royal Commission on the Distribution of the Industrial Population,* Cmd. 6153 (HMSO, 1940). Known as the Barlow Report.
14. The home counties were Bedford, Buckingham, Essex, Hertford, Kent, Middlesex, and Surrey. The region as so defined comprised 5,978 square miles, or nearly ten times the 644 square miles of Greater London.
15. The figures are for factories employing more than 25 persons.

only did the region have a fourth of the country's people but they were the country's most prosperous quarter, with more regular employment, at high wages. An industry locating there could be sure of an adequate supply of labor. Roads and railways radiated from the London center in all directions, and vessels left the port for everywhere. The city offered cheap power and excelled in services to industry of every kind. The more it attracted industry and population, the more attractive it became. "Nothing succeeds like success," the commission was reminded.

Being charged with deciding whether the concentration of the country's population in great urban complexes, particularly the London agglomeration, were in the national interest, the commission assembled the evidence under three headings—social, economic, and strategic. For many purposes, urbanization was desirable; cities could offer better social and medical services, utility services, and educational and cultural opportunities, and a greater diversification of employment opportunities. Many of the evils currently associated with big cities could be overcome with proper planning. Urban mortality rates could be reduced to rural levels. Urban housing could be made livable. Smoke and noise pollution could be overcome. Yet other disadvantages of urban living were unavoidable— particularly the time and costs of commuting, traffic congestion, and loss of access to open space.

From the standpoint of the national economy, urbanization offered opportunities for better utilization of the labor force and for efficiencies in distribution. But it brought some inefficiencies in production and distribution, too; it introduced high land cost factors, and if industry were allowed to choose freely its own location, it could take the best agricultural land—land that, from the standpoint of the nation, would be better left in farming. From the viewpoint of the employer, what he gained through reduced transportation costs he might lose in higher land costs. And for the worker, what he gained through a greater range of job opportunities might be offset by the cost in time and money of commuting.

Strategic considerations were less evenly balanced. Meeting at the very time of the Anschluss, the Sudeten crisis, and Neville Chamberlain's pilgrimage to Munich, the commission could only conclude that dispersal of industry from overcrowded areas was "definitely to be recommended on strategic grounds." (By the time the report was printed, Britain was at war.)

The commission could find no data, however, to tell them the ideal size of a city. Much depended on how well the city was planned: "Mere size need not in itself be a disadvantage, but it is size without system, chaotic growth without the adoption of proper principles of planning . . . that are to be avoided." Even cities of a million or more, under those conditions, were "not necessarily anathema and to be avoided or abolished at all costs." But as for London, there was no question. It was too big, on all three grounds. "It is not in the national interest, economically, socially or strategically, that a quarter, or even a larger proportion of the population of Great Britain, should be concentrated within 20 to 30 miles or so of Central London." The goal should be a "balanced distribution of industry and the industrial population so far as possible throughout the different areas or regions" and in each of those areas or regions there should be "appropriate diversification of industries."[16] On these general objectives the commission was unanimous. And it was supported by testimony from business, labor, and local government officials. Even the London County Council testified that Greater London was already larger than was desirable.

If the ends were agreed, however, there was no consensus on the means. Organized labor wanted authority in the government to determine industrial location. Organized business would accept governmental measures to "encourage" and "discourage," but opposed compulsion. The commission split along the same lines. Seven of the thirteen members would go only so far as to propose a national industrial board that would be empowered to prohibit the establishment in the London region of new factories—except on proof that a proposed activity "could not be conducted on an economic basis elsewhere"—and that would itself recommend what its additional powers should be. The other six wanted a more vigorous program to be enacted without delay, three of them calling for a new government department with far-reaching powers to plan and regulate the location of industry.[17]

16. The quotations are from ibid., pars. 325, 326, and 320.
17. The Barlow Report also endorsed the objective of decentralizing London and other metropolitan concentrations through the development of planned new communities, an idea first advanced by Ebenezer Howard in 1898 and advocated by planners in Britain and elsewhere ever since. A New Towns Act was passed in 1946, and fourteen were started by 1950. Most new towns are located near metropolitan centers, particularly London, and are designed to house the "overspill" from those centers. Hence they are an aspect of intraregional, rather than interregional, population distribution policy and as such are beyond the scope of this study. However, in the development areas, new towns are designed also to be attractive to industry,

The unanimous conclusion that the growth of London should be restrained appeared to be accepted by the country as self-evident. When in 1944 the Churchill coalition government announced its policies for postwar reconstruction, they included a proposal for direct controls. Industrialists would be required to obtain a government certificate for factory construction projects—and construction would be prohibited in some areas.[18] But Parliament reacted negatively when the proposal was presented. Back-benchers expressed the fears of industrialists that "compulsory location of industry" was being authorized,[19] and the government hastily withdrew, observing that the power was not yet needed anyway—since wartime controls were ample for the purpose—and no plans had been made to use it. Yet, two years later, the same powers were granted as an incidental provision of the Town and Country Planning Act of 1947, without objection—or even so much as comment—throughout the whole extensive debate.

Under the 1947 act, projects for factory construction had to be submitted to the Board of Trade for certification that they were consistent with "the proper distribution of industry." The Labour government then in power had made clear that it intended to use the new power rigorously to restrain the growth of London and its metropolitan region. The industrial development certificate procedure has remained on the statute books and has been applied, with varying degrees of stringency by successive governments, throughout the quarter century since 1947.

The Depressed Areas Problem Solved—Temporarily *(1948-58)*

While the prewar initiatives in bringing assistance to depressed areas can be credited mainly to the Conservative government of Neville Chamberlain, nevertheless it was in the Labour party that the policies were most passionately supported. Most of the stricken coal areas sent Labour

and so are mentioned below as a form of industrial development infrastructure. By 1971, 28 new towns had been designated. For a chronology of new town building, a list of the towns with population targets, and a map showing locations, see Marion Clawson and Peter Hall, *Planning and Urban Growth: An Anglo-American Comparison* (Johns Hopkins University Press for Resources for the Future, 1973), pp. 202–06.

18. *Employment Policy*, par. 26.
19. *Hansard*, March 21, 1945, vol. 409, especially cols. 858–60.

representatives to the House of Commons. Indeed, the heart of the party in its early days had been the miners' union; in the lean years following the 1931 election, when the party was reduced to forty-six members in the House of Commons, half of them were members sponsored by the miners.[20] So while Conservative spokesmen tended to talk of the depressed areas in measured economic terms, full of statistics, their Labour opposites were apt to strike a more emotional tone. "We are dealing not with sticks and stones, but with living communities . . . this country will be immeasurably poorer—and it will be a poverty that cannot be measured in pounds, shillings and pence—if those communities, with their sense of belonging and their people with deep roots and traditions, are allowed to die because the House and the Government allow industry to go just where it likes for the sake of a couple of pennies more profit."[21] Committed as socialists to the concept of national planning, the Labourites came to office in 1945 determined to plan the reconversion of the wartime economy so that jobs would be distributed according to where the workers lived. Its powers for that purpose were sufficient. It could finance modern advance factories in the development areas, on well-planned industrial estates (in the U.S. term, industrial parks). And even before the 1947 act, it could stringently control new plant construction in Greater London and its region—as well as in the West Midlands, centering on Birmingham, which had also grown rapidly in prewar years—through the rationing of building materials.

Employing its powers with enthusiasm, the Labour government actually steered into the development areas more than half (51.1 percent) of the new industrial buildings in Britain during the three years from 1945 through 1947.[22] Greater London was held to 5.3 percent and the Midlands to about 14 percent—only a third as much as the two areas had recorded between 1932 and 1938.[23] As of mid-1948, 443 new factories in the development areas had been completed and 530 were under construction. Already, 31,800 workers were employed in the new buildings and the total was to rise to 184,500 when all were finished. Of those, almost two-

20. R. T. McKenzie, *British Political Parties* (2nd ed., Heinemann, 1963), p. 359.
21. James Griffiths of Wales, Labour spokesman on depressed areas legislation, *Hansard*, Nov. 9, 1959, vol. 613, col. 59.
22. *Development Areas*, Second Report from the Select Committee on Estimates, House of Commons, Session 1955–56, par. 11.
23. *Distribution of Industry*, par. 80. The time period given is "since the war," which may not be the same as the 1945–47 period specified in *Development Areas*.

thirds would be in government-financed plants. In addition, some 70,000 were at work in government munitions factories or other facilities converted to civilian production.[24]

Surveying the situation in 1948, the government could well conclude that it had solved the problem. Unemployment in the depressed areas stood at just over 100,000, less than one-third the level of 1939. The rate was about double the national level, but factories yet to be completed or to be brought into full operation would require half again as many workers as were registered as unemployed. When the program was complete, the government told Parliament, "there should no longer be a special danger of heavy localised unemployment in most parts of the Areas."[25]

The financial powers, interestingly, had hardly been employed. The authority to make grants had not been exercised at all. Up to September 1948 the Treasury had contracted to lend only $6 million and had advanced only $4 million. "Lack of finance is rarely the main obstacle," said the 1948 report. "The really important powers . . . are those of building factories for leasing to industrialists, the provision of suitable sites and the improvement of basic services."[26]

To be on the safe side, the government decided not to revoke the classification of any of the existing development areas or reduce their boundaries, even those that were enjoying full employment. In fact, it added two major areas—Merseyside, centered on Liverpool, and the Highlands and Islands of Scotland, unique among the designated areas as a region dependent on agriculture and fisheries.

On the whole, however, the government evidently concluded that its job was finished. The viability of the development areas had been proven, it appeared. Many of the new factories had been built speculatively by the government, but no difficulty had been encountered in

---

24. *Distribution of Industry*, pp. 58–59. In 1966 some 200,000 workers were in factories that had "moved" to the depressed areas in 1945–50 (including branches established at some distance from the parent plants). These figures include enterprises established in the government-financed plants, including converted munitions factories. Brown, *Framework of Regional Economics*, p. 286.

25. *Distribution of Industry*, par. 4 and app. 4, p. 44. The unemployment rates were 4 percent in the development areas as against 2 percent for the country. For comparability with U.S. unemployment rates, British figures have to be adjusted upward by a factor of about 50 percent, which would put the rates in the neighborhood of 6 percent and 3 percent, respectively.

26. Ibid., par. 84.

finding tenants. The assumption appeared to be that the "momentum of development . . . would now be taken over by private enterprise so that Government spending could be allowed to taper off."[27] If problems again arose, the powers were on the statute books and the vulnerable areas retained their eligibility, but meanwhile the powers could be held in abeyance. As it happened, the government was compelled by a shortage of building materials and a balance-of-payments crisis to reconsider its entire range of economic policies. The vigorous industrial dispersal program was terminated, and even the advance factory construction that had been planned was deferred. The government reduced the pressure on businessmen to locate in development areas. It did, however, launch in 1948 a program for dispersal of government offices from London.

In relaxing their regional policy, Odber concludes, the policymakers "both underestimated and partially misunderstood" the underlying problem of the development areas. That was the modernization of the industrial structure of the regions, which could not be accomplished once and for all but "would be a long, slow process involving a steady use of powers under the Distribution of Industry Act."[28] But the indicators continued favorable—on the surface. The new plants in the depressed areas were continuing to expand and increase employment, and although the government was no longer speculating in the building of new advance factories, it was building both extensions to existing facilities and new factories that companies promised to occupy. The basic industries of the development areas—coal, steel, and shipbuilding—were all booming as producers strove to catch up with deferred demand.[29] And the unemployment rate in the depressed areas continued to decline toward the national average; only in Scotland did it remain at double the national rate.

So the Labour government, and the Conservative government that succeeded it in 1951, continued to hold regional policy in abeyance. Annual expenditures fell from over $36 million a year in the 1946–49 period to a low of $11 million in 1952–53 and, after rising above $16 million twice, fell again to $8 million in 1957–58. Most of the expenditure was for expansion and modification of the state-owned factories; loans to entrepreneurs made by the Conservative governments in the 1951–58

27. Odber, "Regional Policy in Great Britain," p. 339.
28. Ibid.
29. McCrone, *Regional Policy*, p. 116.

period averaged less than $2 million a year. When a select committee on
estimates of the House of Commons in 1955 made the first comprehensive study of the subject since 1948, it questioned whether even this level
of expenditure was not too much. It recommended that those development areas that had recovered be declassified, that the Board of Trade
divest itself of at least some of its factories, and that in any case it stop
constructing factories to order for American firms that were rich enough
to finance their own buildings. It belittled the entire factory-building
effort as accounting for only 5 percent of the employment in the development areas. But the Board of Trade held its ground. It would not de-
classify any of the existing areas because, it argued prophetically, they
were still vulnerable to another collapse of their basic industries. And
the government activities, even if they contributed only 5 percent to
industrial employment, still provided the marginal assistance without
which the depressed regions could not have approached the level of full
employment that had been reached in the prosperous regions.[30]

New Difficulties—and New Programs   (*1958–64*)

As the 1950s drew to a close, the country learned that the depressed
areas problem had not been solved, after all. The basic industries were
bound to catch up, at some point, with the backlog of demand. The coal
shortage came to an end in 1958, stocks began to accumulate, and production fell. At about the same time, shipping availability pulled even with
requirements; British shipbuilding output fell by one-fifth between 1956
and 1960. Traditional textiles declined also. These secular declines in the
economy were compounded by a cyclical recession.[31] Unemployment
edged up in the whole country but most sharply in the vulnerable development areas. However, those areas were affected unevenly and many
smaller places outside the development areas were harder hit than many
inside. The result was that the old pattern of development areas did not
reflect with much precision the new distribution of unemployment.

Sensitive to any recurrence of prewar mass unemployment, the Conservative government moved quickly. Prime Minister Harold Macmillan
personally intervened in 1958 to divert a steel mill scheduled for the Mid-

30. *Development Areas.*
31. McCrone, *Regional Policy*, pp. 116–18.

lands and obtain agreement to divide the project between Scotland and South Wales. Control of industrial construction in the South East (the London region) and the Midlands through refusal of industrial development certificates was tightened.[32] Then came a series of enactments by the Macmillan government—in 1958, 1960, and 1963.[33] The new measures, which superseded the Distribution of Industry acts, were called Local Employment acts, and the change in name reflected a change in concept. In order to make all areas suffering from unemployment eligible for aid on an equitable basis, the development areas were abolished and in their place the small districts served by local employment exchanges were made the basis of the system. Districts were designated according to their unemployment figures; a level of 4.5 percent was made the standard for eligibility, and districts moved in and out of eligibility status as their unemployment rose above or fell below that figure (although the Board of Trade might vary the standard if it anticipated either a rise or a fall in unemployment in a particular place). The result was to broaden the application of the incentives by adding new districts throughout the country but at the same time to narrow it, by excluding relatively prosperous communities (usually the larger ones) that might be located within areas of general depression. These larger centers included some of those that had originally been made eligible for benefits because of their superior prospects as centers for an area's development.

Within the eligible areas, old powers were extended and sometimes broadened, and some important new ones were added. At the end of 1963 the range of incentives for development was as follows:[34]

1. *Construction of state-owned factories.* The Board of Trade's power to construct state-owned factories continued unchanged (in 1959 the board had resumed the construction of advance factories cut off in 1948).

2. *Grants for private factory construction.* To equalize advantages for enterprises that preferred to finance their own construction with those that the tenants in state-owned factories received through favorable rental terms,[35] a new system of grants was instituted (by 1963, they were standardized at 25 percent of construction cost).

32. Barry Moore and John Rhodes, "Evaluating the Effects of British Regional Economic Policy," *Economic Journal* (London), vol. 83 (1973), p. 89.
33. For detailed provisions, see McCrone, *Regional Policy*, pp. 131–36.
34. Ibid., p. 145.
35. Rents in government-owned factories were based not on the cost of the fac-

3. *Grants for machinery.* Payments amounting to 10 percent of the cost of machinery and equipment were offered, subject to the condition that employment be increased as a consequence of the expenditure.

4. *Grants for nonfactory building.* The same benefits offered for factory construction were extended to nonmanufacturing enterprises, including hotels, shops, and service establishments in general.

5. *Loans.* The loan provisions of earlier acts were liberalized by removing the requirement that an applicant must first demonstrate that he could not obtain financing from other sources.

6. *Grants for derelict land clearance.* Grants to local authorities were authorized for clearance of derelict land (principally mined-out areas) to make it available for industry.

7. *Tax incentives.* Most important, manufacturers in development districts were authorized in 1963 to depreciate investment in plant and machinery at any rate they chose.

During the period 1960–64 the Conservative government under the first five of these headings spent $335 million—more than triple the rate of expenditure of the Labour government in its peak years of 1947–49. Loans accounted for more than half of the $335 million, and factory construction for most of the remainder. Grants amounted to $55 million. The Board of Trade estimated that the expenditures would result in 154,000 jobs, created at a cost of less than $2,240 per job.[36]

More Controls, More Planning, More Benefits   (1964–70)

As the Conservative government was enacting its measures to revive national assistance to the depressed communities, the Labour opposition was attacking from the left. While chastising the Conservatives for let-

---

tory but on its commercial value, which reflected any disadvantages in its location. Thus, in theory, added costs imposed on companies were offset by the lower rent. Studies cited by Denton, Forsyth, and MacLennan, *Economic Planning and Policies,* p. 302, suggest that added costs imposed on firms moving to the development areas were in fact generally offset.

36. McCrone, *Regional Policy,* p. 145. In addition, an independent Development Commission, created in 1909 to encourage social and economic development of agricultural communities, had been authorized in the postwar period to build small advance factories. In mid-Wales, where much of its attention was concentrated, 1,500 people were employed in 1972 in eighteen commission-built factories, accounting for 3 percent of the area's employment. New town corporations also have authority to build advance factories, and so do local authorities.

ting the program lapse throughout the 1950s (conveniently forgetting that the reversal of policy after the war actually occurred during the Labour administration of Clement Attlee), Labour could only accept the Conservatives' proposals and pledge to do more when they were returned to power. They promised to enact new measures to stem the growth of London. They proposed to introduce a new element of regional planning into industrial development. And they committed themselves to exceed whatever benefits the Conservatives proved willing to extend to the depressed regions. When Labour won their majority in 1964, they had the opportunity to make good their promises.[37]

CONTROL OF OFFICE BUILDING

The "drift to the South" of the British population, if it had been slowed during the immediate postwar years of vigorous dispersal policy, started again during the relaxation of that policy in the 1950s. Between 1951 and 1961 the country's regions of out-migration—Scotland, Northern Ireland, Wales, and Northern England from Yorkshire and Lancashire to the Scottish border—lost a net total of 730,000 people to the South. Of those, 530,000 went to London and its South East region. Between 1953 and 1963 more than half of the new jobs created in Britain were in the South East. Just as the first objective set for the nation by bipartisan consensus in the 1940s—revival of the depressed areas—had not been accomplished, so the companion goal of checking the growth of London seemed headed toward failure.

The reasons were clear enough. Not only had the once-stringent control on factory building in the South been relaxed ("There is a fairly widespread feeling among industrialists that if they hold out long enough the Board of Trade will eventually allow them to build where they like, rather than where it wants them to go," the *Financial Times* observed in early 1959[38]), but London had entered upon its great postwar boom in

37. J. D. McCallum, "U.K. Regional Policy 1964-72," in Gordon C. Cameron and Lowdon Wingo, eds., *Cities, Regions and Public Policy* (Edinburgh: Oliver & Boyd for University of Glasgow and Resources for the Future, Inc., Washington, D.C., 1973), p. 271, has suggested that it was the development areas that "turned out" the Conservatives and elected Labour. In Scotland, Wales, and northern England the Conservatives lost 27.8 percent of their 1959 seats, in the rest of the country only 11.6 percent. If the latter figure had been sustained nationwide, the Conservative party would have retained power.
38. February 6, 1959; quoted in *Hansard*, Nov. 9, 1959, vol. 613, col. 57.

office building. By 1964 a total of 37 million square feet of office space had been built in Greater London since the war, adding more than 40 percent to total capacity. Already, London had three times as much office space as Birmingham, Manchester, Liverpool, Glasgow, and Edinburgh combined, yet proposals for another 25 million square feet had been approved by the London County Council. The South East region, which already had almost half the clerical jobs in the nation, had been increasing its clerical employment at a rate higher than that of any other region, and almost twice that of the development areas.[39]

The government had assumed that the London population could be stabilized through holding down industrial employment alone; "the tremendous growth in offices, service trades and white-collar jobs in industry . . . was not foreseen," a white paper acknowledged in 1963, and the office growth was bringing "formidable transport, housing, and financial problems in its wake."[40] The Conservative government had responded by promising to disperse additional government offices and by creating a Location of Offices Bureau, whose job it was to develop an inventory of available office space outside London and assist firms willing to move from the metropolis to find suitable quarters. Direct controls like those applied to factory construction had been rejected on the ground that when an office building was constructed—unlike a factory—its prospective tenancy and use were in most cases not known, and hence whether it had to be in London could not be judged.[41]

Such a voluntary approach had no appeal to Labour. Their method was direct and drastic action. "We should now put a fence round all these conurbations and put up a sign saying, 'Stop! No further industries must come in here,'" the party's spokesman had declared in the 1959 Local Employment Act debate. "If there is to be no control over the location of industries, then, in a short time, the mass of people in this country will be living in London and all the rest will be derelict."[42] Within the term *industry* he specifically included office buildings. Growth of all kinds would be frozen.

Accordingly, upon assuming power in 1964, Labour first imposed a

39. John Rhodes and Arnold Kan, *Office Dispersal and Regional Policy* (Cambridge: Cambridge University Press, 1971), p. 9.
40. *London—Employment; Housing; Land*, Cmnd. 1952 (HMSO, 1963), pars. 5 and 10.
41. Ibid., par. 18.
42. James Griffiths, *Hansard*, Nov. 9, 1959, vol. 613, cols. 51–54.

freeze on all new projects in the capital, then applied to office construction there the same direct control that had worked successfully (when strictly administered) to curtail factory building—defying the Conservative position that the two kinds of cases were decisively different. The criteria for issuance of office development permits would correspond to those for approving industrial development certificates. To win a permit, said the president of the Board of Trade in presenting his legislation, an applicant would have to show that his project was "essential in the public interest. . . . Mere inconvenience or extra cost [resulting from a location outside London] cannot be accepted as grounds for granting permits." The office building boom, he explained, had been "extravagantly increasing employment in the area, sucking in population from the rest of the country, depopulating other less fashionable areas, and imposing intolerable congestion of all kinds on those who live and work in and around London."[43]

The Conservatives demurred. They reiterated their reason for rejecting such controls when they were in power. Moreover, they argued, the office building market had since then become actually depressed, and rents were being cut. The Conservative approach of encouraging a voluntary exodus through its Location of Offices Bureau had worked: 116 firms had already moved 12,100 office jobs out of central London. Should the city be put in a "straitjacket" and not allowed to change? "It sounds . . . like the cry of despair from parents who tell their children to stop growing out of their clothes."[44]

But the bill passed. The office building controls, applied first in Greater London, were extended to the Birmingham conurbation in August 1965 and, a year later, to the whole of the South East, East Anglia (adjacent to the South East), and West Midlands (Birmingham) regions. By 1967, Greater London's share of the country's new office building construction, which had been running at over one-third of the total for England and Wales, began to decline. Rents rose. The combined effect of the controls, the work of the Location of Offices Bureau, and independent cost factors (no one has attempted to measure the relative importance of these influences) brought about a substantial flow of office jobs out of central London. Estimated at 1,000 jobs a year before the first governmental moves were taken, the figure rose to more than twenty times that num-

43. Douglas Jay, *Hansard*, Feb. 1, 1965, vol. 705, cols. 739 and 733.
44. John Hall, Conservative spokesman, *Hansard*, Feb. 1, 1965, vol. 705, col. 754.

ber by 1968, and to an estimated total of over 200,000 jobs in the period 1963–72. Of these, some 37 percent were relocated out of the city's heart but still within the Greater London conurbation. The remaining 130,000 were relocated outside Greater London. But most of those were to locations not far beyond the greenbelt, still within the region. Only 1 percent of the jobs went to the development areas.[45]

ENTER REGIONAL PLANNING

A heavily criticized feature of the Conservative government's regional policy had been its abandonment of the broad "development areas" as the basis of eligibility for assistance and the substitution of the smaller "development districts." Under this provision of the Local Employment Act of 1960, many of the larger cities that had been seen by the planners as the regional growth centers most suitable for development had been rendered ineligible. In 1963 this anomaly had come under potent criticism from the National Economic Development Council (a tripartite government-management-labor body augmented by academic experts that had been created to advise the government on economic policies).[46] It advocated a return to regionalism, the deliberate development of the relatively prosperous centers of those regions as "growth points," and the planning on a regional basis of the "social infrastructure" necessary to attract industry.

At the same time, two comprehensive studies initiated by the Conservative government itself were reaching the same conclusion. A regional plan for central Scotland, prepared by the Scottish Development Department, and the plan for the North East region of England compiled by a special commission organized from London, both published in November 1963, centered their development programs on "growth areas" or "growth zones."[47] These were the communities with the most favorable

45. Estimates of Gordon C. Cameron, in *Constraining the Growth in Employment of London, Paris and the Randstad—a Study of Methods* (Paris: Organisation for Economic Co-operation and Development [OECD], 1973), pp. 30–32. The Labour government relaxed controls in the 1967–69 period, removing them from East Anglia and the rural parts of the Midlands and raising the exemption limit from 3,000 to 10,000 square feet in the areas where they applied outside Greater London.

46. National Economic Development Council (NEDC), *Conditions Favourable to Faster Growth* (HMSO, 1963).

47. *Central Scotland: A Programme for Development and Growth,* Cmnd. 2188 (HMSO, 1963); and *The North-East: A Programme for Regional Growth and Development,* Cmnd. 2206 (HMSO, 1963).

prospects for industrial development, not necessarily the heaviest centers of unemployment in the region. Public investment—roads, docks, airports, water supply, housing, advance factories—would be concentrated there as the best means to facilitate the development of the entire region. New towns, authorized under legislation of 1946, would be constructed there (five of the eight growth areas in central Scotland were to be new towns). All of the communities of the regions would be gradually refurbished, as funds became available, but in the meantime the selected growth areas would be made attractive enough, both for industry and for community living, to enable the depressed regions to compete with the South.

The Labour party endorsed these concepts, and when it won office in 1964, it restored the regional basis for the provision of development assistance. It reestablished the old development areas, and in the process vastly enlarged them. All of Scotland except Edinburgh, the capital, was included in one area. The two areas on the opposite coasts of northern England were joined in a broad belt extending across the island. The old South Wales area was expanded to cover almost the whole of Wales. A new area in the South West encompassed Cornwall and part of Devon. Altogether, the assisted areas included over 40 percent of the land area of Britain and 20 percent of the population.[48]

Beyond that, the government took the first moves in the direction of a new regional level of government for England, not just for the depressed regions but for the whole country. (Scotland, Wales, and Northern Ireland already had regional status, the former two served by special ministries of the national government and Northern Ireland by its own parliament.) It divided England into eight regions and established two new bodies in each. Stopping short of establishing democratically elected regional assemblies or councils—an idea that had long had some measure of advocacy in Britain—it set up in each region an economic planning council, made up of some twenty-five to thirty citizens (representing industry, labor, local officials, academicians, and so forth) appointed by the government, and an economic planning board, consisting of the senior national officials in each region. The council was to prepare a strategic plan for the development of its region. It was to review annually the government's proposed investment programs and give its advice. It was to be consulted on major decisions affecting the region. And it was given

48. McCrone, *Regional Policy*, p. 126. Maps of the areas of 1945–60, the subsequent districts, and the new areas are on pp. 108, 123, and 127.

a general charter to initiate studies and make its views known. The council had no budget, but the board was to provide it with the necessary staff and with data and information available in the departments. In that sense the board was to serve the council, but since the council had no authority beyond rendering advice, it for the most part served the board, or the board members' superiors in London where the decisions on public investment were made.

EXPANSION OF BENEFITS

The principal program innovation of the new government was the introduction in 1967 of a continuing subsidy to manufacturing industries in the development areas to supplement the capital investment grants to which policy had previously been restricted. This took the form of a wage subsidy—made up mainly of a regional employment premium—in the amount of $5.25 a week for each adult male employed (reduced in 1970 to $3.60) with somewhat smaller sums for women and juveniles. The initial subsidy was estimated at 7–8 percent of the wage bill of the affected industries. It was seen as helpful particularly to the labor-intensive industries that the areas of surplus labor needed, and as a means of making the depressed areas truly competitive.

As for the capital investment subsidies, Labour introduced a new approach. It abolished both the special accelerated depreciation allowances for the development areas and the 10 percent grants for plant and machinery (but not the grant for buildings, which remained unaffected) and in their place offered a differential in a new "investment grant" that was being introduced nationwide. The grant was set first at 40 percent in the development areas and 20 percent in the rest of the country, then raised to 45 percent and 25 percent.[49] By shifting from tax concessions to grants, it was argued, the benefit would not be dependent on profitability in the early years; the new approach would thus be particularly advantageous in helping new entrepreneurs to get started and small firms to expand.

In the programs left unaltered, the government increased spending

49. When the regular tax allowances are added, the total benefits are even higher, but (since tax allowances apply only to the nongrant portion of the investment) the differential is reduced. At the time that the nominal allowances were 40 percent and 20 percent, for assisted and unassisted areas, Thomas Wilson calculated the actual benefits at 53 percent and 40.3 percent. McCallum, "U.K. Regional Policy 1964–72," p. 275.

and tightened controls. It expanded sharply the number of centers for the retraining of workers, and raised the grants paid to employers for on-the-job training. It reinvigorated the factory-building program at the rate of about forty new speculative factories a year. Total expenditures under the assistance programs were running at $550 million–$575 million a year by 1969.[50] In addition, the development areas were getting more than $240 million in infrastructure expenditures beyond what would be their per capita share of total government expenditures for the purpose.[51] More stringent policies were followed in the granting of industrial development certificates in the South. By 1966 the development areas had once again begun receiving more than half the new industrial construction in Great Britain.[52]

Finally, the Labour government refined the classification of areas, expanding the single category of development areas into a gradation of three zones. For the localities of heaviest unemployment—essentially the coal-mining districts whose distress originally gave rise to the British regional program—it reestablished a separate category of "special development areas" and offered liberalized benefits, principally these: a higher subsidy (35 percent instead of 25 percent) for factory construction there; an "operational grant" to new firms during their start-up years, negotiable in amount and related to employment; and free rent up to five years in state-owned factories. At the other end of the scale it responded to the pleas of communities that were suffering some distress but not enough to qualify them as development areas, by establishing a category of "intermediate areas." For fear of detracting from the benefits going to the development areas, however, the intermediate areas were initially kept small. They were granted only a portion of the assistance available to the development areas, mainly the 25 percent building grant.[53]

50. McCrone, *Regional Policy*, p. 144.
51. Gordon C. Cameron, "Regional Economic Policy in the United Kingdom," in Niles M. Hansen, ed., *Public Policy and Regional Economic Development: The Experience of Nine Western Countries* (Ballinger, forthcoming). By adding these and all other "regionally-differentiated" expenditures that could be identified, J. D. McCallum arrives at a grand total of $1.75 billion spent on regional policy in the two years 1968–69 ("U.K. Regional Policy," 1971; processed).
52. McCrone, *Regional Policy*, p. 147.
53. As a specialized approach to a unique area, the government also established in 1965 the Highlands and Islands Development Board with a broad grant of authority to assist in the economic and social development of seven Scottish counties. Its powers to make grants and loans and construct advance factories paralleled those exercised by the national Department of Trade and Industry in other development areas but it also had the power to acquire equity.

Challenge and Consensus   (*1970–72*)

At this point the issue between the parties was not whether Britain should have vigorous regional policies but what they should be. The Conservatives remained unreconciled to the Labour government's substitution of direct grants for the investment subsidies that the Conservatives had previously given through the tax route, through free or accelerated depreciation. They also opposed the regional employment premium. In their view, both the Labour measures tended to "subsidize inefficiency" and "prop up lame ducks,"[54] while tax allowances, since they were offset against profits, could only be earned by enterprises operating in the black. Efficient and profitable enterprises, they argued, were what the country needed. But Labour's position was exactly opposite. The profitable firm, the government contended, was the one that needed subsidy the least. Assistance programs should be designed to help especially the new or struggling industry, the money-loser that without the aid would have to lay off its workers and close its doors.

On this ground, the parties confronted each other in the 1970 general election campaign. Labour Prime Minister Harold Wilson termed the Conservative proposal to abolish investment grants "a callous prescription for creating derelict areas over vast areas of Britain," and spokesmen for industry in the development areas backed the Labour party in defending the regional employment premium as essential to making their areas competitive.[55] But the Conservative party was appealing to the country on a promise to cut waste, control spending, reduce taxes, stop inflation, and "get the Government off the backs of the people," and the investment grants (running at about $1.4 billion a year nationwide) and regional employment premium (about $240 million) were the most conspicuous places where large savings could be made and defended.[56] So, after their victory in the election[57] the Conservatives proceeded as

54. Chancellor of the Exchequer Anthony Barber, Conservative, *Hansard*, Nov. 4, 1970, vol. 805, col. 1097.

55. Wilson speech at Bristol, reported in *Times* (London), May 4, 1970; and statement of the North East Development Council, reported in *Times* (London), June 2, 1970.

56. McCallum, "A Review History." Of the $1.4 billion in investment grants, he estimates that $215 million was attributable to the regional differential.

57. Just as it was the development areas that turned the Conservative government out of office in 1964, McCallum notes, "U.K. Regional Policy 1964–72," p. 283,

planned. They scrapped the nationwide investment grants in favor of tax allowances in October 1970, and announced that the employment premium would be terminated in September 1974, when the seven-year commitment in the original legislation would expire.

These changes were presented not as any reversal of the philosophy underlying the regional programs but only as the means of making regional policy truly "effective." In the new schedule of tax allowances for the nation's industry, regional differentials were provided: the first-year depreciation on plant and equipment could be at any rate up to 100 percent in a development area but was held to 60 percent elsewhere, and depreciation on buildings was authorized at 40 percent in development and intermediate areas while held to 30 percent in the rest of the country before April 1972 and 15 percent thereafter. Moreover, some regional benefits were increased; the grants for industrial building construction (which had remained when the investment grants, covering machinery and equipment, were repealed) were raised from 25 percent to 35 percent in development areas and from 35 percent to 45 percent in special development areas. The operational grants payable in the latter areas were increased to 30 percent of eligible wage and salary costs for three years, and the number and size of those areas were increased. The government promised more flexible loan policies and larger grants for industrial development infrastructure and for clearance of derelict land. Taking all the changes into account, the government contended, the differential benefits that induced a manufacturer to locate in a depressed area would be about the same as under the Labour programs. Nevertheless, comparative figures presented by the government a couple of years later showed that the advantages had been in fact substantially reduced (see p. 64, below).

But the government could not have chosen a less propitious time for the elimination of the investment grants to industry. A slackening of economic activity, which had appeared before the election, continued to deepen, and unemployment rose by 1971 to the highest rate since the depression of the 1930s. Early in 1971 one of Britain's most prestigious companies, Rolls-Royce, went into bankruptcy. Some major shipbuilders verged on collapse. Labour made startling gains in the May local elec-

---

it was the prosperous areas that rejected Labour in 1970. Labour lost only 7 percent of its seats in the development and intermediate areas but 29 percent in the rest of the country. If they could have held their nationwide loss to 7 percent, they would have stayed in power.

tions. "The Government panicked," in the words of one observer. "Prime Minister [Edward T.] Heath made a tour of the regions and came back shaken," said another.[58] A government committed to withdrawal from intervention in the economy quickly became hardly less interventionist than its predecessor. The reversal was dramatized by a minor cabinet shake-up; several junior ministers in the Department of Trade and Industry who had been identified with the philosophy of disengagement were sacrificed and replaced by pragmatists who had no qualms about the role of government.

To expedite aid to areas hardest hit by the economic downturn, the special development areas were enlarged, once again encompassing major cities like Glasgow and Newcastle and their industrial suburbs, and the operational grants to new industries in those areas were liberalized. Entrepreneurs there could now get five years of free rent in the state-owned factories. The intermediate areas were also slightly expanded. Emergency financial assistance was extended to several giant individual firms and $240 million was allotted for additional public works in the regions. A new round of advance factory construction in the assisted areas was set in motion—which, when announced early in 1973, was described as bigger than any previous round, with 940,000 square feet of industrial space.

But, concerned about employment and production nationally, the government moved to help industrialists in the unassisted areas too, by relaxing controls—which, of course, offset to a degree the additional aid being given the development areas. The exemption limit for industrial development certificates was raised from 5,000 square feet to 10,000 square feet in the South East region, and marginal cases that had been decided in the negative during the Labour administration began to be decided in the affirmative.[59] In the other region where they had been stringently applied —the West Midlands—the government announced that they would be

58. Unattributed quotations in this and subsequent chapters are from persons interviewed during the course of this study in 1972 and 1973 who preferred not to be identified.

59. Marginal cases are decided by ministers, or by ministry officials in consultation with them, on the basis of criteria that have never been formalized and made public. Thus it is impossible to document a relaxation of controls. But it is understood by observers, and not denied by participants, that an administrative "relaxation" occurred with the change of government. Comparisons of the proportions of applications for industrial development certificates that are denied are of no help because during a period of stringent administration, many companies—sometimes after informal consultation with government officials—conclude that it would be pointless to present their proposals for formal denial.

freely available (unemployment there had risen to about the national average). Office building controls were also removed from Birmingham and the exemption limit raised to 10,000 square feet in London.

Then the Conservative government, in the Industry Act of 1972, reversed the course it had adopted in 1970. It returned to the use of the direct grants favored by Labour, and offered the regional incentives on a scale beyond what even Labour had dared. They abandoned the regional differentials in depreciation allowances (by extending to the whole country the previous favorable terms allowed the development areas) and provided instead for the development areas "regional development grants" for industrial investment (manufacturing, mining, and construction). These grants superseded and standardized the varied forms of assistance previously available to manufacturing industry in the assisted regions and improved the regional differentials. They were set at 20 percent in development areas and 22 percent in special development areas for both buildings and plant and equipment (reducing the former while restoring the latter). Moreover, companies were permitted to take their tax allowances on investment financed by the grants, so that for profitable companies the 22 percent was equivalent to 30 percent. The grants were automatic, and they were made available not only to new facilities but for modernization even if employment in the facility were not increased —or even if it were reduced. While the regional employment premium would be eliminated after 1974, as previously announced, the rate and phasing of its termination would be determined only after consultation with industry. Beyond these aids that were automatically available, the act also authorized "selective assistance" in the form of discretionary loans, loan guarantees, and grants. They were to be dispensed by a new Industrial Development Executive, staffed by industrialists brought into the civil service, with substantial discretion delegated to regional officials acting on the advice of boards of citizens. The selective assistance would be available to service as well as manufacturing establishments. Finally, the whole of the two planning regions embracing Lancashire and Yorkshire were classed as intermediate areas, adding the major centers of Manchester, Leeds, and Sheffield and bringing the share of the British population living in the assisted regions to 44 percent.[60] In intermediate

60. Adding Northern Ireland the assisted areas include 47 percent of the total United Kingdom population.

areas, the 20 percent grant was available only for buildings, not for machinery and equipment.

The Conservatives calculated the regional differential incentives, in percentages, in development areas as follows:[61]

	Labour program, 1970	*Conservative program*	
		1970	*1972*
Industrial buildings	19.2	25.8	19.0
Plant and equipment	13.7–12.8	2.0	19.0
Typical project	14.8–14.1	6.7	19.0

While the differentials for development areas under the new 1972 program exceeded those offered under the Labour government, the added incentives available in the special development areas as opposed to the development areas were narrowed. The operational grants were eliminated, and all that remained was the difference between 20 percent and 22 percent in the regional development grant. The system of incentives in effect in the various eligible areas in March 1974 is shown in Figure 2-1 and Table 2-1.

With the Industry Act of 1972, Britain after nearly half a century of experimentation with regional policy was very near consensus. The Confederation of British Industries and the Trades Union Congress both endorsed the principles embodied in the act. The Labour party could still express dissatisfaction, particularly on elimination of the regional employment premium, but welcomed the Conservatives' "retreat from dogma," in the words of Roy Jenkins, the deputy party leader.[62] As the Conservative government arrived at a position not far from that on which the Labour party had long been unanimous, there remained outside the national consensus only a minority wing of the Conservative party—a group led by Enoch Powell dedicated to laissez faire in regional policy as well as other economic matters. It was hopelessly outnumbered within the Conservative party in Parliament, but had somewhat more support in the party at large outside the assisted areas. No one in Britain, as of 1974, was predicting that Britain's regional policy would be abandoned

61. *Hansard*, April 19, 1972, vol. 835, col. 116. The typical project had an investment ratio of 20 percent in buildings, 80 percent in plant and equipment.

62. *Hansard*, March 22, 1972, vol. 833, col. 1533. The Labour government that took office in 1974 continued the regional employment premium and doubled the amount, which brought the payments to the same proportion of wages as when the subsidy was introduced in 1967.

Figure 2-1. *The Assisted Areas in Great Britain, Early 1974*[a]

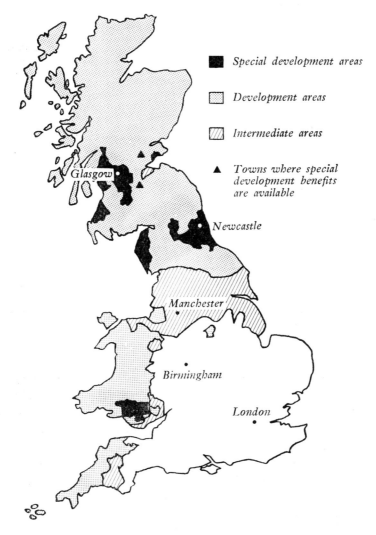

Source: *Local Employment Act—1972*, Report by the Secretary of State for Trade and Industry for the year ended 31 March 1972. (No changes were made in 1973 and the early months of 1974.)

a. The Orkney and Shetland Islands, which are not shown on the map, are classified as development areas.

Table 2-1. *Eligibility for Incentives and Disincentives, by Area,
in Great Britain, Early 1974*

	Area			
Government measure	Special development	Develop- ment	Inter- mediate	Remainder of Great Britain
Regional development grant Percent of cost of buildings allowed	22	20	20	o
Percent of cost of machiney and equipment allowed	22	20	o	o
Selective assistance	yes	yes	yes	no
Regional employment premium	yes	yes	no	no
Industrial development certificates required	no	no	yes[a]	yes[b]
Government factories for rent or sale, with possibility of rent-free period	yes	yes	yes	no

Source: U.K., Department of Industry and Central Office of Information, *Britain for
Industrial Growth—The Facts* (March 1974).
   a. Generally freely available.
   b. Freely available in some areas, such as the West Midlands.

unless and until the long-standing regional disparities were finally removed. But in the nature of things, *some* region or regions would always
be at a relative disadvantage, because the structure of a national economy
is never stable. "I expect to see regional policies at least as strong as the
present ones in force for the remainder of my lifetime," observed a young
civil servant–adviser to Conservative ministers on regional policy. His
view was the prevailing one. Not even Mr. Powell could express optimism
that his arguments in support of a return to laissez faire on matters of
population and employment distribution, no matter how well reasoned,
were likely to reverse the course that history had taken.

The Achievements of Regional Policy

What, then, could the elaborate—and expensive—structure of regional
policies be said to have achieved? The Expenditure Committee of the

House of Commons in 1972, after extensive hearings and analysis of what data the government could provide, concluded in exasperation:

There must be few areas of Government expenditure in which so much is spent but so little known about the success of the policy. The most our witnesses could say was that, although the imbalance persisted between assisted and non-assisted areas, they thought that the situation was better than it would have been without the incentives and controls of some sort of regional policy. Yet no one could say whether this effect was a major or minor one.[63]

In terms of the national objective of population dispersal, the proud boast of the advocates of British regional policy is that, sometime in the 1960s, net migration into the London region was, for probably the first time in British history, brought to a halt. The South East region, which includes the capital, lost between the censuses of 1961 and 1971 a net of 37,000 persons through migration to other parts of the country and to foreign countries, and the trend has been accelerating; between mid-1971 and mid-1972 the net loss was 29,300, which represented slightly more than half of the region's natural increase of 58,400.[64] This was in part, however, a statistical artifact, for the adjacent regions, East Anglia and the South West, have the country's highest rates of regional population growth, and among the areas growing most rapidly are the fringes of the London metropolis, which has outgrown its defined regional boundaries. The London region still has the heaviest stream of in-migrants, but they are more than offset by Londoners retiring to southwestern and East Anglian coastal towns or moving to long-distance commuter centers in the adjacent regions. Together the three regions gained 308,000 persons through migration in the 1961–71 decade, and another 22,000 in 1971–72. So while the drift to the South has been dispersed within the South, it has not been stopped.

Scotland lost 325,000 persons through out-migration in the 1961–71 decade; the northern region of England 108,000; the northwestern region 114,000; Yorkshire and Humberside 70,000. Only Wales, with a net loss of 4,000, seemed to have approached stability. Scotland lost 95 percent of its natural increase during the decade, the North 62 percent, the North West one-third. The annual migration figures for 1971–72 suggest the trend may have slowed a little: the loss that year for Scotland was 25,800,

63. *Public Money in the Private Sector*, Sixth Report from the Expenditure Committee, House of Commons, Session 1971–72, par. 172.

64. Since London is the principal recipient of foreign immigrants, the net loss of interregional British migrants was greater than 29,300. The figures on migration are from U.K., Government Statistical Service, *Abstract of Regional Statistics 1973* (HMSO, 1973), tables 10 and 11, pp. 18–20.

Figure 2-2. *Unemployment Rate in British Regions of High Unemployment as Ratio of National Rate, 1954–72*

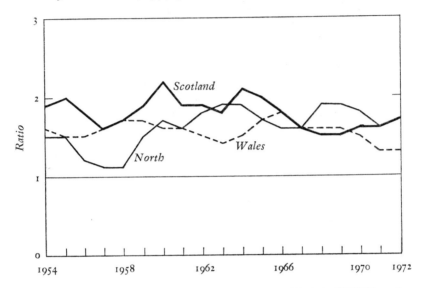

Source: U.K., Central Statistical Office, *Abstract of Regional Statistics* (HMSO), various years.

the North 6,700, the North West 16,000, and Yorkshire and Humberside 3,600, and Wales actually showed a net in-migration of 5,300. But it is too early to judge whether the new trend will be sustained or whether it is primarily a consequence of the cyclical recession in the country's economy during that period.

Nor have the regional programs solved the problem of depressed area unemployment that brought them into being. As Figure 2-2 shows, unemployment in the regions that have been the prime beneficiaries of regional policies has remained consistently above the average for Britain as a whole and the relationship in 1972, after a decade of vigorous regional policy, was not significantly improved over what it had been in the 1950s when regional policy was in abeyance.

Yet, obviously, neither of these sets of data is an absolute criterion for judging the effectiveness of regional policy. The question is, how much more population drift to the South would have occurred if vigorous regional policies had not been pursued? How much higher would the unemployment rates of the depressed regions have been? These ques-

Figure 2-3. *New Industrial Construction in Regions of High and Low Unemployment as Proportion of Total for Great Britain, 1954–70*[a]

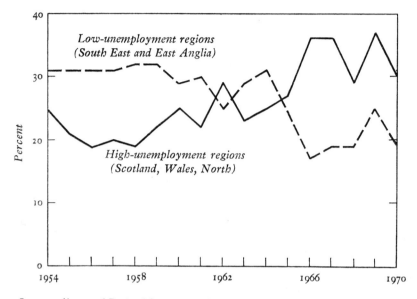

Source: *Abstract of Regional Statistics,* various years.
a. As determined by square-footage ratios.

tions cannot be answered precisely, but estimates have been made of the employment consequences of the new enterprises that government programs have steered into the development areas. Figure 2-3 shows the dramatic consequences of the invigoration of regional policy in the 1960s. The share of new industrial construction going into the London region and neighboring East Anglia was cut from over 30 percent a year to below 20 percent in four of the last five years of the 1960s, while Scotland, Wales, and the northern region of England rose from a combined share of around 20 percent to well over 30 percent.

Such a shift in investment was sure to have employment-generating and hence population-stabilizing consequences. Since the complaint of the Expenditure Committee about the scarcity of evaluative data about British regional programs, the results of three careful studies by British economists have become available. A. J. Brown, estimating the employment equivalent of the extra share of new industrial building going to the development areas, concludes that the regional programs were bringing the development areas by the late 1960s at least 30,000 jobs a year that they would not otherwise have gotten. The additional jobs in service occupations created by the 30,000 workers and their families brought the total to 50,000, "and the number could be considerably greater than this." Using an alternative approach (called "shift-share"), Brown compared employment in each major industrial classification in the development areas with what it would have been if each category had grown in those areas at only the national average rate. On this basis, he finds an excess growth of around 70,000 jobs a year for the period 1961–66, which he attributes to regional policy.[65]

Using a somewhat more elaborate version of the shift-share approach, Barry Moore and John Rhodes confirm that the development areas have experienced a growth in investment and employment substantially greater than would have occurred if their industries had expanded at only the national average rate. And they conclude that the excess growth began to appear in 1963, precisely when regional policy was invigorated. The extra investment, building up gradually year by year, had reached $220 million per year by 1970, and totaled by that time $700 million– $1 billion. The additional employment by 1971 they calculated at 150,000 in manufacturing industries, plus an estimated 70,000 jobs in service and other industries, for a total of 220,000 over the eight-year period. The fact that these gains coincided with the period of strong regional policy, whereas no excess growth occurred during the 1950–63 period when regional policy was weak, leads them to conclude "that a 'regional policy effect' has been legitimately identified."[66]

Robert S. Howard has calculated that companies moving to the depressed areas in the period 1966–70 brought an average of 24,000 new jobs a year. Since such movement was virtually nonexistent during the 1950s when regional policy was weak, he attributes the entire employment increase in migrant firms to regional policy. To this he adds 10,000 as the growth of existing firms beyond the national average for their respective industry groups, and applying the multiplier for employment

65. Brown's methodology and conclusions are set out in *Framework of Regional Economics*, pp. 292–301 and 317–18. His evaluation was part of a comprehensive review of British regional policy financed by the government and conducted for the National Institute of Social and Economic Research.

66. Moore and Rhodes, "Evaluating British Regional Policy," p. 99. They excluded shipbuilding and metal manufacturing in their computations since those industries were affected more by other national policies than by regional policy as such.

generated in service industries, he arrives at a total of 58,000 as the annual increase in employment brought about by regional policy in the late 1960s.[67]

In the absence of policy, Brown concluded, the migration flow to the South would have been twice as high. Unemployment in the development areas would have been 1–1.5 percentage points higher (Moore and Rhodes calculated 1.8 percent), which would have added 0.5 point to the national unemployment rate. That would have meant a loss of output in excess of $500 million a year, plus some uncalculated amount for lower labor force participation in the depressed areas.[68]

But how much, if any, of the $500 million gain in the gross national product may measure waste? Do measures like the industrial development certificate system that force manufacturers to locate their plants in places they would not freely choose impose resource costs on the economy? Lord Stokes, the chief executive of British Leyland Motor Corporation, was vehement in his testimony before a subcommittee of the Expenditure Committee: "You have cost us a fortune by making us set up factories in places which are quite unsuitable to have factories. You ruin our business, we try to make it survive." His company's factories were scattered in seventy-three locations, including Scotland and Wales, whereas the company would have preferred to concentrate its operations in the Midlands. "We had to put a factory up at Liverpool and we have to cart the bodies down to Coventry, so every night of the week there are hundreds of loads of car bodies coming down from Liverpool." Parts for a truck are carried from England to Scotland for assembly at a cost of $43 and another $96 is spent to bring the truck back to its market in southern England. "We send forth 30-ton lorries up from the Midlands every night to Scotland." In all, Lord Stokes estimated that the industrial development certificate policy was costing his company $180 million over a ten-year span, an amount far exceeding the total of the grants the company received for dispersing its factories.[69] Chrysler later told the same committee that locating a plant in Scotland instead of in Coventry cost it $19 million over eight years. "Our cars would be cheaper and we would sell more" if the expansion had taken place in Coventry, contended Gil-

---

67. Unpublished study, Department of Trade and Industry, 1973.
68. *Framework of Regional Economics*, pp. 336–37.
69. *Public Money in the Private Sector*, Minutes of Evidence, vol. 2, pp. 197–203 (May 19, 1971).

bert Hunt, the company's managing director.[70] Chrysler's parts flow
from England to Scotland and back again in what has been called "the
longest assembly line in Europe." Several other companies, however,
testified that their added costs in the development areas were more than
offset by the subsidies granted through the regional programs.[71]

In rebuttal to the automobile companies, government witnesses
pointed to the social and economic costs occasioned by congestion.[72] To
allow the automobile industry to site all its expansion in the Midlands
"would have created quite extraordinary serious problems of housing and
almost intolerable problems of skilled manpower," said one official. "I
am not sure it is right to assume that if manufacturers were allowed to
expand in an unfettered way in the area of their choice they would necessarily impose no penalty upon themselves, because they would contribute to an increasing congestion of every kind in that area," said another. "The essence of the problem here is that one may be imposing
private costs in certain circumstances in order to achieve certain public
benefits," said a third.[73] Brown has assembled evidence suggesting that
the supposed productivity increases arising from concentration of related
manufacturing enterprises and population in large centers are largely
mythical; what looks like higher productivity is often no more than a
higher-priced output reflecting higher operating costs. Quite apart from
the effects of government policy, the trend in individual industries in
Britain, he observes, has been toward dispersal rather than concentration.[74] The results of several studies of Scottish industry, Gordon C.

70. *Regional Development Incentives,* Minutes of Evidence and Appendices,
House of Commons, Session 1972–73, pp. 44 and 49.

71. *Regional Development Incentives,* Second Report, Session 1973–74, par. 34.

72. They also challenged the automobile companies' figures, which were un-
audited and unsupported by the detail that would be needed, said the committee's
report, in order for the conclusions to be "fully accepted." Ibid., par. 35.

73. Testimony of Sir Frank Figgures, director-general of the National Economic
Development Office; Sir Antony Part, Treasury Department; and P. Le Cheminant,
Department of Trade and Industry, ibid., vol. 3, pp. 523, 553, and 665.

74. Brown, *Framework of Regional Economics,* pp. 147–56. All of the estimates
of the employment effects of regional policy are based on comparison of the rate
of job creation in the development areas during periods before and after regional
policy was strengthened in the early 1960s. The spontaneous trend toward decentralization was presumably operative during both periods; hence the increase in the
rate is attributed to regional policy. Moreover the spontaneous dispersal of industry
prior to the 1960s was primarily from more congested to less congested areas within
the prosperous southern and Midlands sections of England, so that the subsidies and
other elements of regional policy can be credited with bringing about decisions to
disperse plants to more distant locations in the depressed areas; Howard, in unpublished study.

Cameron reports, "all seem to point to the conclusion that the costs of developing in an assisted area are not significantly different from operating in a prosperous core region." For the typical company higher transportation costs, of the kind cited by the automobile manufacturers, were not a significant fraction of total costs. But in view of the "conflicting evidence, . . . we cannot measure the loss of output, and perhaps more critically of exports, due to a higher cost level imposed on companies."[75]

If total benefits were difficult to calculate, apportioning them among programs was even more difficult. The Expenditure Committee complained in particular that little effort had been made to quantify the comparative value of spending for infrastructure and spending in direct subsidies.[76]

Yet even the exchequer costs themselves were uncertain. Direct expenditures for regional programs could be calculated—they amounted to about $650 million in 1971–72—but several types of expenditure were concealed in other figures. These included differential expenditure on infrastructure and assistance to particular industries, such as coal and shipbuilding, which while national in scope were concentrated in the assisted areas. On the other hand, the expenditure total took no account of "clawback"—that is, the increased tax revenue generated by the assisted projects and the reduction in unemployment benefits—which Moore and Rhodes calculated at close to $400 million a year during the period 1963–70.[77]

The Expenditure Committee itself, after reviewing all of the cost and benefit data offered by Brown, Moore and Rhodes, Department of Trade and Industry economists, and others that had been made available since its 1972 report, expressed no less frustration the following year:

> There are significant areas of obscurity where the light has still to shine. . . . Much has been spent and much may well have been wasted. Regional policy has been empiricism run mad, a game of hit-and-miss, played with more enthusiasm than success. We do not doubt the good intentions, the devotion even, of many of those who have struggled over the years to relieve the human consequences of regional disparities. We regret that their efforts have not been better sustained by the proper evaluation of the costs and benefits of the policies pursued.[78]

75. Cameron, *Constraining the Growth in Employment*, pp. 23–25.
76. *Regional Development Incentives*, Second Report, pars. 104–05.
77. Ibid., pars. 9 and 12.
78. Ibid., par. 170.

The Question of Selectivity

The suspicion that the British regional programs are unnecessarily wasteful was widely held in the country in the early 1970s. In the view of some supporters of regional policy, the one thing that could eventually destroy the national consensus in favor of that policy is its cost, which was expected to exceed $1 billion a year in direct assistance when the Industry Act was in full operation.[79] "The consensus could vanish fast," said a senior official, "when some future government feels itself under compulsion to cut back spending and is looking for somewhere to get a big chunk of money quickly." The danger is heightened to the degree that any of the spending appears unnecessary to achieve the ends sought. This has raised, as a particular aspect of the cost-effectiveness problem, the question of whether substantial sums could be saved if regional benefits were administered more selectively. Advocates of greater selectivity point to the assistance being given to the oil industry and its suppliers to establish facilities in Scotland, for example, as an unnecessary expenditure for the purpose sought; since the oil is being pumped off the Scottish coast, the facilities would be established in the region in any case. And they point out that the investment in Scotch whiskey distilleries would surely take place in any event, for "where else, indeed, could Scotch be made?"

Ideally, if cost were the only criterion, each company would be given only the marginal amount of assistance necessary to induce it to locate its investment in the desired area. A company that would locate there anyway—like the oil companies in Scotland—would get none. A project that could be induced for only 5 percent of its investment would get 5 percent, another might get 10 percent, while only those that needed the maximum grant of 20 percent or 22 percent would get it. In a system of

79. The government estimated that regional development grants would reach an annual level of $650 million by 1976–77 and the special assistance loans and interest relief grants on private loans would reach $140 million. Ibid., par. 11. The regional employment premium would add another $230 million–$240 million at the pre-1974 rate, and the doubling of the premium in 1974 will put the total annual subsidy well over $1 billion if the grant and loan estimates prove accurate. The special assistance loans are offered at 2 percentage points below the market interest rate and may be interest free for up to three years. In the first year of the act the usual forgiveness was for one or two years. The tendency appeared to be toward using the interest subsidization of private loans as the principal form of aid, since that procedure requires less outlay of government funds.

uniform grants, by contrast, the maximum aid level necessary to induce the firm at the margin to locate in the development area provides a windfall to every one that would have located there with a lesser incentive or none at all.

In other countries, such as France and Italy, officials do negotiate the level of assistance to be granted in individual cases, and most grants are in amounts well below the authorized maximum percentages. But in Britain, to place such discretion in administrative officials has been rejected as counter to the ideal of equity. Where the public treasury is concerned, the argument has been, all citizens are entitled to equal treatment. Discrimination on the basis of need would penalize the efficient, reward the inefficient, and alter competitive relations within an industry. A standardized benefit available to all is simplest to organize and supervise, and it enables an entrepreneur to make precise cost calculations in planning his investment. So the assistance programs, up to the Industry Act of 1972, tended to set standard levels of benefits available to all. All factories received the same rate of subsidy. Modernization projects were given the same benefits as new construction. Even the requirement that a subsidized project must increase employment was removed, so that installation of labor-saving equipment received the same assistance as investment that created employment.

The authors of the 1972 act sought a device that would introduce selectivity in some benefits but would, at the same time, be accepted as meeting the test of equity. The solution they chose was a form of collective and semipublic decision making. The regional officials who administer the "selective assistance" provisions of the act—that is, reduced-interest loans with flexible interest payment moratoriums—are required to act on the advice of boards of local citizens. In practice, the board has to agree before the loan is made, because any approval given over the board's objection would become a matter of public knowledge and a potential source of embarrassment. In the first two years of the program's operation, this structure of shared responsibility appeared to be providing an acceptable way of bringing an element of discretion and selectivity into the loan program while protecting the applicants against arbitrary and inequitable decisions. But the approach was being applied to only a relatively minor part of the total regional assistance expenditures. If it contained a suggestion as to how the major program—the regional development grants—might ultimately be made more selective, there was no public indication that the suggestion was being pursued by the leadership of either major party.

London and the Service Sector

Whether the drift to the South can be stopped appears to depend mainly on what happens in that sector of the economy that was somewhat belatedly recognized as crucial in the mid-1960s—the nonmanufacturing, or service, sector. Since the invigoration of the regional program in the 1960s, the development areas have more than held their own in manufacturing; between 1965 and 1971, when employment in manufacturing declined by 428,000 in the country, only 15,000 of the loss was accounted for by the three regions made up wholly or predominantly of development areas—Scotland, Wales, and northern England. Almost half of the total loss was in the South East region centered on London. But in the service sector, the picture was quite the opposite. The three depressed regions lost 64,000 jobs while the rest of the country gained 55,000.[80]

The government's regional policy had been based all along on the assumption that service jobs were geographically related to the basic industries of manufacturing, agriculture, and mining, and that if manufacturing were dispersed, service jobs would therefore follow. The theory was correct for a large part of the service sector—retail distribution, transport and communication, and so on. But many service organizations, like manufacturers, serve a national market. This is especially true in the most rapidly growing employment categories in the whole economy—professional and scientific employment; insurance, banking, and finance; and public administration and defense.

The success in dispersing factories had resulted from the combination of controls and incentives, but neither instrument was nearly so powerful in dealing with service industries. The office development permit system set up to parallel the industrial development certificate mechanism was gradually dismantled, by governments of both parties, until in 1973 it applied only to the London conurbation. Even when in its fullest operation, this control succeeded only in pushing developments a short distance out of London or Birmingham; the number of relocations into the

---

80. The service sector is defined here as employees in all classifications except agriculture, forestry, fishing, mining, quarrying, and manufacturing.

development areas has never been significant. Indeed, despite some of the rhetoric that surrounded its introduction, the permit system was never administered primarily as a regional development measure, as were the industrial controls, but essentially as anticongestion measures; they have been the responsibility not of the government department charged with industrial dispersal but of the department charged with physical planning. Since much of the South East is not congested, the planners have found no good reason to deny office buildings in the peripheral parts of the region that would take the pressure off central London—provided the developments were properly planned. The next step in that logical sequence is to rely on planning controls entirely, and so the permit system came to be scrapped—except in the London region, the one locality where the existence of congestion could hardly be denied.

The control program in London presents the government with a continuing dilemma. The virtual ban on new office building construction during the early years after Labour imposed controls resulted in rents climbing to what Londoners claim are the highest levels in the world. This threatens London's ability to compete for the headquarters and European branch offices of financial institutions and other multinational corporations that the City of London has been counting on to make it the financial and commercial capital of the European Community, and, said one official, "the Lord Mayor is screaming." To restrict building means that existing office space is allocated among competing claimants on the basis of who can afford to pay the highest rentals, and this is seen as being neither equitable nor in the country's broader interest. Yet to permit unrestricted expansion would be to reverse the policy of deconcentration of jobs and population to which Conservatives as well as Labourites are firmly pledged. Accordingly, the Conservative government that came to power in 1970 tried to steer a middle course between holding down construction and holding down rents. It announced in 1972 that controls would be retained but in their administration "special account would be taken of the importance of enhancing the prospects of London as an international financial and commercial centre."[81] In practice, this has meant a relatively free policy in allowing buildings intended for known tenants, particularly corporations constructing their own office buildings, while speculative buildings have been uniformly dis-

81. *Industrial and Regional Development*, Cmnd. 4942 (HMSO, 1972).

allowed. The government, troubled by the double standard, weighed the adoption of some means by which a limited number of speculative buildings might be permitted—perhaps through an auction method—but took no action. The net result, however, was a considerable relaxation of the early stringency. Authorized new space in 1970–72 amounted to a net of over 20 million square feet in central London and 60 million in the South East as a whole—well over twice as much as in the last three years of Labour.[82] The permits did not measure the square footage that would actually be constructed, of course, because the projects still had to be cleared through the local planning process. In the jurisdiction of the Greater London Council, less than half of the space awarded development permits had by 1973 received planning clearance.[83]

An incentive system for service dispersal as strong as that available for manufacturing has not been devised. For a time in the 1960s, the building grant was available for a nonmanufacturing enterprise on the same terms as for a factory if it provided at least fifty jobs and did not exist mainly to serve local needs. The major inducement for location of factories, however, was not the building grant but the grant for plant and machinery, which on the average accounts for 80 percent of manufacturing investment. A comparable inducement for the location of a corporation headquarters would therefore require a much higher building grant than the one that was offered for factories. That idea has been rejected by successive governments, partly because of the high cost and partly because the experience of the 1960s showed that a building grant in any feasible amount would not be likely to lure any significant volume of office jobs out of London; speculative office builders would be loath to proceed in development areas without evidence of demand from prospective tenants, but London tenants would have little inducement to create demand because the grant would be given to the builder, not to them. Recognizing that a new approach must offer incentives directly to tenants, the government in June 1973 introduced for the first time a significant subsidy for them—a grant of up to $2,000 for each office employee transferred to an assisted area, and a rent subsidy covering the full cost of three years' rental in an intermediate area and five years' in a development area.[84]

82. Cameron, *Constraining the Growth in Employment*, table 4.

83. *Economist* (London), March 24, 1973.

84. Rhodes and Kan, *Office Dispersal*, pp. 84–97, recommend a selective incentive system, extension of the office development permit system to all of the South East and the Midlands, and a program of advance office building construction.

In one part of the service sector, of course, the government has complete control. That is the part made up of the government's own activities. In 1962 the Conservative government initiated a plan to disperse 14,000 government jobs out of the London area; the subsequent Labour government continued that program and decided also that new government activities would, wherever possible, be headquartered outside the capital. As the consequence, the number of headquarters-type jobs in central London (that is, excluding those in offices serving only London or its region) has remained approximately constant while the number outside of London has almost doubled.[85] In 1970 when the Conservatives returned to office, they commissioned a study that resulted, in 1973, in recommendations for the dispersal of another 31,000 jobs, which would leave only a third of government headquarters employment in the inner city, and another 20 percent in the suburbs and elsewhere in the South East. The author of the plan, Sir Henry Hardman, concluded that the development areas were so far from London that relocation there would result in unacceptable loss of efficiency, and he was able to recommend only 1,200 jobs for Scotland and 2,100 for the northern region.[86] But the Labour government, when it announced approval of the plan in August 1974, raised those figures to 7,000 and 4,500, respectively. The 12,000 proposed by Hardman for movement from London to other locations in the South East was reduced to 850. The civil service unions responded by "threatening militant action."[87]

Despite this bold decision by the new government, the sense of urgency that originally surrounded—and to a remarkable extent still surrounds—the industrial dispersal program seems to be lacking in consideration of the service sector. The pressure from the depressed regions is less; they still think of development primarily in terms of factories. And the means are unclear; few people are confident as to how to go about decentralizing service activities like banking and insurance. But the important factor appears to be a subtle and gradual change in both official and public attitudes about the need for a vigorous policy for restraining the growth of London—a need once taken for granted by all concerned, including the capital's own local politicians. Echoes of the old rhetoric

85. Cameron, *Constraining the Growth in Employment*, p. 35.
86. *The Dispersal of Government Work from London*, Cmnd. 5322 (HMSO, 1973).
87. *Economist* (London), Aug. 3, 1974, p. 18.

about congestion in the capital can still be heard—but few words of genuine alarm. Little fresh enthusiasm is evident for doing anything about it, and what there is is largely canceled by those who warn against doing too much about it.

One reason for this reversal of the public attitude appears to be the drastic scaling down of the projected increase in the country's total population. In the mid-1960s, British planners foresaw the necessity of accommodating an increase of 16 million in England and Wales in the period between 1971 and 2001—to reach a total population of 66 million. Alarmed at the prospect, the government launched studies of several seacoast areas to determine whether major new conurbations might be built there to help absorb the millions of additional Britishers. When the South East planning team was organized, it assumed the need to plan for a possible 4.5 million additional persons in its region alone. But then the outlook changed. The birthrate turned down and has continued steadily downward. By 1972 the estimate of 66 million at the end of the century had been revised to 55 million. To accommodate the additional 200,000 a year that is now in prospect, no urgent measures seem required. Moreover, the new estimates of population growth, like those of the mid-1960s, are widely expected to prove too high. In 1972 the natural increase for England and Wales was only 131,000, down from 216,000 the year before and 373,000 in 1966–67; and as emigration and immigration were in approximate balance, the total increase was less than 0.3 percent. The South of England can absorb some additional population, and if the natural increase is approaching zero, then perhaps internal migration need not be so vigorously discouraged. No British government has ever proposed to try to halt interregional migration altogether or to set anything like precise population targets for particular regions—not even governments that have been most vigorous in trying to stop the drift to the South.

Successful planning in the London region is a second factor serving to reduce pressure for measures to curtail growth. The original demand for restraining growth was a reaction not just to bigness itself but to the way in which London was getting bigger. In the prewar years London had grown through the usual process of urban sprawl, the formless spreading of the conurbation over the open countryside. But since the war, in a triumph of urban planning, sprawl has been conquered. London is now girdled by a greenbelt preserved in perpetuity against development; the city proper has been losing population and will continue to do so, because of planning controls on the use of limited land and the reduction of residential density. Beyond the greenbelt, growth is confined to areas designated by the planners, largely in new towns and other clusters separated from one another by protected open space. Under these circumstances the South East region is seen still to have considerable capacity to absorb population in an orderly distribution pattern. Those who would be appalled at the thought of adding another half million people on the edge of the London conurbation do not feel the same concern at the addition of that number in well-planned new towns in Hampshire or East Anglia. The new population can be added there without significantly aggravating anybody's feeling of congestion—particularly if the new towns can be largely self-contained and commuter traffic to and from London is therefore not significantly increased. The planning team for the South East asserted that the region could "cope satisfactorily" with a population increase of even more than 4.5 million in this century while preserving the amenities of the countryside and even promoting greater agricultural productivity.[88]

Finally, the very success of policies to restrain metropolitan growth has created new problems that cast doubt on those policies. A Greater London Council committee warned in 1969 that "there must come a point" when the continuing decline in London's labor force "could be positively harmful to the . . . many industrial and commercial concerns which have good cause to be in London and cannot be moved elsewhere without high cost or significant loss of efficiency."[89] Among concerns that might be affected were the multinational enterprises that London wished to attract. In order to free labor the council would still encourage the relocation of "nonconforming" industry, and it was spending substantial sums of its own money to purchase sites for redevelopment. But the composition of the freed labor force did not necessarily match the changing job requirements. The dockers could hardly be retrained in any great number for office jobs, and as they and other skilled industrial workers were forced out of the city by the loss of industrial employment, they were being replaced in substantial proportion by low-skilled and

88. South East Joint Planning Team, *Strategic Plan for the South East* (HMSO, 1970), pars. 10.4–10.6.
89. *Report of the Strategic Planning Committee* (Greater London Council, March 7, 1969), p. 2.

low-paid immigrants. London was seen as "going the way of American cities"—changed in social, economic, and racial composition, its tax base eroded while the demand for services rose.

This problem of structural dislocation extended to the rest of the South East as well. British policy remained one of discouraging manufacturing in the entire region; a firm forced out of London was not to be allowed to come to rest within the region, even in one of the new towns that the government itself was fostering, if it was considered "mobile"— that is, if it could not prove that it was dependent on a South East location in order to be competitive. First priority in relocation still went to the assisted areas. So as industry migrated, substantial pockets of jobless workers were left stranded, not only in London but elsewhere in the South East. If the region's unemployment *rate* was low, its unemployment *total* still exceeded that of any of the assisted regions. The representatives of the London and South East workers began to talk in terms reminiscent of those who had spoken for the displaced coal miners of the 1930s. Was it equitable and humane that they should be uprooted from their homes and forced to migrate north? Inevitably, London politicians reacted as Scottish and Welsh politicians had responded a generation earlier. The Greater London Council reversed its position and the cry of "work to the workers" was heard again.

With the objective of controls on London called into doubt on so many counts, the Conservative government found it easier to respond to a political and administrative fact of life: direct controls are inevitably onerous and unpopular. Giving assistance to investors in the development areas has been the pleasant part of regional policy; that makes friends among the beneficiaries without arousing enmity elsewhere. But denying industrial development certificates is just the opposite; it makes enemies among those denied permission, and their employees, with no offsetting gain of friendship in other places. "How do you tell a man he can't build an addition to his plant when he says he has the land and wants to employ a thousand people, and the people need jobs?" asked a member of Parliament. "We've had to say, 'No, mate, you can't have it,' but it's tough." Moreover, the experience has been frustrating, because the entrepreneur can expand by crowding more activity into his existing space or by buying or leasing vacant facilities elsewhere in the region—which may be less suitable, less efficient, and less pleasant for the employees. Or he may simply wait—one company waited seven years—until the government relents. One study showed that four-fifths of the projects that were denied industrial development certificates in the West Midlands and the South East eventually went ahead anyway.[90]

As part of its effort to reduce controls on the economy when it came to power in 1970, the Conservative government liberalized the administrative rules governing issuance of industrial development certificates and office development permits, intending that the regions of high unemployment be helped primarily through direct assistance. Nevertheless, the policy of restraining the growth of the South East was by no means abandoned; industries that were truly mobile still could not be located there. Conservatives still defended the system of industrial development certificates as essential to prevent inflationary pressure on the London labor market. The Labour party has been more consistently in support of the certificate system, and in 1972, while out of power, it even suggested a new and additional measure of restraint—a "congestion levy" imposed on all employment in zones declared "congested." This would function as a kind of negative regional employment premium to "provide active encouragement to firms to move from congested areas."[91] Whether the whole of the South East would be considered congested was not made clear.

If the tone of urgency has disappeared from discussion of the growth of London and its region, political support seems nevertheless sufficient to prevent any abrupt and overt change at any time soon in the official policy of restraint, at least on industrial development. Not only does the policy have the backing of the assisted areas, which include almost half the country's population, but it has had—and probably will continue to have—the support of a majority of the public in the South East as well. Small town and suburban dwellers, in particular, treasure their green countryside and resist the intrusion of new factories, with their accompanying truck traffic and pollution. It is public opinion in the suburban counties that has preserved the London greenbelt against the pressure of developers, even beyond the point that might be dictated by what the planners consider sound planning principles. The combined political weight of these groups will probably suffice to sustain the objective of restraining the growth of employment and hence of population

90. Brown, *Framework of Regional Economics*, p. 303.
91. Labour party, *Labour's Programme for Britain* (1972), p. 117. As of late 1974, the new Labour government had not acted to institute such a tax.

in South East England, for a long time to come. But perhaps greater reliance will be placed on planning procedures as the essential tool—possibly supplemented by a congestion tax—and less dependence on the direct control devices of industrial development certificates and office development permits.

The Issue of New Regional Institutions

When the Labour government in 1965 created England's first country-wide system of regional institutions—the economic planning councils (made up of private citizens and local officials, usually twenty-five to thirty in number) and economic planning boards (made up of senior government officials)—the action was presented as only the first in a series of steps to be taken to devolve decision making to the regions. Ultimately, there was to be an elected regional government, with limited powers. But the further steps were not taken, and before Labour left office it appeared to have lost much of its enthusiasm for the original experiment. During its term in office, the Conservative government retained the boards and councils but did not commit the country to any further devolution.

The institutional weaknesses of the economic planning councils are many. They lack legitimacy: the members are intended to be representative of industry, labor, local governments, and other interests concerned with economic development but they are nevertheless appointed by and wholly responsible to the national government. They lack authority: they are appointed to advise, and are given no power to decide anything. They lack resources: they have no budget, and when they need assistance they are obliged to call on government agencies to assign staff to them as an additional and usually secondary duty. They are even inhibited from communicating with individuals and groups outside the council, because much of the information they receive as council members about matters pending for national government decision is given them in confidence. "Some able people" who were attracted to the councils in 1965 "quickly lost interest when they found that they were given no real authority or influence," a royal commission observed in 1973.[92]

92. *Report of the Royal Commission on the Constitution, 1969–1973*, Cmnd. 5460 (HMSO, 1973), vol. 1, par. 280.

The economic planning boards, similarly, have no decision-making power. They are a device that occasions regional officials to meet and exchange information more often than they otherwise would—which is useful—but the line of responsibility from each official to his London superior remains as before, and there is no pooling of departmental powers in any official form of collective responsibility at the regional level.

When the councils set out on their initial task—the preparation of regional "strategic" plans—London could offer them nothing beyond the most general guidance as to how regional economic planning was to be accomplished and, inevitably, each went its own way. The result was a diverse set of documents. In general, they were strong on inventories of resources and diagnoses of problems but weak on innovative and specific solutions; one was described by a critic from another region as "not much more than an industrial development brochure." The plan developed by one region, the West Midlands, was formally rejected by the Department of the Environment.[93] Since then, the councils have carried out some supplementary studies but "their light now burns dimly,"[94] as they work without funds or staff of their own, neglected by the central government.

Recognizing the weaknesses of the councils, the Labour government, when it decided in the late 1960s that the time had come for truly comprehensive and specific regional planning, had to turn elsewhere to get it done. It turned, naturally, to where the authority, the legitimacy, and the staff resources all lay—to the national and local administrative bodies. For the second round of regional planning, governments have relied on "joint planning teams"—that is, temporary, ad hoc task forces made up of professional planners and other experts drawn primarily from national and local governmental staffs. Each team works under the general direction of a steering committee from the region, on which the economic planning council is represented. The first such venture, which has become the model for the others, produced in 1970 a highly specific plan for the South East.[95] The plan amounts, as it were, to a population distribution plan for London and its surrounding counties, plotting the size and location of new towns, the location of industry and of greenbelt,

93. Jesse Burkhead, "Federalism in a Unitary State: Regional Economic Planning in England," *Publius*, vol. 4 (1974), p. 51.
94. William Thornhill, *The Case for Regional Reform* (London: Nelson, 1972), quoted in ibid., p. 51.
95. *Strategic Plan for the South East.*

and so on. Accepted by the local authorities and approved by the national government, the plan is being enforced by both governmental levels to channel the region's growth. Planning teams were subsequently organized for the North West, the West Midlands, East Anglia, and Scotland, and the rest of the country would be covered as regional officials of the Department of the Environment won the necessary local interest and cooperation.[96] But when regional plans are completed, no body exists at the regional level to keep them up to date and monitor their execution—except for the economic planning councils and boards with their recognized inadequacies.

A modest proposal to establish effective and continuing regional planning machinery was put forward in 1969 by the Royal Commission on Local Government in England. It suggested the conversion of the planning regions into "provinces" and the replacement of the economic planning councils by "provincial councils." Of the council members, 75–80 percent would be elected indirectly (by the local governmental authorities), the remainder appointed. The new councils would assume the responsibility for "strategic" land-use planning and would have a reserve authority to administer any functions that might be considered regional in scope. But since the decisions as to what was regional in scope would be made by a council dominated by representatives of local authorities, it could only undertake functions that were in effect delegated by those authorities.

Some within the Labour government then in power were prepared to go much further. Anthony Crosland, the minister of local government and regional planning, proposed directly elected regional governments with authority for health and water supply as well as planning. But no action was taken, and when the Conservatives assumed power the next year they shelved the proposal pending its review by another royal commission that had been set up specifically to consider the question of devolution of power from Westminster, particularly to the separate "nations" of Scotland and Wales.

That commission, reporting in 1973, stopped short of even its predecessor's recommendations on regionalization. While recommending the creation of legislative assemblies for Scotland and Wales, it found that "there is no public demand for English regional assemblies with legislative

96. The West Midlands team is made up almost entirely of local authority planners, in a departure from the "joint" pattern.

powers, whether under a federal system or otherwise" and that the range and volume of regional functions were not sufficient "to justify an additional tier of elected government." Accordingly, the majority recommended "regional councils" much like the ones proposed in 1969, composed predominantly of members elected by local governments but with one-fifth appointed by the central government to represent industry, commerce, trade unions, education, and other interests. The councils would "play an important part in the formulation of broad economic and land-use strategy" for the regions, would review and comment on local plans, and would appoint members to ad hoc regional bodies created to provide particular governmental services. But they would themselves administer no services, and they would be dependent on the local authorities for funds and staff.[97]

The initial reaction of the national authorities to this proposal was cool. From the standpoint of both the political leaders and departmental officials, regional bodies appointed by and wholly responsible to London —such as the existing economic planning councils—have distinct advantages over councils made up predominantly of locally elected members, whether those members are chosen directly by the people or indirectly by local governments. The existing councils have provided for ministers a useful source of advice, particularly on spending plans; probably every council can point to at least some instance where its review resulted in a timely change in a proposed project or in spending priorities. A minister in doubt as to the best course of action on a particular matter has had available a competent sounding board of regional opinion, enabling him to float trial balloons in private and thus, if they were shot down, to avoid public embarrassment. At the same time, the councils have been safe, from London's viewpoint. While they have sometimes been assertive about their "right" to review government proposals in advance of their adoption—a right accorded them in their initial charters —their claims have not been enforceable whenever government departments believed they had good reason for withholding information. The

97. *Report of the Royal Commission on the Constitution, 1969–1973*, vol. 1, pars. 1195–1209. This position was taken by eight of the thirteen members. Two members, who did not sign the report, proposed strong and directly elected English regional governments with legislative powers; two recommended regional assemblies without legislative powers but with the members directly rather than indirectly elected, and one wanted no regional instrumentalities beyond coordinating committees of local authorities.

councils have been independent enough to serve the government's purposes, but not so strong and independent as to confront the government
—as locally elected councils might. An elected council might, indeed, fall
into the hands of the political opposition and, if it disagreed with the
government on an issue, it might take its case to the people and marshal
public support against the government.

The commission's proposal, if it disturbed the central authorities,
was presumably well calculated to mollify the other strong potential
source of opposition—the local governments—by giving them control.
As would be expected, the local authorities have traditionally fought
any suggestion for a new regional level of government that might assume
any local governmental powers or impose a new layer of supervision and
review between them and the national government. They find the traditional channels of national-local relationships familiar and on the whole
satisfactory, if not always devoid of aggravation.

But critics of the system contend, quite properly, that comfort for
national and local officialdom should be one of the lesser objectives of
institutional design. Measuring the system by other criteria, they find it
defective. These critics, who include the two-man dissenting minority of
the Royal Commission on the Constitution, contend that an additional
level of government can be justified by the range of functions for which
the national government is too remote and the local governments (even
as recently reorganized into larger units) too small—functions now administered by field offices of central government agencies and by the
many ad hoc authorities that exist in the various regions. The latter, the
commission itself found, were widely criticized as making their decisions
"behind closed doors . . . without the restrictions that would be imposed
by a framework of public accountability."[98]

Economic development as such was not discussed in the reports of
the two royal commissions. Those studies recognized that one of the
purposes of regional land-use planning would be to facilitate economic
growth through the design of industrial infrastructure, but whether
a new level of government might have a major role in inducing private
investment to utilize the infrastructure was not discussed in the reports,
nor has it been the subject of much active consideration elsewhere. Occasionally a voice is heard to suggest that a body made up of a region's

98. Ibid., par. 872.

own leadership, with funds at its disposal—such as the "selective assistance" authorized by the Industry Act of 1972—would have greater capacity than central governmental officials stationed in the regions to conceive projects, stimulate local entrepreneurship, and overcome obstacles to development.[99] The Labour government, before it left office in 1970, was considering the establishment of an economic development corporation, patterned on Italian models (see chapter 4), that could not only make loans but provide equity capital, engage directly in enterprise, and make expenditures for infrastructure; at that time, it contemplated a single national body, but sentiment later turned toward proceeding with separate regional corporations for those purposes instead. The party's official promise before the election in the winter of 1974 was only for "regional machinery with sufficient powers, expertise and finance to enable each region to decide how best to promote development, and to co-ordinate regional planning activity."[100] That language presumably meant something considerably stronger than the existing economic planning councils, but it is loose enough to permit a Labour government to move in the direction of regional governments, regional public corporations, or any variation or combination of the two.

Nevertheless, the finding of the royal commission that no great public demand exists in England for any kind of regional organization remains a fact of British life. Given the general apathy, even a determined Labour government, supported by the party's long-time commitments to decentralization and to regional development, may find it politically difficult to try to improve much on the present mechanisms in the face of the combined resistance of the local authorities and national government officials who would sense a threat to their own influence and authority.

The Prospect of Stability

After four decades of experimentation, Britain's policies for dispersal of economic activity and of people appear to have entered a period of

99. In proposing the creation of legislative assemblies for Scotland and Wales, the Royal Commission on the Constitution excluded economic development functions, such as those carried out in the regions by Department of Trade and Industry officials under the Industry Act, from the list of activities that might be devolved from the central government to the new governments.

100. Labour party, *Labour's Programme for Britain*, p. 18.

stability. The differences between the parties are narrow, and the changes are likely to be minor, whichever party is in power. Labour is on record in favor of some measures to strengthen the industrial dispersal policy—a system of regional development corporations, perhaps, and a congestion tax imposed on development in London—but the basic system of subsidies and controls will remain. Moreover, many circumstances—the magnitude of the other problems pressing Britain, the loss of the sense of urgency about the growth of London, the lack of widespread advocacy of any particular institutional or program reforms—suggest that innovation in regional policy will have a low claim on government attention.

Insofar as there is pressure to modify the program, it would appear less likely to come from the advocates of a more intensive effort than from those who will continue to raise nagging questions about the cost-effectiveness of the present measures, as reflected in the 1972 and 1973 reports of the House of Commons Expenditure Committee. Yet the impulse for reform is slowed by the absence of concrete proposals as to just how costs can be reduced without impairing benefits. If one thing seems clear above all others, it is that no leadership exists for any move to curtail significantly the impact of those benefits, or the scope of the policy objectives that they serve. The Expenditure Committee itself shows no diminution of support for the long-accepted goals. In the closing paragraphs of its 1973 report, this all-party committee warned against relaxing regional policies either because of the prospect of new assistance to lagging areas from the European Community or because of national prosperity. On the former prospect, it observed: "It would be a dereliction of duty for any British government to relax its own pursuit of effective regional policies in the hope of early salvation from across the Channel." And on the latter: "In our view governments should pursue regional policies with the greatest intensity precisely when the growth of the economy makes disparities less obvious. There is never an occasion to relax."

CHAPTER THREE

France: Breaking the Parisian Monopoly

Strengthening the economic capacity of the regions and cities of France leads to a better distribution of power. It creates the conditions for regional action, and thus for a new form of local democracy. . . . Economic growth in itself is not the final objective. The success of territorial planning is to create conditions that permit the French, there where they are, in their community, their department, and their region, to exercise the responsibilities that determine their future.—Olivier Guichard, Minister of Territorial Planning, Public Works, Housing, and Tourism, 1973[1]

THOSE who have followed the history of French policies to influence the distribution of population are likely to say that it all began with a book: *Paris and the French Desert*,[2] published in 1947. Perhaps the title of the book, as much as its content, crystallized opinion. The phrase, the "French desert," became part of the language, identifying the "two-thirds of France" that J. F. Gravier declared were "in decline and moving slowly toward death."

Gravier's powerful polemic set out the figures: The entire growth of France over three-quarters of a century, a population gain of 4.5 million between 1861 and 1936, had been absorbed by two urban agglomerations—Paris and Marseille. More than two-thirds of that growth was in Paris. If five urban departments were excluded, the rest of France, occupying 96 percent of its land area, had lost a net of 1.5 million people. Sixty-four of metropolitan France's[3] ninety departments in 1936 had

1. Le Ministre de l'Aménagement du Territoire de l'Équipment du Logement et du Tourisme and la Délégation à l'Aménagement du Territoire et à l'Action Régionale (DATAR), Foreword, *La Politique d'Aménagement du Territoire* (1973). Cited hereafter as DATAR, *La Politique.*

2. J. F. Gravier, *Paris et le Désert Français: Décentralisation—Équipement—Population* (Paris: Éditions de Portulan, 1947). Quotations and statistics that follow are from pp. 23–24, 62, 64, 76, 137, 192, and 414.

3. Metropolitan France is that part of France located in Europe, as distinct from its overseas colonies and possessions.

fewer people than in 1896, twenty-five had fewer than in 1801. Meanwhile, Paris had become one-seventh of the nation. "One thinks of the caricatures of the Parisian journals of the Second Empire," wrote Gravier, "that showed Paris as about to devour France."

Gravier offered the reasons: "Urban development since the industrial revolution has been expressed in France essentially in the formation of a Parisian monopoly—intellectual, artistic, financial, commercial, industrial, demographic." Paris was the capital of a highly centralized state. Higher education was concentrated there. Headquarters of the major corporations were there. And it was even the country's manufacturing center, accounting for 30 percent of employment in chemicals, 44 percent in printing, 45 percent in automobiles, and 49 percent in electrical machinery. Between 1896 and 1931, industrial employment rose by 63 percent in Paris, 18 percent in the rest of the country.

And he called for action: "Between decadence and renaissance, between the invasion of the desert and the colonization of the interior, between progressive decomposition and the total life, the indivisible life of the national community makes it necessary to choose once and for all, not only through discourse but through action." Political leaders and other spokesmen for the "French desert" took up the cry.

A National Approach to "l'Aménagement du Territoire"
(1944-54)

The government had already been struggling with the problem of interregional balance. Studies had been initiated as early as 1944, and at the end of the war an "industrial decentralization mission" had been assigned the task of trying to persuade war-damaged industries in the Paris region to rebuild elsewhere. But the mission had neither funds to subsidize the movement of undamaged equipment nor power to prohibit rebuilding in Paris, and confronted with the necessity of a rapid reconstruction of the country's industrial potential, it could accomplish little. Indeed, some war-damaged industries in other localities were attempting to relocate in Paris. Requests for industrial construction permits in the Paris region amounted to 35–40 percent of the total for the country.[4] New and comprehensive measures clearly were needed.

They were contained in an official scheme that "burst like a rocket"

4. Jean Faucheux, *La Décentralisation Industrielle* (Paris: Berger-Levrault, 1959), p. 20.

on the national scene early in 1950.[5] The minister of reconstruction and
housing, Claudius Petit, proposed that France adopt a national approach
to *"l'aménagement du territoire,"* or territorial planning,[6] with decentralization as its aim. That was a new concept. Individual cities had been
planned before, and even metropolitan areas, but planning the distribution
of people and activity on a national scale was something else. The proposal was greeted with skepticism and irony—the suggestion for decentralization ran against the "irreversible" trend toward concentration
of activity and population and against the necessities of production, the
skeptics argued. The aim was utopian, a "misty dream." Better *"laissez
faire . . . laissez profiter."*[7]

The Petit report defined *l'aménagement du territoire* as "the search,
in the geographical setting of France, for a better distribution of people"
in relation to natural resources and economic activity. More than that, it
was a search for a distribution that would best serve the welfare of the
people in the noneconomic aspects as well—the living environment, the
working environment, opportunities for recreation and for culture.[8]
As a ministry official later explained, its objectives were "to dam up the
current that carries all the vital forces of the country toward the great
centers; to re-create the sources of life in the regions whose resources are
underutilized and which, despite rich possibilities, tend to become
deserted; to restrain the development of the great agglomerations; to
emphasize the underdeveloped zones of the country."[9]

Of particular importance, in the light of later policy, was the emphasis on "cultural decentralization." Efforts to develop economic activity would be fruitless, wrote Petit, if intellectual and artistic life were

5. Ibid., p. 27.
6. *Aménagement du territoire* has varied translations. The government office
la Délégation à l'Aménagement du Territoire et à l'Action Régionale (DATAR)
translates its own name as the "Territorial Planning and Regional Development
Agency," while the French government information office renders the term as
"town and country planning." Rémy Prud'homme prefers the broader term "regional
policy" ("Regional Economic Policy in France, 1962–1972," in Niles M. Hansen,
ed., *Public Policy and Regional Economic Development: The Experience of Nine
Western Countries* [Ballinger, forthcoming]; Kevin Allen and M. C. MacLennan
translate it as "regional development," *Regional Problems and Policies in Italy and
France* [London: George Allen and Unwin, 1970]).
7. Faucheux, *La Décentralisation Industrielle*, p. 18.
8. Quoted by Joseph Lajugie, "Aménagement du territoire et développement
économique régional en France (1945–64)," *Revue d'Économie Politique* (Paris),
1964, p. 282.
9. M. Randet, in a report presented to an international conference in Edinburgh,
1954, quoted by Lajugie, ibid., p. 283.

neglected. Accordingly his plan envisaged the selection of a dozen cities that had the potential to become "seats of an intense intellectual and artistic life, true provincial metropoles animated by flourishing universities around which could be assembled certain of the great schools massed until now in Paris."[10]

With the approval of the Petit report, territorial planning on a national scale became a part of the broad structure of national planning that France had adopted at the end of the Second World War. Henceforth, the objectives of restraining the growth of Paris, of developing the underdeveloped regions, of improving the balance between the capital and the "French desert" would be pursued consistently by successive French governments, with a steadily increasing emphasis, constantly more elaborate techniques, and growing resources.

The beginning, however, was modest. Initially, the government's principal action was to establish a loan fund to finance the development of well-located and well-equipped industrial parks in the provinces, as well as housing for workers, but the fund's resources and the power to acquire sites were limited. In 1953 a second fund was established to provide loans for the relocation from Paris of firms in the engineering (machinery) industry and to offer partial rebates of some taxes to a broader range of decentralizing firms.[11] Transportation charges were also adjusted to favor the less prosperous regions, government agencies and nationalized industries were pressed to decentralize, and moral suasion was used to influence private investors. But, altogether, the currents flowing toward Paris were not dammed. By 1954 only nine industrial parks had been established, and while the government could claim that 52 important factories, with 19,500 employees, had been located in the provinces by Parisian industries with the assistance or cooperation of various agencies, during the same period 270 industrial expansion projects had been undertaken in the Paris region.[12] Of new factory space authorized in France in the years from 1949 through 1955, the percentage going to Paris was 36, 34, 24, 35, 31, and 33, respectively.[13]

10. Quoted by Joseph Lajugie, "Décentralisation Industrielle, Reconversion, Aménagement du Territoire," *Revue juridique et économique du Sud-Ouest* (Bordeaux) série économique, 1956, no. 2, p. 31.

11. Allen and MacLennan, *Regional Problems and Policies*, p. 153.

12. Lajugie, "Décentralisation Industrielle," pp. 35–36.

13. Faucheux, *La Décentralisation Industrielle*, p. 192; Allen and MacLennan, *Regional Problems and Policies*, p. 152.

From "Empirical and Partial" to "Systematic and Coherent"
(1954-55)

Then an economic recession struck France. "Cries of distress" reached Paris from local administrators who "saw more factories close their doors and vitality subside in their communities, in their departments, and in entire regions, some of which had been lethargic already."[14] As it happened, the crisis touched relatively lightly the expanding industries of the Paris region, such as electronics, chemicals, and drugs, but it struck hard at textiles, leather and shoes, ceramics, foundries, and other traditional industries that dominated the economic life of many localities and some whole regions. The Paris-provincial disparities were accentuated. Now was the time for the officials charged with *l'aménagement du territoire*—backed by industrial development groups, regional planning bodies, and research organizations that had sprung up in the provinces since the war—to come forward with a comprehensive program to carry out their mission.

The years 1954 and 1955, wrote Joseph Lajugie, marked a "decisive turn" in French regional policy, the "empirical and partial efforts" gave way to "a systematic and coherent policy," employing much greater technical and financial resources. Moreover, regional policy became accepted as an integral part of national policy for economic expansion.[15] Some of the new program measures were patterned after those of Britain, whose experiments had attracted the attention of the French planners, but others went well beyond what Britain or any other country had tried and set the course that others were to follow later.

First of all, the objective was clarified. In their single-minded concern with pushing industry out of Paris, government agencies had paid little heed to where the decentralized factories had come to rest. Most of them, as might be expected, had not gone far. They tended to settle in a ring of smaller cities within a hundred miles of Paris, and to a lesser extent elsewhere in the North and East of France. Very few had established themselves in the rural southwestern half of the country. If the flow of economic activity and population into the Paris agglomeration itself had been partially checked, the flow into the larger Paris basin had not been stemmed at all. In 1955 the National Assembly made explicit the objec-

14. Faucheux, *La Décentralisation Industrielle*, p. 35.
15. Lajugie, "Aménagement du territoire," pp. 290-91.

tive of balanced growth, as among all regions. Giving the government temporary power to legislate by decree in the field of regional policy, it declared an objective of facilitating the development of "regions suffering from underemployment and insufficient economic development," particularly by assisting agricultural reconversion, establishment of new industries, and expansion of tourism.[16]

A series of decrees issued in 1954 and 1955 laid out a comprehensive program, including these elements:[17]

1. *Control of industrial construction in Paris.* The government assumed power to achieve through direct controls what it had failed to accomplish by persuasion—the limitation of industrial construction in the Paris region. Henceforth, establishments employing more than fifty persons or occupying more than 5500 square feet could not expand their facilities by more than 10 percent without governmental approval. The economic necessity for location of the facility in the Paris region (such as its relation to the Paris market, or to scientific establishments or research centers that could not be found elsewhere) would be examined, and approval would be denied to "activities that are not directly linked to the life of the great agglomerations and can be established elsewhere." The "continuous and sometimes massive influx of new population into the already congested great cities," the decree contended, aggravates the burdens placed on the cities and the nation to provide housing, pure water, transportation, and other facilities and services. The decree would, however, be administered with "all necessary flexibility."[18]

2. *Investment grants.* In zones of "serious and permanent underemployment or of insufficient economic development," new or expanding industrial enterprises could receive up to 20 percent of their capital investment in the form of government grants. These "critical zones" were at first narrowly defined, covering only single communities or

16. Law of April 2, 1945, quoted by Lajugie, "Décentralisation Industrielle," p. 44.
17. Decrees 54-1121 and 54-1122, *Journal Officiel,* Nov. 16, 1954; Decree 54-1231, *Journal Officiel,* Dec. 12, 1954; Decree 55-36, *Journal Officiel,* Jan. 8, 1955; and Decrees 55-873 to 55-883, inclusive, *Journal Officiel,* July 2, 1955. The measures are summarized in Allen and MacLennan, *Regional Problems and Policies,* pp. 157–66; Faucheux, *La Décentralisation Industrielle,* pp. 53–134; and Lajugie, "Aménagement du territoire" and "Décentralisation Industrielle."
18. Decree 55-36.

groups of communities, like the small "development districts" designated in Britain a few years later.[19] They were of three kinds: communities of exceptionally high unemployment, those where high unemployment was anticipated because of imminent factory or mine closures, and communities with important surpluses of rural manpower. The amount of the grant was negotiable and in practice came to 8–12 percent.[20]

3. *Loans.* Direct loans were authorized for firms decentralizing outside the Paris region. The interest, fixed at 5.5 percent in 1955, was 2–3 percentage points below the market rate. The maximum term was twenty years, and a moratorium on interest payments during the first two or three years was authorized. Alternatively, firms able to obtain private loans could be paid an interest subsidy, bringing their effective interest rate to 4.5 percent or less.

4. *Tax relief.* Firms decentralizing to the critical zones were authorized a reduction in the transfer tax on buildings acquired for industrial purposes—from 16.5 percent to 4.7 percent, for a tax saving equivalent to 12 percent of the cost of the building. Local communities were also authorized to exempt the firms from part or all of local taxes for up to five years.

5. *Manpower programs.* Assistance was offered decentralizing firms in retraining and rehousing workers, and transportation and relocation allowances were authorized for workers and their families moving from Paris with their firms.

6. *Advance factories.* Assistance given to local communities and local private or mixed public-private groups to establish industrial parks and worker housing was extended to cover the erection of factory buildings on a speculative basis, as in the British "advance factory" program, and the limited loan funds previously available for these purposes were increased. In the critical zones, special grants up to 20 percent of the cost of necessary public facilities were also authorized. Subsequently, the

19. Thirty-three zones are listed in Faucheux, *La Décentralisation Industrielle,* pp. 218–21. Twenty-six are listed in Pierre Bauchet, "Regional Development Policies in France," in U.S. Department of Commerce, Area Redevelopment Administration, *Area Redevelopment Policies in Britain and the Countries of the Common Market* (1965), p. 119. Faucheux's list includes some added after 1955. The zones were scattered over the country, most in the underdeveloped southwestern half but some in the North and East.

20. Bauchet, "Regional Development Policies," p. 122; Lajugie, "Aménagement du territoire," p. 327.

power to acquire sites for industrial parks through condemnation was established.

7. *Regional action programs.* A system of regional action programming was instituted to coordinate the action of the diverse governmental agencies, local communities, and private enterprises receiving government assistance. The ninety departments of the country were grouped into twenty-two (later revised to twenty-one) regions, and planning groups of senior civil servants were organized to prepare regional economic development programs that would identify the key projects necessary for an economic take-off in each region and set priorities among them. The planning groups, based in Paris, were to receive information from national government representatives and local groups within the region. To systematize the advisory participation of private groups, committees for economic expansion were to be organized on a departmental, multidepartmental, or regional basis, representing in their membership a broad range of interests. (In 1957, a set of regional physical plans was called for to parallel the economic development programs, and in 1958 it was made clear that the two should be combined.)

8. *Regional development companies.* To counter the centralization of the country's credit resources in Paris, regional development companies were authorized. With capital largely subscribed by the large Parisian banks, the companies were authorized to acquire equity (up to 35 percent) in firms located in depressed regions and (in 1956) to make loans to, and underwrite long-term borrowing of, the firms in which they had an interest. Loans could be made at interest rates below the market level, with the government subsidizing the difference (about 1.25 percent in practice). The central government exempted the regional development companies from income taxes and guaranteed their shareholders a minimum dividend.

9. *Decentralization of government activities.* Government agencies and nationalized or state-controlled industries, which together accounted for one-third of the nation's investment, were directed to identify which of their operations might be decentralized from the Paris region and to present timetables for moving them.

With this battery of programs, France had put in place what was, for its time, the most systematic and comprehensive approach to the problem of population distribution of any free country in the world.

A Decade of Limited Results (*1954–62*)

The decrees of 1954–55, Joseph Lajugie wrote shortly afterward, had administered a "psychological shock" to the country and were bringing into being, "little by little, a new climate."[21] But looking back on the period from the perspective of almost a decade later, he concluded that "the resistance of the administrative, professional, and psychological structures, that acted as so many powerful brakes upon the centrifugal movement, had without doubt been underestimated."[22]

The program brought quick results, however, in one crucial respect—in limiting the construction and expansion of factories in the Paris region. The capital region's share of new factory construction in France was brought down from 33 percent in 1949–55 to 27 percent in 1956, to 20 percent the next year, and to 10 percent by 1963 (see Figures 3-1 and 3-2).[23] Moreover, a considerable amount of existing factory space was being abandoned or converted to other uses in the Paris region—a trend stimulated after 1960 by a special grant authorized for industrial firms that gave up their premises in order to make the buildings or the sites available for public purposes, including housing. Between 1960 and 1963 the region saw a net loss of factory space, as abandonments qualifying for grants exceeded the amount of new space constructed.[24] Controls were tightened in 1958 by a decree that subjected conversion of non-industrial premises to industrial use to the same requirements as new construction. In 1959, permits were required for construction of large office buildings. And in 1960 a special fee of $4 per square foot was imposed on all new construction in the region.

The controls imposed on the growth of Paris were the target of repeated attacks "in the name of the great principles of economic liberalism . . . but also, without doubt, in consideration of the private interests hampered by this regulation."[25] Yet the Economic and Social Council,

---

21. "Décentralisation Industrielle," p. 56.
22. "Aménagement du territoire," pp. 303–04.
23. Data on new industrial construction, derived from building permit records, cover only projects over 5500 square feet.
24. Niles M. Hansen, *French Regional Planning* (Indiana University Press, 1968), p. 58.
25. Lajugie, "Aménagement du territoire," p. 321.

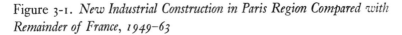

Figure 3-1. *New Industrial Construction in Paris Region Compared with Remainder of France, 1949–63*

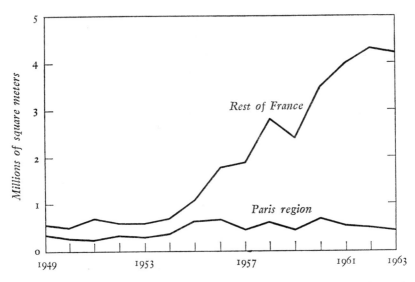

Sources: Jean Faucheux, *La Décentralisation Industrielle* (Paris: Berger-Levrault, 1959), p. 192; Niles M. Hansen, *French Regional Planning* (Indiana University Press, 1968), p. 58.

Figure 3-2. *Percent of France's New Industrial Construction Concentrated in Paris Region, 1949–63*

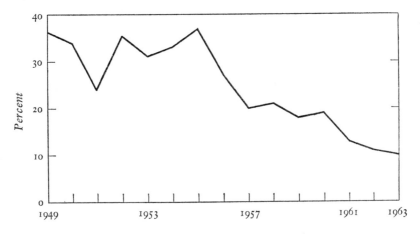

Sources: Same as for Figure 3-1.

on the occasion of a regional policy debate in 1957, not only supported the existing controls but asked that they be extended to other "over-populated" agglomerations.[26]

Some of the relative decline of factory construction in Paris would undoubtedly have occurred in the absence of governmental action, for the increasing congestion of the Paris region and the rising costs of operation there would cause industrialists to look elsewhere. Yet the fact that the region's share of new building dropped abruptly rather than gradually, and that the drop coincided with the imposition of controls and establishment of incentives, suggests strongly that governmental policy was the major factor. Controls were probably much the more important, for the use of incentives developed slowly and remained on a small scale by present European standards. By 1961, $44 million had been disbursed in loans to enterprises and the regional development companies had guaranteed another $98 million. Investment grants totaled $41 million and loans for industrial parks $30 million. Exemptions from national taxes amounted to $8 million, in addition to an uncalculated amount of local tax benefits.[27]

The problem, however, was to get the factories barred from Paris to distribute themselves over the country in a balanced manner. Except for those categories of assistance reserved for the small critical zones, the incentives were available to enterprises locating anywhere in the provinces; the regional development companies, for example, blanketed all of France outside of Paris. Of the 200,000 jobs represented in 1,031 industrial operations listed by the government as having been decentralized from the Paris region up to December 1961, more than half—109,000—were concentrated in the five regions of the Paris basin abutting on the Paris region. The seven regions of the Southwest, the Mediterranean, and the Massif Central—the least industrialized and poorest parts of the country—received only 18,000.[28]

Moreover, any net loss of factory employment in the Paris region was more than made up by new office jobs. The Commission on Production and Exchange of the National Assembly could well conclude that "the decentralization of industrial and tertiary activities in the Paris

26. Ibid. The Economic and Social Council is an official body representative of various economic and social groups and interests.
27. Bauchet, "Regional Development Policies," pp. 129–33.
28. Ibid., p. 137.

region has scarcely been begun, and such transfers as have taken place have simply been toward the periphery of the region, complicating still more the difficult problem of the suburbs. . . . The balance shows nothing positive. On the contrary, the movement is aggravating the concentration in the ring around Paris and thwarting all the efforts at liberation which have been undertaken."[29]

The 1955 proposal that the government set an example by decentralizing some of its own activities had meanwhile come to little. By 1960, President Charles de Gaulle and his advisers recognized the need for some new "psychological shock" in this area. They found the answer in the transfer to the provinces of a dozen of the great Parisian centers of higher learning. Mining and civil engineering schools would go to the Lyon–Grenoble–St. Etienne area, the aeronautics center to Toulouse, public health to Rennes, telecommunications to Nantes, maritime engineering to Brest. At the same time, plans for creation of new specialized centers in law, public finance, the various sciences, and the humanities in a dozen provincial centers were announced. The goal of a psychological shock was unquestionably achieved: the schools launched a vigorous counterattack, mobilizing their powerful associations of graduates to join them in fighting the "provincial exile." But the government held its ground and the decentralization took place.[30]

France's Third Plan (1958–61) declared a balanced distribution of population to be one of the country's general objectives and supported the declaration with a careful argument.[31] It discussed the undesirable social consequences of industrial and population concentration in the capital and of the accompanying depletion of the provinces. It pointed out the economic burden: to provide essential services, including housing, for each new family in the Paris region cost an estimated $12,000, compared to $8,000 in the provinces. These extra costs France could not afford to bear in its competition with the other countries of the European Common Market, none of whom had a metropolis of corresponding size. Finally, the pressure on scarce supplies of land and labor in the capital

29. Quoted by Hansen, *French Regional Planning*, p. 58.
30. Lajugie, "Aménagement du territoire," p. 322–24.
31. This paragraph is based on Allen and MacLennan, *Regional Problems and Policies*, pp. 168–70. The Third Plan was the latest in the series of schemes produced through France's unique system of indicative planning, adopted immediately after the war, whereby expansion goals are set for each segment of the national economy.

was one of the principal sources of the inflation from which the country was then suffering.

Yet the 1962 census figures confirmed that the flow of the nation's population to Paris had been slowed little, if at all. Since the previous census eight years earlier, the Paris region had grown at a rate almost double that of the rest of the country. Almost a third of the nation's total population growth was in the capital and its suburbs—although this was less than the region's two-thirds share during the 1936–54 period. Its 15 percent rate of gain in the 1954–62 period was exceeded only by the region that includes Marseille and the Riviera. The only other regions growing faster than the national average were Upper Normandy in the Paris basin, the region centered on Lyon, and industrialized Lorraine in northeastern France.

Given the strength of the commitment to the national objective that had been established in the early 1950s, the paucity of result during the period up to 1962 was bound to lead to a demand from the assisted regions, backed by the government planners, for a redoubling of the effort. Paris had its boosters too, but through the 1950s and into the 1960s the decentralizers clearly had the upper hand. So while the programs launched in 1955 were being administered, the planners had been refining their concepts of how the government should go about the task of planning and controlling population distribution—*l'aménagement du territoire* on a national scale—more systematically and more effectively. The result was the design and enactment, in the period 1962–66, of an elaborate system for regional planning and regional action that still has no parallel anywhere in the world.

The Regional Planning and Action System (1962–66)

The scheme for regional action programs initiated in 1955 had been unsatisfactory on many counts. A score of effective planning teams could not be established all at once, and the work proceeded region by region at a variable pace; the last of the programs was not completed and published until 1966. When they appeared, they were disappointing. Most of them were little more than inventories of problems and lists of hoped-for projects. Priorities, time schedules, and means of financing and exe-

cuting projects were vague. But even had they been specific, no mechanisms existed to carry out the conceptions contained in the programs.
The region itself was a new and artificial geographical concept. Created
for the purposes of planning, the regions were without tradition, governmental structure, social organization, or even, in many cases, a sense
of community; in some of the regions, local authorities and other spokesmen actively protested the way in which the departments had been
grouped together. The regional plans were not incorporated in the national plan. The various operating agencies of the government had their
individual programs, administered separately on a nationwide basis
through independent field organizations.[32] The Economic and Social
Council, as early as 1960, found that regional planning and coordination
were being hampered by "indifference, incomprehension, refusal to co-
operate, and even ill will."[33]

The first reform was a series of steps initiated in 1959 to fix the regions
more firmly into the country's administrative structure. The prefect of
the region's principal department was designated as the region's coordinating prefect.[34] All of the departmental prefects and top regional
officials of various agencies were organized as an interdepartmental conference with the coordinating prefect as chairman. Government agencies
dealing with regional matters were ordered to conform their field organizations to the new regional boundaries. Not a radical change in the
structure of local government in France, but nevertheless the first change
of any kind since the departments and prefectures were created by
Napoleon a century and a half before.

At this point, responsibility for the regional action programs could
be devolved from Paris to the regions. The interdepartmental confer-

32. In France almost all local community public works are carried in the ministries' budgets, since they receive some assistance, averaging about 25 percent, from
the national treasury. Hence the issue of decentralizing planning and decision-making
responsibilities covers a far wider range of governmental activity than would be
the case in the United States or Britain; the question is largely one of whether and
how to devolve on regional or local authorities the power to make the kinds of
decisions that, in the United States and Britain, have always been made at the local
level.

33. Quoted by Hansen, *French Regional Planning*, p. 79. See also Lajugie,
"Aménagement du territoire," pp. 303–04; and Allen and MacLennan, *Regional
Problems and Policies*, pp. 219–23.

34. The prefect is the principal national government (Ministry of the Interior)
official in each department. He is responsible for supervising local government and
coordinating the work of officials of the field offices of other ministries.

ences, under leadership of the coordinating prefects, were instructed to complete or bring up to date their regional programs. They were also told to prepare regional investment programs to be incorporated in the Fourth Plan (1962–65). Their contribution to this "regionalization of the national plan" was limited, however, by the continued unwillingness of the central ministries to relinquish any real responsibility for decision making, by the inadequacies of data, and by difficulties in establishing satisfactory relations with the private committees for economic expansion who were supposed to be consulted in the process.[35]

In 1963 came the key action to provide a point of leadership and coordination for the whole regional planning system. Premier Georges Pompidou established in his own office the Délégation à l'Aménagement du Territoire et à l'Action Régionale (DATAR), headed by one of his closest associates, Olivier Guichard.

Despite all the measures that had been taken, the premier explained, the record of regional action "still remains insufficient." Thus, in 1961, 10 percent of the French departments—the richest—had gained more than a third of the new industrial installations, and the large cities had received nearly three-fourths of the new installations in their departments. Hardly a beginning had been made in the creation of new employment centers, and only limited results had been obtained in the deconcentration of public services and of industries dependent on the state. "The rural world suffers particularly from the regional disparities that threaten to become more acute if the measures necessary to the decentralization of the country's economy are not clearly effectuated."[36] Responsibilities related to regional policy had been divided among government agencies, and an interministerial committee had not been sufficient to coordinate them.

DATAR was therefore superimposed on the governmental structure as an instrument of "coordination and impulsion" and of oversight. It was charged with making sure that the necessary elements of regional policy were brought together for governmental decisions and that the decisions were then executed by the appropriate ministries. It would have recourse to the premier's authority when necessary. It would act as an executive agent for the interministerial committee. DATAR would be the point of contact for the coordinating prefects and the interde-

35. Hansen, *French Regional Planning*, pp. 91–92.
36. Decree 63-112, *Journal Officiel*, Feb. 15, 1963.

partmental conferences in the regions. It was also given responsibility
for coordinating the execution of a number of major developmental
projects contained in the national plan—such as development of tourism
and recreation facilities on the southwestern Mediterranean coast—and
it was given a small fund, amounting to about $50 million a year, to be
used for initiating key projects in regional plans ahead of when they
would otherwise be scheduled.

The reorganization laid the basis for an attempt at full integration
of the regional and national planning processes in preparation of the
Fifth Plan, covering the period 1966–70. The coordinating prefect in
each region was renamed "regional prefect" and given clear responsibility for the regional-level stages of the process—although he was
obliged to consult at each stage with a regional economic development
commission (an official body of forty to fifty persons representing local
governments, business, labor, and so forth, that succeeded to the advisory
role of the private regional committee for economic expansion) and the
interdepartmental conference (renamed the Regional Administrative
Conference). While the job of regional prefect remained an additional
duty for the prefect of the region's principal department, he was provided a small staff of assistants for the regional planning job.

The contents of the prefect's submission were defined with more
precision than in the previous period. The first part of his report was
to be a long-range analysis, looking twenty years ahead, based on hy-
potheses as to general trends supplied to him. The report would project
population and employment trends, analyze the prospects of economic
development, identify long-range problems, suggest a general development strategy for the region, and outline requirements for education,
training, and various types of public investment. This general analysis
was to be accompanied by detailed estimates of labor supply and demand
for the 1966–70 period and a tabulation, with priorities indicated, of the
public investment necessary to bring public services up to national standards. The prefects' reports and recommendations were synthesized with
those of the ministries in the Fifth Plan.[37]

An element of decentralization was introduced also into the execution
of the plan. For projects whose exact location and nature did not have
to be decided in Paris, the prefect was given in each annual budget of

37. Allen and MacLennan, *Regional Problems and Policies*, pp. 230–31; Hansen,
French Regional Planning, pp. 96–101.

each ministry an "envelope" of credits and the decision as to location, timing, and character of the specific projects left to his determination in accordance with the region's plan.

A Regional Strategy Evolves (*1959–70*)

At the same time that the processes of regional planning and regional action were being elaborated, the concepts and objectives of regional policy were being refined.

If the object of regional policy were to stop the flow of people toward Paris, it soon became apparent that the original "critical zones" as areas for special attention were badly defined. As conceived in 1955, they were the small districts of heavy unemployment, some of them in the industrialized areas of the North and East that had suffered economic dislocation and needed to be rescued. As the planners examined the migration flow and looked ahead, however, it was clear that the problem of surplus population was centered not in industrial communities but in the rural half of the country, the West,[38] and it was not localized in particular communities there but was endemic. In the preparatory work for the Fourth Plan, the planners projected manpower supply and demand in the several sections of the country and concluded that to prevent the inundation of Paris would require a heroic effort to build the West.

So the concept of basing regional policy on potential as well as actual manpower surpluses—that is, on projections of labor supply and demand as well as on current unemployment—was gradually introduced into regional policy. In 1960 the benefits available to the critical zones were made available also to regions or localities that were defined not only by the old criteria of actual unemployment or underemployment but by the number of young people who would be leaving school in relation to job opportunities, and the prospective release of manpower from agriculture due to increased productivity.[39]

38. The West—the area south and west of a line drawn diagonally approximately from Le Havre to Marseille—has 56 percent of the land area but only 37 percent of the population and 24 percent of employment in manufacturing and construction. Jacqueline Beaujeu-Garnier, "Toward a New Equilibrium in France?" *Annals of the Association of American Geographers*, vol. 64, no. 1 (March 1974), p. 113.

39. Bauchet, "Regional Development Policies," pp. 112–13; Allen and MacLennan, *Regional Problems and Policies*, p. 191.

The Fourth Plan, when it appeared in 1962, completed the shift in policy. The whole of the West of France was recognized as a problem area. To halt out-migration there (a complete halt, however, was not seen as possible) would require 90,000 additional nonagricultural jobs between 1960 and 1965 beyond those currently anticipated. "The industrialization of the West is one of the great tasks which the Fourth Plan proposes to the ambition of the nation."[40] Civil and military departments were called on to locate public installations there. Emphasis was placed on industrial training for rural young people entering the labor force. The plan called for light industry, which was least affected by transportation costs, to locate there.

Incentives to industry were not made available equally throughout the West, however, and this reflected another element of the evolving French strategy: the emphasis on "growth poles," or growth centers. In 1959, several major cities in the West had been designated as "special conversion zones" to receive even larger benefits than the earlier "critical zones"—uniform 20 percent investment grants for new industries and 15 percent grants for expansion of existing industries (compared to the variable 8–12 percent for the critical zones)—and in 1960 the critical zones were abolished. The plan continued five special conversion zones in the West where industry was to be concentrated. There, extra expenditures on infrastructure would be made as an inducement to industry. The cities would be renovated generally through redevelopment schemes, and highways, ports, other elements of communication and transportation systems, universities, research centers, and training centers would be developed there. Such expensive investments in infrastructure, made speculatively in advance of the location of industry, obviously could not be made in every community without exorbitant cost and waste through scattering, the plan argued. The most likely locations had to be selected and the expenditures made accordingly, then industry induced to go there. Development of the growth poles would, it was hoped, have a stimulating effect on smaller cities, or "secondary poles," in the regions.

In 1964 the logic of the two approaches was combined. Incentives would be extended to broad areas of the country and graduated according to the severity of the problem, as in Britain, but—in contrast to Britain—they would be higher in the growth centers. So the entire coun-

---

40. *IVe Plan*, p. 130, quoted by Hansen, *French Regional Planning*, p. 205.

try was divided for the purpose of graduated benefits into five zones. Zone 1 consisted of the whole of the West, where long-term development was the goal. There investment grants of 10 percent for new industrial establishments and 5 percent for extensions were available everywhere, but in eight urban growth centers the grants would be double those amounts. Zone 2 included a half-dozen declining industrial districts in the North and East where investment grants would be available until such time as the industrial structure had been adapted and growth restored. The amount of the grant was not a fixed share of the investment, as in zone 1, but was determined in individual cases according to the number of jobs created and the type of industry, with preference to those industries that would diversify the economic base. In both these regions, tax benefits were also offered to new and relocating industry. The rest of France outside the Paris basin was divided between zones 3 and 4—sections where industry was not declining sharply but should be stimulated to some degree in the interest of balanced national growth. There tax benefits (greater in zone 3 than in zone 4), but not the investment grants, were available. Zone 5, the Paris basin, was denied any of the incentives.[41]

In the Fifth Plan (1966–70) the growth center concept was carried to its logical conclusion. Eight French cities (or in some cases combinations of two or more adjacent or neighboring cities) that were judged to have the greatest power to compete with Paris in attracting investment, jobs, and population were designated as *métropoles d'équilibre*—literally, counterweight metropolises—an idea that had been discussed in academic and planning circles for several years. Selected on the basis of a point system devised by the central planners (giving weight to the size of population, availability of services to industry and commerce, availability of services to the general population, and influence over the surrounding territory),[42] they formed a ring around the periphery of the country, all outside the zone of Parisian domination and collectively adjudged capable of generating centrifugal forces powerful enough to offset the forces pulling actively toward the capital. Each was conceived as having

41. For a map of the areas and a more detailed listing of benefits for each, see Allen and MacLennan, *Regional Problems and Policies*, pp. 209–13.
42. The criteria and resulting rankings for thirty-two cities are set out in ibid., pp. 194–202. Also see Hansen, *French Regional Planning*, p. 230, and Joseph Lajugie, "Le schéma français d'armature urbaine," *Revue juridique et économique du Sud-Ouest* (Bordeaux), série économique, 1969, no. 1, pp. 9–13.

a zone of influence of about the same area as the zone dominated by Paris as a regional center. But the eight—Lille and two adjacent cities in the North, Nancy-Metz and Strasbourg in the Northeast, Lyon–St. Etienne and Marseille in the Southeast, Toulouse and Bordeaux in the Southwest, and Nantes–St. Nazaire in the West—had a combined population less than that of Paris. They ranged from 1.5 million in Lyon–St. Etienne (to which Grenoble was later added) to 350,000 in Toulouse, compared to the nearly 8 million in Paris. As financial centers, the eight combined were one-tenth as important as Paris.[43] The disadvantages of the regional centers were enormous, but those centers were still the best the provinces could offer as potential counterweights to Paris. The designation of the metropoles, observe Allen and MacLennan, "marks a total victory for the school of thought which considers regional development possible only if efforts and privileges are concentrated in those parts of the region where growth is feasible. All the *métropoles* are towns which have been selected on the basis of their importance to the economies of their region and not to their need, whether of employment, increased income, etc."[44]

Top priority in public investment, under the Fifth Plan, was to be given the needs of the metropoles.[45] City centers would be renovated and attractive central sites laid out for office complexes. Metropolitan plans would be developed by special teams established by the new regional authorities.[46] New housing would be expedited. Airport requirements would be met. The need for subways in the larger metropoles would be appraised. Government research would be further decentralized, and private research establishments encouraged to locate in the metropoles to serve as a magnet for other enterprises. Where 58 percent of government research investment under the Fourth Plan was in Paris and nearby Orléans, they would be limited to 35–40 percent under the Fifth Plan, and ten large provincial centers would be raised to 50–55 percent from 22 percent. Enrollment at the University of Paris was to be cut from 33 percent of the national total in 1964 to 26.5 percent by 1973. Specialized hospital facilities would be developed. So would cultural institutions. The metropoles were conceived as administrative, cultural,

43. Estimate of A. Lewin, quoted by Hansen, *French Regional Planning*, p. 239.
44. *Regional Problems and Policies*, p. 198.
45. This paragraph is based on Hansen, *French Regional Planning*, p. 236.
46. Known as organisations d'études d'aménagement d'aires métropolitaines (OREAMs). A similar approach was later used for regionwide plans in some regions.

and service centers, rather than industrial complexes; those that had not been eligible for inducements for industrial expansion remained ineligible.

As service and administrative centers, the *métropoles d'équilibre* were seen as being at the top of an urban hierarchy in their respective regions, just as Paris was at the top of a hierarchy for the country. Below them would be middle-sized, or intermediate, cities, that would offer less-specialized services, and at a still lower level would be the rural service and trading centers. Priorities in public expenditure would follow the hierarchy.

The system of industrial incentives adopted in 1954–55 was maintained in its general outlines, though occasionally modified in its details, throughout the 1960s and into the 1970s. The most important new approach added was a "decentralization indemnity," adopted in 1964, which provided to firms moving out of Paris a reimbursement of up to 60 percent of the cost of disassembling, transporting, and reassembling industrial equipment. The level of investment grants was also liberalized, with the maximum raised from 20 percent to 25 percent, and the benefits available to designated centers in zone 2 were standardized at the same level as for zone 1.

Paris and the Tertiary Sector (*1962–*)

But French policy, like that of Britain, could not for long be wholly single-minded. It was relatively easy in France, as across the Channel, to accentuate the positive and popular side of regional policy—the granting of benefits to the areas to be developed. The negative side, the imposition of controls on Paris, was bound to prove less popular with those directly affected, and hence to come harder. True, adoption of limits on factory construction in the metropolis had presented no great difficulty despite their stringent application, but that was because those controls did not run counter to the aspirations that the influentials of Paris held for their city. They saw the capital's future not as a thriving factory center, but —much as London's leaders saw their metropolis—as the commercial, financial, and cultural heart of Europe. Anything that threatened the rise of Paris to that destiny would arouse resistance. So once more the service, not the industrial, sector would be the test.

The conflict between enhancing and decentralizing Paris at the same time was apparent as early as 1962, when the Fourth Plan threaded a narrow path between the two objectives.[47] The plan reaffirmed the need to restrain the growth of Paris in the aggregate, but it emphasized the need for selectivity and discrimination in exercising the restraint. On the one hand, activities that had to be in Paris because of the city's role as a European center must be encouraged to establish themselves and grow. On the other hand, activities that could operate as well elsewhere should still be pressed to leave. What brought the two objectives into harmony was the proposition that only by emptying the city of unnecessary jobs could room be found, at acceptable social and economic costs, for the ones that in the interest of the country's leadership role in Europe had to be there.

But the "compatibility" of the goals has always been easier to state in principle than to work out in practice, and the necessity constantly to reconcile them has led to a kind of adversary process within the French government, in which DATAR frequently finds itself in opposition to other agencies supporting specific planning targets or particular projects. It has also led to a certain ambivalence in French policy, as decisions and official statements sometimes emphasize one of the objectives and sometimes the other.

The first great clash came in 1965, over the physical plan for the Paris region. The Paris boosters advocated a plan for regional development to accommodate 18 million people by the year 2000—about double the population at the time. DATAR contended that the capital should plan for only 10 million, or 12 million at the outside. The delegate general for the Paris district (a kind of regional prefect) chose a range in the middle, 13–15 million. DATAR appealed the issue to President de Gaulle, who upheld the prefect. This was commonly interpreted as a defeat for DATAR in one of the first great tests of its decentralization philosophy. Yet defenders of DATAR contend, reasonably, that if it had not carried the issue all the way to the president of France, the Parisian business community would probably have been able to get its 18 million figure into the plan unopposed.

The Fifth Plan (1966–70), developed at the time of this controversy, reflected the policy conflict and the manner of its resolution. In its discussion of the Paris region the plan had little to say about controls on

47. Allen and MacLennan, *Regional Problems and Policies*, p. 171.

the capital's growth. Its emphasis was on the proper physical planning of the region so that growth could be accommodated with maximum amenity and least cost. Half of the region's growth would be channeled into five new towns of up to half a million population each, to be built in a ring around the Paris conurbation. To meet the argument that the high cost of services in the metropolis was a drain on the whole country, it established the goal of imposing on the Paris region's residents something closer to the true costs of its services, including transportation, water supply, and sewerage.[48]

An official of the French planning office explained that in the Fifth Plan

where Paris is concerned we . . . discarded the official line of the past fifteen years urging the need to arrest its growth, since we realized that this kind of talk might affect the city's own economic potential. The policy is now to recommend moderate growth coupled with modernization. I may also add . . . that the aim in this instance is not to contain the growth of Paris by means of regulations. . . . So far as possible we would like to eliminate such regulations in favor of economic measures, which would mean that Paris would bear its development costs, or as we say in the Plan, getting back to real costs where Paris is concerned. Thus the extremely heavy deficit of the Paris area's public transport system would no longer be borne by the entire country, a larger share being assumed by Parisians.[49]

Nevertheless, the ambivalence remained: the Fifth Plan also strongly reiterated the goal of building the lagging regions; it set a target of 35–40 percent of new industrial jobs in the West, and it established the *métropoles d'équilibre* as counterweights to Paris. The "victory" of the Paris expansionists in 1965 had aroused the provinces, and their political strength supported DATAR and its decentralist allies within the government in making sure that in the sections of the plan dealing with the provinces—if not in that dealing with Paris—the commitment to decentralization would be firm and unmistakable. The plan was consistent enough internally if the projected Paris population were regarded not as a target but as a forecast of what might happen and should be prepared for—not as a goal of government policy but as a contingency plan in the event of the failure of government policy.

48. Ibid., pp. 179–80.
49. M. Viot, of the Commissariat Général du Plan, in Organisation for Economic Co-operation and Development, "Salient Features of Regional Development Policy in France," report of a conference held in October 1965 (Paris: OECD, 1967; processed), pp. 8 and 13.

Clearly, that was the DATAR point of view. Its objective was to see that the contingency was never realized, if that were possible. But, equally clearly, the Paris building community looked on the population figure as a target. And they had important support from the sponsors and the managers of the new towns that the regional plan created around Paris. The new towns had definite population goals—not just forecasts. In support of those goals, infrastructure investments were being made, and if the goals were not achieved those expenditures would be wasted. So the new towns, backed by at least a segment of the Paris regional officialdom, complained of the government's discrimination in favor of the provinces in its incentive systems.

But DATAR pressed ahead, and by 1967 it succeeded in winning approval for a comprehensive—if initially cautious—program to bring about decentralization of the tertiary, or service, sector. The means would be essentially those that had been used successfully to disperse the country's industry, and they would be applied in a truly discriminatory fashion. The European headquarters of multinational corporations would still be welcomed and encouraged, but to make room for them the operations of domestic corporations serving only France would be invited, urged, and subsidized to leave. The approach was threefold.

A new incentive system was designed especially for the service sector. An investment grant of 5–15 percent (20 percent in exceptional cases) was authorized for firms that would transfer, or establish, outside the Paris region functions of an administrative or research or development character. But, consistent with the theory that service activities are at the heart of any growth center strategy, the incentives were limited to activities being located in thirteen urban centers, the eight *métropoles d'équilibre* and five other cities with important regional functions.[50] To qualify, a project would have to create a hundred jobs in an administrative activity, or fifty in design or research or in a firm's head office.

In order that office space vacated by firms decentralizing from Paris could not be freely reused, or manufacturing facilities be freely converted to activities in the tertiary sector, a system of permits was introduced for occupancy of office space in the region exceeding 32,000 square feet. Responsibility for administering these controls, in addition to the existing controls on office building construction, was assigned to

50. The five were Rennes, Dijon, Clermont-Ferrand, Rouen, and Nice. In 1972 four others—Caen, Cannes, Montpellier, and Besançon—were added.

a new decentralization committee, whose membership was balanced about evenly between nominees of DATAR and representatives of other ministries.

While offering incentives and armed with the power of restraint, DATAR turned its vaunted powers of persuasion on the big tertiary employers to induce them to take advantage of what was offered. As the principal initial targets, it chose the banks, insurance companies, and other financial institutions whose total national employment was 244,000 persons in 1954 and 415,000 in 1968—almost half in the Paris region— and was expected to grow to 540,000 by 1975. "DATAR claims to regard business planning as a contract between State and company," observed the *London Sunday Times*. "Every permit and every grant can be regarded as a political decision, and firms who play ball can be looked after. . . . DATAR publishes innumerable documents . . . acting as a propaganda machine such as no British civil servant has ever dreamed of."[51]

"We Have Attained the Unattainable"

Ten years after the creation of DATAR, that organization was able to proclaim the achievement of the first goal of *l'aménagement du territoire:* the centuries-old drain of population from the provinces to Paris had at last been brought to a halt. During the period between the censuses of 1962 and 1968, net migration from the provinces to Paris had fallen by three-quarters, to just above 10,000 a year, and the trend was still downward. "It is not impossible," said DATAR's tenth anniversary report, written in late 1972, "that at this hour we have already reached the end of the first stage that to some appeared unattainable ten years ago— that is, a balance in the population exchange between Paris and the provinces."[52] Thereafter, DATAR officials in their private and public statements began to drop the qualifying clauses; by all signs, the unattainable had indeed been attained.

Disparities in the growth rate between Paris and the provinces had

51. November 26, 1972. While many of the financial institutions were government owned or controlled, this did not make DATAR's task any easier. Some said it made the job harder, because of the institutions' "powerful connections" within the government.
52. DATAR, *La Politique*, p. 10.

clearly narrowed between the censuses. The Paris region was still growing faster than the national average, but its share of the national growth had dropped from 31 percent in the 1954–62 period to 24 percent in the years 1962–68. Second among the twenty-two regions in rate of growth in the previous period, Paris had now fallen to fourth. Perhaps most significant, all of the eight *métropoles d'équilibre* but one (Lille) had growth rates exceeding that of Paris. Toulouse had grown twice as rapidly as had the capital. The Lyon and Marseille regions together had gained more people in the six years, in absolute numbers, than had the Paris region. Altogether, provincial cities of more than 200,000 had a combined increase of 13 percent in population (those between 20,000 and 200,000 grew even faster), compared to Paris' 8 percent.

The metropolis still grew faster than the national average in the 1960s because of a net immigration of 50,000 a year from abroad. Paris was still the principal reception point for foreign immigrants, particularly from North Africa, Spain, and Portugal, many of whom pick up menial jobs in the service industries vacated by Frenchmen leaving Paris or rising in the social scale. The 1968 census showed 832,000 foreigners living in the Paris region, almost half again as many as in 1962. More than 35 percent of foreigners from countries outside the European Community living in France were in Paris. Government policies were attacking this problem also; restrictive measures cut immigration almost in half between 1970 and 1972, from 210,000 to 120,000, and the goal was to further reduce the figure to 80,000 a year.

No French studies comparable to those published in Britain attempt to measure how much of the new trend toward dispersal of the native French could be attributed directly to governmental policies. One school of thought, represented both in Paris and in the provinces, attributes the slowing of Paris' growth to the sheer discomfort, inconvenience, and high cost of living in the capital: Paris can no longer readily attract from the countryside an abundant supply of native labor, and employers have accordingly been deterred from making investments and creating jobs there.

That Parisians have been dissatisfied with their city for some time is evident from the polls. In a 1959–60 survey of preferred place of residence, only 44 percent of the Paris respondents chose Paris or its suburbs —a degree of satisfaction with their surroundings markedly less than that shown by the people of rural areas, small towns, or provincial cities.

Nor did Paris exert much of an attraction on provincial residents; only about one in sixteen of the respondents outside Paris chose Paris as his ideal home. "If the expressed aspirations could be satisfied," wrote the analysts of the data, "Paris would cease to grow."[53] The same authors in 1964 asked a cross-section of provincial residents: "In a general sense, do you believe that conditions of existence are better in the country, in a small town, in a large provincial city, or in Paris?" Ten percent of the respondents chose Paris. The large provincial city was the choice of 25 percent, the small town 28 percent, and the countryside 27 percent (10 percent expressed no preference).[54] In 1963, more than two-thirds of the residents of the Paris region in a national sample thought the growth of their city should be curbed.[55]

In the 1963 survey those who deplored the size of Paris cited pollution, traffic congestion, noise, and deficiencies of public transportation as their chief complaints. Ten years later, government officials said that the complaints appeared to be much the same, except that the housing problem—the unavailability of housing at reasonable cost in or near the city center and the bleakness of forbidding housing blocks being erected on the outskirts—would probably be added among the prime causes of dissatisfaction. "There can be no family life when one has to ride trains and buses for two hours in each direction to and from work, which is not at all uncommon," observed one; "and in the new suburbs there is no community life either—not of the kind that French people know and value in smaller places." In 1973, Parisians spoke frequently of a steady deterioration in the level of public services as the city has grown—again mentioning public transportation as the leading example.

The 1968 census data appear to confirm the growing disenchantment, for while migration into Paris had actually risen, out-migration had increased even more, by about 50 percent. In-migrants exceeded out-migrants only in the age bracket between fifteen and thirty-four. Beginning with the thirty-five through forty-four bracket, the flow out of the Paris region exceeded the movement in, with the differential at its

53. Alain Girard and Henri Bastide, "Les problèmes démographiques devant l'opinion," *Population* (Paris), vol. 15 (April–May 1960), as quoted by Hansen, who summarizes the poll results in *French Regional Planning*, pp. 34–36.

54. Alain Girard, Henri Bastide, and Guy Poucher, "Mobilité Géographique et Concentration Urbaine en France," *Population* (Paris), vol. 19 (April–May 1964), p. 256.

55. Hansen, *French Regional Planning*, pp. 35–37.

highest in the fifty-five through seventy-four age range.[56] Since Paris has been a relatively tight labor market throughout the period, those of the out-migrants who were in their prime working years presumably left voluntarily. Apparently the attraction of Paris to teenagers and young adults wears off rapidly as the young people enter careers and assume family responsibilities; many leave at that point if they can find opportunity elsewhere—220,000 of the out-migrants were active members of the labor force—while another large group leaves the capital on retirement.

It is the timing of the expansion of employment opportunities in the regions outside Paris that suggests that government policies were the crucial factor in the dispersal of investment, and hence of population, that occurred. From the end of the war until 1955, the Paris region consistently accounted for one-third or more of the country's new factory facilities. But after that year, as the total annual volume of industrial construction soared upward, *all* of the increment was steered away from Paris (see Figures 3-1 and 3-2). The capital region's share of new factory construction fell from 33 percent to 10 percent between 1955 and 1963 and remained at or below that level throughout the subsequent decade. Because 1955 was the very year that controls were imposed on new factory building in the Paris region and the first incentives for dispersal were introduced, it is difficult to avoid attributing to government policy the sudden and decisive reversal of a solidly established trend—just as the British analyses of investment location saw in coincident timing the reason for crediting the appearance of new dispersal trends to shifts in government policy.

New factory construction in the Paris region was in fact less than enough between 1962 and 1968 to offset the loss of factory jobs through conversion of industrial space to other uses. Net employment in the secondary sector (manufacturing and construction) dropped slightly in the six years, by 11,000 jobs, while increasing by 522,000 in the rest of the country. Since then, the trend has been reversed, as secondary em-

---

56. Pierre Bertrand, "Le déséquilibre des migrations Paris–Province s'atténue," in *Économie et Statistiques* (Paris), vol. 6 (March 1970), especially p. 10. Bertrand's figures are for the age of the migrant at the time of the census rather than at the time of the migration. Since the migration took place at any time during the six-year intercensal period, the migrant was, on the average, three years younger at the time of movement than he was in 1968. That would mean that out-migration exceeded in-migration beginning with the age bracket 32–41.

ployment rose during 1968–71 at a rate of 25,000 jobs, or about 1.5 percent, a year. Tertiary employment rose even faster.

The Balancing of National Growth

Restraining the growth of industry in the Paris region would not fully serve the purpose of national policy if the result were merely to divert the growth to the neighboring regions of the Paris basin, as had been the disappointing consequence of the initial efforts in the 1950s. The other objective of national policy, declared at the outset and reaffirmed in a series of ever-stronger policy statements in the 1960s, was to balance the national growth and stem migration by guiding industrial development into the rural areas of the West (as well as declining industrial centers of the Northeast) that were the sources of the pressure on Paris.

On this facet of policy, the government in 1973 was also claiming success. "The new industrial activities have especially profited the West of the country and the regions of conversion," said Guichard in DATAR's decennial report. "The population of the least favored regions has grown as fast as, if not faster than, that of other regions." The ten regions lying west and south of the Le Havre–Marseille line had gained a net of 200,000 workers during the 1962–68 period compared to a loss of 400,000 during the preceding intercensal period—and this despite the accelerated movement of workers out of agriculture.[57] The Fifth Plan had set a specific target for those regions—35–40 percent of all new industrial jobs compared to the previous 25 percent—and by the beginning of the 1970s that target was being closely approached, if not met. The Sixth Plan (1971–75) reaffirmed the targets. The West was to achieve an industrial employment growth rate of 2 percent a year, almost twice the national average and somewhat higher than the rate achieved in the 1960s. For Brittany, the region with the greatest surplus of rural manpower, the plan's targets called for an increase of 40,000 nonagricultural jobs, or 8,000 a year, and during the first two years of the plan a total of 15,000 were created. Out-migration from that province had fallen by two-thirds.[58]

57. DATAR, *La Politique,* p. 5.
58. Ibid., p. 10.

This did not mean that competition for the growth of industry had been wholly resolved in favor of the outlying underdeveloped regions. The five regions abutting the Paris region are still the major beneficiaries of the restrictions on factory building in Paris, even though the investment grants are generally not available there.[59] Between 1962 and 1968 their industrial employment rose at a rate twice the national average, and 34 percent of the national increase in industrial employment was located there. By the end of the decade, however, there was a slight turn downward in favor of the more distant provinces; the five regions' share of the country's new factory construction, which had averaged 26 percent in the 1963–67 period, fell to 25 percent in 1968 and 23 percent in 1969. It was not clear whether this represented the beginning of a significant and lasting trend, but in any case the government took some further steps to encourage it. In 1972, industrial activities moved from Paris were made ineligible to receive the decentralization indemnity if they were relocated within the basin.

DATAR officials remark, with a mixture of pride and chagrin, that their goal of balanced growth was being achieved with one of the smallest regional programs in Europe, in terms of budget expenditure. Investment grants had reached a level of only $80 million in 1970 and $60 million in 1971, less than a quarter of what was being spent in comparable grants in Britain.[60] Because of the limitations of available funds, the grants could not be automatic, as in Britain, but had to be administered with a high degree of selectivity. Those over $2 million, and usually over $1 million, were acted on case by case and scaled down to fit the budget. A ceiling related to job creation ($3,000 per job in new plants in 1973, $2,400 in extensions) kept the actual subsidy for capital-intensive enterprises well below the authorized maximum of 20 percent and—unlike the British program—entirely excluded modernization projects that did not increase employment. In 1971 the effective ratio of the grants was a

59. The five regions cover more territory than the Paris basin as the latter is defined for purposes of the industrial incentives program. Half a dozen small areas on the edges of those regions farthest from Paris are included in the zones eligible for grants. Statistics are assembled by regions rather than zones.

60. This comparison disregards Britain's regional employment premium, which would make the differential even more striking. The French regional investment subsidies were considerably less than the $360 million in the French budget for the coal industry in 1970 and the $1.2 billion for agriculture, according to Jérôme Monod and Philippe de Castelbajac, *L'Aménagement du Territoire* (Paris: Presses Universitaires de France, 1971), p. 66.

little more than 10 percent of the almost $600 million in capital expenditures for assisted projects, which were to provide jobs for 46,000 workers. Direct government loans amounted to $60 million in 1969 but fell below $13 million by 1971—explained by officials as due to the adequacy of credit from other sources. Loans by the regional development corporations were running in the late 1960s at a rate of about $55 million a year. DATAR's special fund for key development projects—roads, industrial parks, manpower training, and so forth—amounted to between $50 million and $60 million a year (raised to $80 million in 1972–73 by the addition of part of the proceeds of a new tax on Paris building).

In each of these categories except the regional development corporations, from half to two-thirds of the assistance was directed to the West. Of new employment receiving some form of government assistance—which DATAR estimated at one-third of all new employment in the eligible areas—the West received about two-thirds, the depressed industrial areas of the North and East one-third.

In France, however, budget expenditure can sometimes be the least important element of policy. "The state always has some means of applying pressure" on major private industries, said a DATAR official. The requirement of approval for factory construction in the Paris region opens the opportunity for government-industry negotiation. As in Britain, a limited expansion in the capital area may be permitted on condition that most of the expansion be located elsewhere. The government can encourage the choice of a particular region, or it can insist at least that the relocation be outside the Paris basin, in one or another of the assisted areas. Finally, a commonly recognized element in the effectuation of government policy is the close informal ties that have existed between the leaders of government and of industry—they have been members of the same "establishment," especially during the period after 1958 when General Charles de Gaulle and his Gaullist successors and their allies held continuous power. "The executives of a major industry would not think of making a key decision in which they knew the government was interested, like location of a big plant, without first talking it over with their friends in the government," observed one official. The importance of informal influence is likewise emphasized by researchers who have questioned company executives about the reasons for their locational decisions.

In two instances, using all these varied means of inducement, pressure, and control, the planners set out to concentrate particular industries in selected regions of the West. The decision was made to marry one of the most promising, rapidly growing industries—electronics—to the western area with the greatest supply of surplus rural manpower, Brittany and its neighboring regions. So higher education facilities in telecommunications were moved from Paris to Nantes, the area's metropole, and civil and military research and military training in those specialties were likewise moved to the West, to serve as magnets for private industry. More than half of the new electronics plants established since 1955 in France are in the West, with a heavy concentration in Brittany.[61] The industrial sector's share of that region's labor force rose from 22 percent to 27 percent between 1962 and 1968, a proportional increase higher than that of any other region (although from the second lowest base). Similarly, Toulouse in the Southwest, where aircraft manufacture had been concentrated before the war, was designated as the country's aerospace center and the government's research and development activities in that field were concentrated there, which accounts for Toulouse's record as the fastest-growing of the *métropoles d'équilibre.*

The policy of regional concentration has not been extended to other industries, however. Motor vehicle manufacture, heavily concentrated in Paris until 1964, has been dispersed to many areas. The dangers of overreliance on a single industry—dramatized recently in Toulouse by cutbacks in aerospace production—have apparently convinced the planners that diversification is to be preferred, as a general rule, to concentration.

The key to the successful use of incentives, controls, and pressures in the systematic pursuit of the decentralization objectives is, it seems clear, the institutional one—the existence and authority of DATAR. Its power rests not on its size (in 1973 it consisted of but forty officials) nor on its operating responsibilities (the only program it operates directly is the allocation of its small fund for infrastructure expenditures) but on its recognized status as the premier's personal agent for territorial planning and regional action.[62] It has been both a symbol of the government's continuing commitment to the goals of decentralization and balanced growth and an activist agency that can compel the rest of the

61. DATAR, *La Politique*, p. 18.
62. In 1972 DATAR was placed in the Ministry of Territorial Planning, Public Works, Housing, and Tourism, but DATAR officials said its status, role, and method of operation were not changed.

government to pay constant heed to that commitment. It participates in the regionalization of the national plan, in budget decisions, and in the work of the various interministerial committees whose policies have a bearing on regional objectives. Led and staffed by zealots, it has been described as a "continuing lobby" within the government for decentralization—one with ready access to the premier. While it inevitably loses some battles with the economic and finance ministries on issues where the goal of decentralization may appear to be in conflict with other goals —like maximization of the gross national product and enhancement of the competitive position of France—it is in a position to wage its struggle on something like equal terms.

The Retreat from the Growth Center Concept

The overt favoritism in the policy of concentrating public expenditures in growth centers—especially as embodied in the *métropoles d'équilibre*—was bound to draw protest. Much of it came, naturally enough, from the large cities that had failed of designation as metropoles, but their complaints could not be wholly written off as the inevitable disgruntlement of losers. Some of the winners at the time of their designation had shown little sign of spontaneous development as true economic and cultural centers of the large areas they were now expected to influence, and the effort to convert them into regional metropolises by the fiat of government planners had an element of artificiality. In polycentric regions with two or more major urban complexes, the metropole that was chosen often had no decisively better claim to the designation than did a rival city, and the choice was in fact a narrow one between cities of the same general size, each of which had its own direct links with Paris. Sometimes rival cities in these areas were jointly designated as a metropole even though they had little physical or functional unity. In other cases the designation of one city as a metropole, with some unclear kind of primacy over its competitors, seemed an arbitrary and quite unnecessary attempt to insert an intermediate layer between the other major cities and the capital.[63]

A more widespread concern was that, if the metropole idea worked,

63. For specific examples, see Hansen, *French Regional Planning*, pp. 244–45; Allen and MacLennan, *Regional Problems and Policies*, pp. 202–04; and Beaujeu-Garnier, "Toward a New Equilibrium?" p. 123.

it would only repeat on a smaller scale the folly of overconcentration that had given rise to the whole dispersal movement on the national scene. Harking back to Gravier's theme of two decades earlier, Lajugie was writing in 1969: "The problem is to direct the distribution of [the] population, over the national territory, in the direction of an urban-rural balance . . . that will not substitute for 'Paris and the French desert' a collection of 'Bordeaux and the Aquitain desert,' 'Toulouse and the Garonnais desert,' etc."[64]

If one reason for checking the growth of Paris was to avoid the higher costs of public services in large agglomerations, the same reasoning argued for checking the growth of the other, smaller conurbations that were already experiencing some of the pains of congestion that had afflicted the capital. "By the time a city reaches a million, it has to have a subway," remarked one central planner. The Lyon agglomeration was already well over that figure, and Marseille was approaching it, and both had subway plans in progress. Was it wise policy to encourage those metropoles, or had the time come to pursue a policy of restraint instead?

The government in 1972 indicated, in a somewhat half-hearted and tentative way, a change of course for Lyon. For purposes of the industrial incentive program, Lyon and its environs were put in the same least-favored zone (zone 5) as the Paris basin. That meant that manufacturing industries moving from Paris to Lyon would lose the tax benefits and decentralization indemnity paid them if they established themselves elsewhere outside the Paris basin. Moreover, the tax benefits and the indemnity were made available, for the first time, to industries relocating out of Lyon. And controls on construction of new industrial facilities, comparable to those in effect in Paris, were imposed. Yet administrative responsibility for approval of the new construction was not assigned to the central government officials in the capital who administered the controls on Paris but was left in the hands of regional officials, and they applied such a permissive standard that the controls were subsequently abandoned. Nor were special building permit fees levied to hinder expansion, as they were in Paris. And the policy of encouraging tertiary activities in Lyon was continued, for it was still looked to as the city most likely to develop as a magnet strong enough to effectively counter the attractions of Paris. Thus the incentives paid for relocating non-manufacturing activities from Paris to Lyon remained in force.

64. Lajugie, "Le schéma français," p. 33. Gravier and Bauchet, among others, were expressing the same concern. Hansen, *French Regional Planning*, p. 240.

But the logic, as well as the pressure, for a broader approach was inescapable. If the growth of Paris could only be checked through the development of counterweight metropoles, then the growth of the metropoles themselves could be restrained only through the development of lesser counterweights, forming a circle around each metropole just as the latter formed a circle around Paris. And so, late in 1971, the emphasis of French policy suddenly shifted from the *métropoles d'équilibre* to the cities at the next lower level in the urban hierarchy—the *villes moyennes*, or medium-sized cities. A series of pronouncements, from the premier and other officials, began to extol the virtues of the *villes moyennes*, and measures began to emerge to give them a new importance as growth centers and an enhanced capacity to fulfill that role.

High on the list of virtues cited was the quality of small-town life. The great cities, Premier Pierre Messmer told an audience in 1972, were the source of today's increasing social tensions. "All the problems there are difficult," he said, "long and uncomfortable transport journeys, polluted atmosphere, the lack of green space, crowded housing, uneasy human relations." The government was striving to cope with those problems: in recent years, from one-third to one-half of all its public works expenditures had been in the Paris region. Yet all the expenditures had not accomplished much beyond preventing the situation from getting worse. It was the *ville moyenne* that offered a "calmer and better ordered" life, where people lived close to their work, where "escape to nature" was easy, where places of amusement and recreation were accessible. Instead of the anonymity of the big city, it offered neighborliness and easily formed friendships. Moreover, the trend in industry was away from "gigantism" toward plants of a more human scale, employing usually only a few hundred people, that were well suited to location in smaller cities.[65] In provincial cities, DATAR estimated, the cost of public facilities per capita was only a third to a half of what it was in the Paris region, and within the provinces the costs were lowest in the smaller places.[66]

So the government late in 1972 accorded the *villes moyennes* a share of the priority status previously reserved for the *métropoles d'équilibre*, which thereby lost most of the advantages that they had had under that designation. (What those advantages had amounted to in terms of extra

65. "Animation et Développement des Villes Moyennes," address at a conference at Nice, Oct. 22, 1972.
66. DATAR, *La Politique*, p. 77.

budget expenditure is not clear. No special appropriation was made, and since the policy was in effect only a short time, it is unlikely that any great volume of infrastructure investment was diverted to the metropoles from where it would otherwise have gone.) "An urban strategy relying on the large metropoles cannot succeed in organizing the totality of the urban phenomenon," explained DATAR. "It is therefore natural that after having developed the *métropoles d'équilibre*, the public authorities shift their concern to the promotion and the growth of the *villes moyennes*."[67] It is noteworthy that DATAR could speak of the development of the metropoles as a goal that had already been accomplished.

The government thereupon announced that the subsidy paid for the relocation of tertiary sector activities from Paris to the metropoles and other designated cities would be available to help finance moves to any locality in zone A (a combination of the former zones 1 and 2). The same equality of status was not granted the medium-sized cities in the other zones, but seven of them had been earlier made eligible along with the metropoles. Similarly, the maximum subsidy of 25 percent for new industrial construction was authorized for the whole of zone A, large and small cities alike. Despite the resonant endorsement of the *villes moyennes* as sites for small plants, however, they could (with certain designated exceptions) receive the maximum rate only in projects with an investment of $1 million or more, while it was permissible for projects of any size in the metropoles.

The favoritism accorded the metropoles in urban development and in the expenditure of national funds for infrastructure was also extended to the *villes moyennes*. The metropoles remained the hope for developing effective counterweight attractions to Paris as major centers of tertiary activity, but much of the necessary expenditure for that purpose—as DATAR indicated—had already been made. So attention devoted to the development of air transportation facilities, universities, and other services could now be shifted from the metropoles to smaller communities. The need for institutions of higher and technical education would receive priority attention. Comprehensive redevelopment plans, like those being prepared for the metropoles, would be developed for the *villes moyennes* to serve as the basis for a formal contract between the local and central governments that would govern the direction and

67. Ibid., p. 76. Beaujeu-Garnier writes that the "policy of 'métropoles d'équilibre' has been virtually stopped in France." "Toward a New Equilibrium?" p. 123.

tempo of the community's development. By 1974 a dozen contracts had been signed and many more were in prospect.

In the planning, great care was to be taken to see that the smaller communities avoided the mistakes of the larger cities. They would not be permitted to disfigure themselves with buildings out of scale with the architectural harmony that gave to the smaller French cities their distinctive charm. Emphasis would be placed on "cultural decentralization" —music, theater, fine arts, museums. Yet no standard plan of development would be imposed. Initiative in making proposals would be left to the local elected officials and those of the new regional governments, so that the diversity of the smaller cities would be preserved.

In all of this, what constituted a *ville moyenne* was never defined exactly, and what the new emphasis on them would ultimately amount to was far from clear. While the term is translated in French government publications as "medium-sized cities," the identifying feature of the *ville moyenne* was not one of size but of function: it was a city that filled the role of service center for a surrounding hinterland. Typically, it would be in the 50,000–100,000 population bracket, but larger centers that had missed designation as metropoles would be included, and many smaller cities that functioned as service and administrative centers would qualify. By the same token, suburban or dependent cities that were part of larger agglomerations, no matter what their size, would not have independent status as *villes moyennes*. Presumably, what cities became the beneficiaries of the new policy, and what the benefits would actually be, would in practice be determined in the regional planning and budget allocation processes. And their development would be a slow process, restrained by the time required for the preparation of growth plans and by the availability of funds for public works investment.

In its retreat from emphasis on developing big cities, the government has also been offering a degree of favoritism to the country's most rural areas, designated in 1967 as "zones of rural renovation." Subsidies are granted in these zones, which include more than a quarter of the country's territory, for industrial projects involving investment of as little as $60,000 and creating as few as fifteen jobs or, if the project is "of special interest," even less—compared to minimums of $100,000 and thirty jobs in urban projects. Minimum requirements for grants for expansion of existing plants are scaled down correspondingly. The rural areas are also the beneficiaries of a special rural renovation fund plus

Figure 3-3. *Zones for Investment Subsidies and Controls in France, 1973*

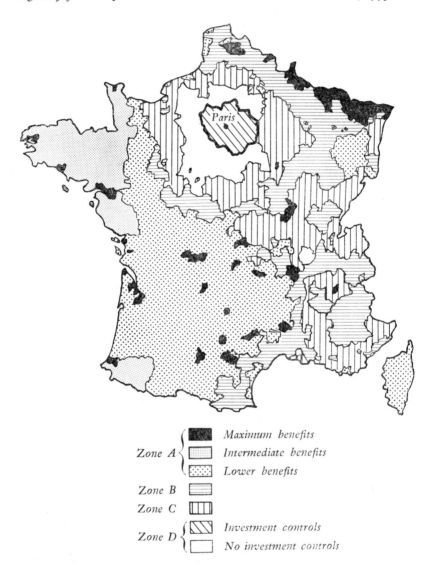

Source: La Délégation à l'Aménagement du Territoire et à l'Action Régionale (DATAR), *Regional Investment Incentives* (1972). The boundaries remained unchanged in 1973.

other extra expenditures, which amounted in all to some $70 million in 1972; these funds are mostly devoted to agricultural projects, including irrigation, but also include expenditures for communications, education, and development of tourism.

With these and other adjustments, the French pattern of eligibility for various kinds of incentives to industrial development had achieved by 1973 a bewildering complexity, which is indicated in Figure 3-3 and Table 3-1. Basically, the country was divided into four zones. Most of the western half of the country was assigned to zone A, which offered the greatest benefits, and the Paris basin to zone D, which offered none. But the rest of the map was a patchwork, as individual communities and small districts were allocated among the zones through the application of planners' criteria as to needs and prospects for development. Moreover, zone A was divided, in effect, into four subzones with different scales of benefits, reflecting what remained of the old discrimination in favor of larger cities and some new discrimination in favor of Brittany, the extreme Southwest, and areas along the northeastern border. Cutting across the zones were distinctions applying to particular programs. Rural renovation areas, with their more generous incentives for small plants, were found in several sections of zone A. Some tax benefits were available only in the western parts of zone A but not in the east—a remnant of the time before the system was "simplified" by the consolidation of the old zones 1 and 2 into the new zone A. Within zones B and C, the grant for the relocation of tertiary activities from Paris was available for those moved to the metropoles and certain other designated metropolitan areas but not to the rest of the zones. And Lyon, in zone D, was eligible for grants in the transfer of tertiary activities from Paris, also in zone D. Within the Paris basin part of zone D, there was also discrimination in the use of a new "disincentive"—a graduated building permit fee—among four subzones. Beyond all this, the administrators of the grant programs had wide discretion to make exceptions; if particular areas of zones B and C had exceptional employment problems, they could be treated as though they were in zone A.

By 1973, then, the country that a half dozen years earlier had been perhaps the prime exponent of the philosophy that aids to industrial development should be concentrated in a relatively small number of large growth centers had gone a long way toward the other extreme. The *métropoles d'équilibre*, which embodied the epitome of the growth cen-

Table 3-1. *Availability of Industrial Development Incentives in Various French Zones, 1973*

Zone	Grants for industrial investment	Grants for relocation of tertiary activities	Decentralization indemnity	Tax benefits	Subsidies for personnel training and personnel moving expenses
Zone A					
Areas of maximum benefit	Up to 25% for new plants, 20% for expansions[a]	Up to 20% for investments over $2 million; smaller percentage for smaller projects	60% of cost, up to $100,000 indemnity; up to 60% on larger projects	(a) Local governments authorized to exempt from business tax for five years; (b) transfer tax reduced from 14–17% to 2%; (c) accelerated depreciation;[b] (d) reduction by half of capital gains tax on land	Partial cost of training program; entire cost of moving expenses of employees plus relocation indemnity
Areas of intermediate benefit	15% for new projects up to $1 million and 12% for expansions; variable up to 25% and 20% for larger projects	Same as above	Same as above	Same as above[b]	Same as above
Areas of least benefit	12% for both new and expansion projects up to $1 million; variable up to 25% and 20% for larger projects	Same as above	Same as above	Same as above[b]	Same as above
Zone B					
Designated major metropolitan areas	None	Same as above	Same as above	a, b, and d (above) only	Same as above
Remainder	None	None	Same as above	a, b, and d (above) only	Same as above

Zone C

Designated major metropolitan areas	None	Same as zone A	For transfer from Paris and Lyon areas only	a and b for transfers from Paris and Lyon areas only; d (above)	Same as above
Remainder	None	None	Same as zone A	Same as zone C metropolitan areas	Same as above

Zone D

Lyon area	None	Same as zone A	None	None	None
Paris and Paris basin	None	None	None	None	None

Source: France, la Délégation à l'Aménagement du Territoire et à l'Action Régionale (DATAR), *Investment Incentives in France* (1972).

a. The areas are further divided between those where the maximum grant is automatic up to $1 million of investment and variable above, and those where it is automatic up to $2 million.

b. Only in western parts of zone A.

ter concept, were no longer being given overt preference over other major cities beyond what intangible advantages the name might bring, and the former gradation of incentives according to the size of the city, with the largest getting the most generous assistance, had been equalized to the point where only a few remnants of that distinction remained. All of this subjected the new pattern to the kind of criticism that had given rise to the growth center strategy in the first place—if the available funds were spread over too many communities, then fewer would receive the investment that would enable them to succeed in attracting industry, the whole program would be less effective, and much of the effort and expenditure would be wasted. Some of the planners—or "technocrats," as they are called—had resisted for these reasons the abandonment of the earlier policy. But the planners were divided and, in any case, the political imperatives were clear.

The Problem of Decentralization and Regional Institutions

While Britain still struggles with the question of how to decentralize the making of decisions in the developmental process, France has given its answer—for the time being, at least. A new set of regional institutions came into being at the beginning of 1974, with responsibility for regional planning and, to a degree, for implementation of the plans.

The new institutions represent the culmination of the move toward regionalization that was begun in the 1950s. The concept of "regionalization of the plan" that was introduced with the Fourth and Fifth plans was further refined with the Sixth Plan (1971–75).[68] The regional prefects, acting with the advice of their regional economic development commissions (CODERs), were required to prepare elaborate plans, in three stages, corresponding to the stages of the national plan. First was a report on the general directions of regional development, compiled from studies made by working parties of government officials, CODER members, and independent experts. These reports contributed to the first stage of the national plan—that is, the report on the country's gen-

68. The procedures and their rationale are set out in detail by Jacques Antoine, "La préparation du VIᵐᵉ Plan dans sa dimension régionale," *aménagement du territoire et développement régional* (Institut d'Études politiques, University of Grenoble), 1968.

eral directions, or "options," that was submitted by the government to, and approved by, the National Assembly. Starting from the approved national options, the regional officials defined more precisely the contents of their plans at the same time that national commissions were refining particular segments of the national plan. The two sets of proposals were reconciled in the national plan approved by parliament. Then the regional plan was translated by the regional authorities into a schedule of public expenditure—by object, by source of funds, and by year (for the first two years), all consistent with the national plan.

In theory, then, the whole planning process envisioned the merger of two approaches—that of sectoral commissions, closely associated with national ministries, that reviewed problems and prepared national plans for sectors of the country's economic and social life, and that of the regional bodies that prepared multisector analyses and plans for the country's geographical subdivisions. The reconciliation took place in stages, so that regional thinking could influence national thinking, and vice versa, at each stage. The major decisions embodied in the final product were, of course, influenced more by the national ministries and sectoral commissions than by the regional reports. The decisions were made by the central government, whose basic organization was sectoral, and it was at the national level, moreover, that the broadest perspective existed. As a national objective, for example, the dominance of Paris in higher education had to be broken, and if the regions did not plan for enough expansion of their institutions to achieve the necessary decentralization—as was the case—then expansion had to be thrust upon them by national decision. By the same token, since to develop every region's ports would be an economic waste, the national government had to determine where investment would be concentrated, whether or not that decision might take the heart out of the economic development plans of the regions not favored. The regional plans tended to be discredited by their optimistic assumptions, adopted for advocacy purposes; the total of the regions' initial forecasts of long-range population growth far exceeded the prospective national population, and had to be cut back by the central planners. Yet, to the extent that a regional point of view and sound proposals were developed during the course of the planning process, ample opportunity was given for that view to be expressed and it could not be dismissed in Paris without consideration.

Moreover, if the national point of view prevailed in the major decisions, the regional view could well prevail in the smaller ones. Some share of the decisions formerly made in Paris on the distribution of projects among communities ("In the old days, we didn't ask to build a high school; we were told by Paris to build it") was left to regional judgment. The regional prefect had his envelope of credits, to be distributed geographically in accordance with his plan, and so did the departmental prefect. The discipline of the whole process compelled a systematization of thinking at the regional level—individual projects were to be related to broad developmental objectives, economic and social plans were to be made consistent with land-use and transportation plans, the general direction of development of each of the various cities that made up the urban hierarchy within the region was to be defined, and priorities of expenditure—among sectors, within sectors, and geographically—had to be considered and determined. At its best, the setting of priorities introduced cost-benefit considerations—if not refined calculations—into decisions that previously had been left to the interplay of political forces. The members of CODER and the working parties found themselves called on to think in regional terms and to relate that thinking in turn to national ideas, and the several hundred participants in these bodies in each region, if no one else, received a civic education that would presumably make a contribution to regional and national life progressively as time went on.

The process, nevertheless, has been severely criticized. The theme of many of the complaints has been that the sound concepts of the regional planning system have been blocked from realization by faults in the structure of the institutions at the regional level and the techniques that grew out of the structure.[69]

Since the man in charge of the entire operation at the regional level, the regional prefect, was a central government official, to transfer powers from Paris to him, it is argued, was not decentralization to a truly regional body at all. It was only deconcentration within the central government, quite a different thing. Power remained where it always was—in Paris.

The CODER, as a strictly advisory body, failed in many cases to

69. The discussion of structural and procedural weaknesses of the planning process relies primarily on Pierre Grémion and Jean-Pierre Worms, "L'expérience française de régionalisation au cours des années 60" (1972; processed); and Grémion's earlier "Regional institutions in the French local political and administrative system," in E. Kalk, ed., *Regional Planning and Regional Government in Europe* (The Hague: International Union of Local Authorities, 1971).

develop vitality. Influential individual members with projects or ideas to promote preferred to present them directly to the prefect, who had the power and the responsibility, rather than to their colleagues on the CODER, who did not. Without a budget or staff of its own and meeting only when the prefect had documents to review, the CODER rarely initiated studies and recommendations. If in reacting to the prefect's proposals the CODER expressed disagreement, the prefect could always transmit that body's recommendations with a private communication rebutting them. "The feeling in the regions," said one observer, "is that they go through motions. They send petitions to the King, but the King decides." One small sample of interest group leaders expressed "uniform dissatisfaction with the results of their participation in the CODER."[70] Not only is the structure of the CODER similar to that of the British regional economic development councils, but so are the deficiencies.

In preparation of the Sixth Plan, each regional prefect was authorized a small staff, to be composed of people who could bring a broad and impartial regional perspective to their work. But it was easier to create the positions than to fill them. The hope that able young members of the civil service elite would seek long-term assignments in the regions did not materialize in significant numbers; careers, except in the prefecture corps, were still made in Paris, and service in the provinces was seen as only a detour. So the regional prefects were forced to rely on persons made available for short-term assignments from Paris or on staff borrowed temporarily, often part time, from various agencies in the regions —not necessarily generalists or even planners by experience and temperament, but specialists whose primary loyalty remained to the agencies where they expected their career advancement.

Like their borrowed staffs, the regional prefects themselves were not planners by background, experience, or training. Traditionally, the prefect's role had been a political and mediating one. As the official at the pivot point of a complex and highly centralized system of intergovernmental relations, it was his job to keep peace among local governments and interest-group constituencies and between them and the central government. Thrust into the planning process, he brought to it the skills

70. Paul Godt, "Regionalization and Interest Groups in France" (Ph.D. dissertation, New School for Social Research, 1971), p. 173. "It appears evident that the CODER were created, in part at least, to replace the Expansion Committees with a consultative organ more easily controlled by the government." Ibid., p. 179.

of the diplomat, politician, and peace officer, not those of the cost-benefit analyst. And his inevitable tendency was to use his new staff in the same way—as negotiators and mediators rather than as planners in any professional sense. So the plans reflected the balancing of political pressures and considerations of equity in the distribution of benefits perhaps more than they reflected objective planning criteria. And in the apportionment of the prefect's envelope of credits, "distributive justice" is even more likely to be the criterion, and the plan itself may be disregarded.

Meanwhile, the regional prefect himself was being bypassed. First, by the other departmental prefects, who were never reconciled to the notion that the prefect of the largest department should be "both judge and interested party." Second, by the big-city mayors and other local influentials who could exert their influence directly in Paris—often as members of the senate or the chamber of deputies—and felt they had more to lose than gain by subjecting their claims to the scrutiny of a CODER or a regional planning staff. Third, by the field personnel of the various ministries, each of whom had his own channel of communication to his home office in Paris.

"The situation," observed Grémion and Worms, "can be summed up in a phrase: The planning process has not transformed traditional institutions or administrative practices; it is these institutions and practices that have transformed the regionalization of the Plan."[71]

Like a more ambitious decentralization scheme of General de Gaulle that was defeated in a popular referendum in 1969,[72] the new regional structure of 1974 reflects the compromises that had to be made with the institutions at the national and local levels that inevitably resisted the creation of independent and powerful regional bodies that might threaten them. Thus, while the new regional legislative body—the regional council—will consist of elected officials, those officials will be holders of national and local elective posts. All senators and deputies in the national

71. "L'expérience française," p. 22.
72. The defeat was not a repudiation of the concept of regionalization as such. The regionalization proposal, considered popular, was combined with a less popular proposal to reform the senate, and the composite reform measure was offered by de Gaulle with a declaration that he would resign if it were rejected. Conceived by de Gaulle as a means of obtaining a popular vote of confidence, and by the country as a referendum on his leadership and tactics, perhaps more than on the substance of the reforms, the proposals were rejected by the narrow margin of 53 percent, and de Gaulle resigned his office and retired. (The Paris region already had a regional assembly, with limited taxing powers, under separate legislation.)

legislature from the region will be members of the regional assembly, comprising half its number. The other half will be local elected officials —mayors and members of departmental councils. A second new body in each region is the economic and social committee, an advisory group like the CODER that it replaces—representing business, labor, agriculture, academic expertise, and so on.

Both bodies are to participate in the planning process, in an advisory role, but in combination they can be expected to enjoy more prestige and exercise more influence than could the CODER alone. They will be consulted annually on the government's public expenditure program in the region. Beyond that, the regional council will have power to raise and expend its own revenues, though its taxing authority is severely restricted—$5 per capita, which is but 2–3 percent of what city governments commonly raise through local taxes. And its executive officer is still the regional prefect, who remains a departmental prefect as before. The evolution of regional institutions would appear to be handicapped by the fact that the exercise of regional responsibility is still a secondary duty for all concerned—for the prefect as well as for the members of the regional council.

The new structure is widely criticized as freezing a pattern of regions that are too many and too small. Some of the most respected regional planners and economists in the country have been advocating consolidation of the twenty-one regions into not more than ten, approximating the number of *métropoles d'équilibre* and corresponding to a regional map used by central government planners for some purposes—and closer in scale, incidentally, to the British regions. But just as the combined opposition from above and below kept the new regional institutions from developing independence through separation from national and local government, so it kept the regions themselves small and numerous to prevent their development as potentially more menacing rivals.

If the steps taken so far disappoint the most avid advocates of decentralization, they still represent a substantial departure from the traditions of one of the world's most centralized democratic governments, and they provide a basis for further devolution as the new institutions develop a regional outlook and the regional planning process is improved. The resistance will continue, too. But a country that had progressively centralized its decision-making processes over a span of several centuries has at least reversed its course. Those committed to a thoroughgoing revision of the entrenched governmental practices are also reconciled to seeing their results not in years but in decades.[73]

The Continuing Ambivalence about Restraining Paris

The 1968 census made clear the necessity for controlling the expansion of tertiary employment in Paris if the growth of the region's total population was to be effectively restrained. While the capital region had registered an absolute decline in manufacturing and construction employment since the 1962 census, the number of service jobs had increased by 285,000, at a steady pace of 2 percent a year—amounting to almost one-fourth of the total national increase in that sector.[74] In the nation as a whole, for every 10 additional jobs in the secondary sector in the 1954–62 period, 14 had been added in the service sector. But in the 1962–68 period, the ratio had increased to 26–10, and in the Sixth Plan the projected ratio was 32–10.

The tightening of controls on construction and occupancy of office space in Paris in 1969 coincided with the beginning of an office building boom. Promoters discovered that they could obtain a greater rate of return from office buildings than from residential housing, and knowing that controls were coming (the decree authorizing the institution of controls had been issued in 1967), they moved rapidly to get their projects under way ahead of the restraints. The decentralization committee charged with controlling the burgeoning activity proved quite unable to stifle it. Pressures from promoters, from the ministries concerned with economic growth, and from politicians and those with influence on them were predictably severe, and the decisions of the committee could be appealed to the minister in charge and even to the cabinet. Approved new construction, which exceeded 8 million square feet in 1969 (compared to a level of half that amount in the mid-1960s),

73. France's new president, Valéry Giscard d'Estaing, committed himself to the principle of decentralization in his campaign in 1974. After taking office, he held a cabinet meeting in Lyon to dramatize that commitment—the first such meeting held outside Paris in modern history. France should not be seen as "a single magnetic center with a gray zone all around it," he said in Lyon. *New York Times*, Sept. 12, 1974.
74. The tertiary—or service—sector in France includes transportation and communications, commerce, banking, insurance, public services, and military.

passed 13 million in 1970 and 15 million in 1971. Well over half the nation's new office building construction was being concentrated in the capital region. The accompanying rise in tertiary employment was principally responsible for a sharp increase in the Paris region's share of the country's total jobs. That share had risen from 21.0 percent to 21.4 percent between 1962 and 1968 but by 1971 it was up to 22.6 percent. Indeed, no less than 86 percent of the country's total employment growth was in the capital region, compared to 29 percent in the 1962–68 period. And whereas factories were dispersed around the periphery of the Paris agglomeration, the office building promoters wanted their structures as near as possible to the heart of the city, portending congestion and transportation problems more severe than any that had ever come about from the earlier concentration of manufacturing employment.

By 1972 the committee was able to impose a ceiling of 6.5 million square feet on speculative building, which it apportioned geographically, plus 0.5 million reserved for the five new towns being developed on the outskirts of the agglomeration. On that basis the committee was able to reject about half of the applications from speculative building promoters. But critics of the program contended that the 6.5 million square feet allowed (when added to more than 3 million built by firms for their own use) was not highly restrictive—it was close to the amount that, considering that demand had slackened, would actually have been constructed in the absence of controls. In 1973, however, the ceiling was again reduced, to 3.75 million square feet, plus 2.75 million for the new towns.

Meanwhile, the administrators were using their authority to approve the occupancy of office buildings as a means of putting a damper on the expansion of firms such as banks and insurance companies that had large clerical operations that could feasibly operate at a distance from the headquarters. DATAR entered into discussions with individual companies, and in its 1973 report was able to enumerate concrete results. Sometimes it had negotiated agreements—as it had done earlier with manufacturing firms—that would permit limited expansion in Paris contingent on much greater expansion in the provinces.

Meanwhile, the incentive system introduced in 1967 was liberalized to make the benefits offered to service establishments roughly equivalent to those offered manufacturing. In areas eligible for investment grants for factories, corresponding incentives were granted for new investments in the tertiary sector from any source—not just for firms or activities relocating from Paris—provided the projects were related to regional development (thus excluding supporting activities of a purely local character, such as retail establishments and restaurants). The same ceiling of $3,000 per job that applied to manufacturing projects, and the same minimum requirements for job creation, were applied to tertiary projects. The amount of the grant was standardized, at 10 percent for administrative and management services, 15 percent for executive and design or research services, and 20 percent for head offices, scaled to reflect the more important value of "high-level" activities in stimulating the development of provincial cities.

Finally, a system of graded building permit fees was introduced in the Paris agglomeration in 1972. With the dual purpose of decentralizing services to the provinces and dispersing them within the Paris region, the fees, which had been uniform at $4 per square foot throughout the region, were lowered to $2 a square foot in certain redevelopment areas in the eastern suburbs and raised to $8 in central and western Paris and in the western suburbs. Half of the receipts went into DATAR's special fund for regional development. In addition, a special payroll tax was levied on employers in Paris and its inner suburbs to shift more of the cost of the capital's public services to the local residents.

But from every sign the consensus that had prevailed for a generation on the need for stringent policies to restrain the growth of manufacturing in Paris did not extend to office building. The builders, speculators, and other interests with a financial stake in Paris' growth had not opposed with any vigor the policies for factory dispersal; indeed, they had to some extent favored those measures because a Paris free of factories would be an even more attractive place for development as a great administrative and financial center. But dispersal of the administrative and financial functions was something else, and real estate and building interests, along with tertiary employers and a large segment of the local officialdom, were aroused in defense of the growth of the service sector. Establishment of the European Economic Community gave them, like their counterparts in London, a telling argument; if Paris were not encouraged and helped by the national government to develop as a financial center of Europe and an administrative center for the growing multinational corporations, then it would lose the race to Frankfurt and Düsseldorf, Amsterdam and Brussels. And with the entry of Britain into the

Community, they could argue that only a flourishing and unrestrained Paris could hope to rival London in the provision of financial services or as a site for corporate headquarters.

DATAR had its counterargument, of course—the same one that had been used a decade earlier:

There is no incompatibility of principle between the pursuit of a decentralization effort extended with caution to the financial institution sector, on the one hand, and the presence in Paris of activities functionally linked to an international financial center, on the other.

It is, on the contrary, only to the extent that the financial center of Paris can be relieved of services and employees that are neither necessary nor useful to it that it will be technically possible to create the material conditions that will give to the center of Paris the maximum chance to enlarge its international financial role.[75]

In 1973 the ministry of finance was supporting a proposal by the financial community to build a "City of London" in downtown Paris. DATAR was attempting to get the sponsors to analyze the proposed activities of the center and break them into three parts, in keeping with the government's dual-objective philosophy—those that were an essential part of a financial capital and belonged downtown; those that needed to be near the capital but could be located in one of the new towns on the outskirts; and those that could be dispersed to the provinces. If this issue could not be solved through negotiation, then it would go to the cabinet and the president for decision. And backers of the project could recall President Pompidou's attitude on a similar issue some years before: in announcing the government's approval of a huge office-building complex proposed for Montparnasse on the edge of downtown Paris—described by one planner as a "planning disaster"—the president declared that "Paris is not a museum."

The conflict—and the ambivalence—in French policy is well reflected in DATAR's brochure designed to attract foreign investors to the underdeveloped regions of the country. One year the booklet explained that as part of its program to reduce the "imbalance" between Paris and the underdeveloped parts of the country, the government was "controlling the growth of the Paris area." But the next year it made a significant addition to that statement: "Nevertheless, as part of its new international policy, the French government fully encourages investors to select Paris,

75. DATAR, *La Décentralisation du Tertiaire: Les Banques et Les Assurances* (1972), p. 4.

or other regional capitals, as the site for their European headquarters, research centers and international departments. Indeed, *the French capital offers an inviting climate for these operations.*[76] This, at the very time that DATAR was pressing French firms to remove their headquarters and research centers to the provinces, and the government was offering incentives to that end.

The inevitability that difficult decisions are carried to the political level of the government, even to the president himself, and that political considerations then tend to dominate decision making and distort the equity of the whole system has led some officials to advocate a shift from controls to "penalty taxation" as the means to stem the growth of Paris. The recently-increased building permit fees—amounting to 3–5 percent of the cost of office buildings in the zone where the fees are highest— have done little to restrain construction. Theoretically, the fees could be raised to a point where they would effectively curtail building—perhaps to 10–15 percent or even higher, as has recently been done in the Netherlands (see Chapter 5, below). That would leave the allocation of space among users to the market rather than to the decisions of administrative officials—or politicians. But, while control through taxation would remove politics from the system, it would drive up the costs of office space and services to the very institutions that the government wants to attract to Paris and put the French capital at a disadvantage in the international competition. Presumably, also, it would result in the exclusion of some useful services from Paris while admitting others that, while not directly useful to the national objectives, could pay the cost of being there. In any case, this proposed alternative to direct controls does not yet appear to be beyond the talking stage.

"Only the Hard Ones Are Left"

As a new president of France, Valéry Giscard d'Estaing, took office in 1974, French dispersal policy appeared in need of vigorous reaffirmation and new departure.

During its first two decades, the policy could claim both operational effectiveness and political success. Since the imposition of controls, the

76. DATAR, *Investment Incentives in France* (March 1971), p. 3, and (August 1972), p. 4. Italics added.

Paris region had been brought down to less than one-third of its former share of the nation's factory construction, and a rising proportion of the construction diverted out of Paris had been steered into the underdeveloped areas that national policy sought to favor. The historic balance of migration to Paris from the provinces had been reversed. And this had been accomplished at a rate of expenditure so moderate that almost no complaint was heard about the cost.[77]

Politically, support was virtually unanimous. The Gaullist party and its allies, in control of the government continuously since 1958, have never wavered in their official commitment to the objective of dispersal, and the principal opposition, the Socialist-Communist alliance, demands more, not less, planning and control. Never has there been any significant segment of French opinion in favor of abandoning the dispersal objective altogether—no political bloc proposing a return to laissez faire, like the Powell wing of the Conservative party in Britain.

Nevertheless, as *l'aménagement du territoire* entered its third decade, signs of a break in the political consensus were appearing. The backsliding was not on the issue of whether France should have a dispersal policy; few would suggest that the country might return to the days of a quarter century ago when it had no policy at all. Nor were the general outlines of the policy in question. The issue was whether the government would prove to be sufficiently united and determined to conceive and carry out the measures that would be necessary to make that policy effective.

"The trouble," said one planner, "is that the easy-to-move industries are gone. There's nothing but the hard ones left." The hard ones were, of course, the tertiary establishments. As in Britain, the government had underestimated—or simply failed to foresee—the powerful forces in the middle and late 1960s making for growth and centralization of corporate administration and banking, insurance, and other commercial services of all kinds; like the British, the French were caught off guard by the surge in clerical employment in their capital, and the imposition of controls was tardy. As across the Channel, the resistance to dispersal in the tertiary

77. Perhaps because the cost of the incentive programs is so modest, their cost effectiveness has not been closely analyzed. Prud'homme, in "Regional Economic Policy in France," assembles data that suggest (1) that the incentives have not been a great influence on actual locational decisions, (2) that investment subsidies favor capital-intensive types of investment, and (3) that DATAR policy has been oriented toward assisting the lagging regions by inducing large corporations to locate branch plants there, whereas experience indicates that the expansion of small, established plants offers a greater employment potential.

sector had proved far tougher than that encountered in the move to decentralize manufacturing. And the techniques were less simple to apply; it was one thing to decide that a large automobile plant could produce as efficiently in Bordeaux as within the shadow of the Eiffel Tower, but quite another to pass judgment on the need for a myriad of diverse tertiary activities to be in Paris.

Moreover, as in London, the very success of French policy in dispersing manufacturing was finally arousing a significant backlash from the capital's working class. In the 1973 legislative elections, Communist candidates in the capital's "red belt" of industrial suburbs exploited the loss of factory jobs as a campaign issue, and while the national party did not take up the cry, the issue remains. As in London, to shift unemployed industrial workers to office jobs has not proved feasible, and fears are expressed that even a moderate economic turndown could bring an unemployment crisis in the capital that would undermine the whole dispersal policy and discredit DATAR's decentralizers as a coterie of zealots who have moved too far too fast.

What worries the advocates of dispersal is not that the policy will be openly reversed, but that it will fail through ambivalent administration. In the face of the new centralizing pressures, even a continuance of the present range of measures apparently will not suffice to achieve the settled national objective. To cope with the hard-to-move industries, more stringent measures will be necessary.

One test of the government's determination will be its action in regard to its own offices located in the capital. Studies of possible decentralization of government agencies have been long in preparation, and officials talk of a coming showdown on that issue that will give a measure of the commitment of the new French leadership. The relocation of the headquarters of some major private or government-controlled tertiary institutions would be a step of immense importance. In Germany, notes Beaujeu-Garnier, "powerful banks are located in Frankfurt as well as in Munich, Cologne, and Hamburg. In France, on the contrary, the merger of important companies (both national and international) over the past few years has increased the temptation to establish large new head offices in Paris. Lyon has been deprived of nearly all its head offices, and Paris' proportion of the turnover of the largest companies seems to have increased."[78]

78. Beaujeu-Garnier, "Toward a New Equilibrium?" p. 124.

Any dramatic new initiative by the government would surely command political support in the country approaching that accorded the initiatives of the past. The combined political weight of the "French desert" still exceeds that of Paris, and any organized demand from the capital for a slackening of dispersal policy can be counted on to raise even stronger counterdemands from the provinces for its strengthening. And the sentiment of Paris would in any case be divided—the antigrowth attitude of a majority of Parisians seems unlikely to change—while that of the provinces would be united. Finally, the objective facts remain: whatever the evils of centralization that produced the national consensus that has prevailed for more than twenty years, they can only be intensified if further centralization is permitted to take place.

On balance, then, the stronger pressures on French political leadership should be for a continuance and strengthening of dispersal policy. The questions, as the government of President Giscard d'Estaing settled into place, were whether it would muster the will to respond and whether it could find the means.

CHAPTER FOUR

Italy: Two Societies, Two Economies

The development of the southern regions constitutes the fundamental objective of the national economic plan.—Law 853, 1971

Overcoming the North-South dualism must be the central and dominant objective of the whole economic policy of the country.—Paolo Emilio Taviani, Minister of Budget and Economic Planning, 1971[1]

IN NOVEMBER 1949, landless peasants moved onto the fields of an absentee-owned agricultural estate in Calabria, the province that occupies the toe of the Italian peninsula, and staked out claims. The land they sought had been promised them in the Italian constitution of 1947, they contended, but the constitutional provisions for land reform had not been carried out. Premier Alcide de Gasperi's government had proposed legislation, but it had not passed. Now the peasants were taking matters into their own hands.

The Communist party, which had shown an alarming strength in the parliamentary election the previous year, had been urging direct action by the peasants and now it championed the squatters' cause. The land seizures spread quickly through Calabria, into Sicily and other provinces of the underdeveloped and impoverished southern half of Italy, and north to the very outskirts of Rome. De Gasperi went to Calabria, where he talked with the peasants and made the inevitable pledges. Not only would land reform be expedited, but the highest priority would be given to southern Italy's enormous need for help to eliminate the disparities between that region and the rest of the country. In January he announced a ten-year plan for regional development.

The "southern question" had been high on the government's agenda ever since formation of the new Italian republic at the end of the Second

1. July 9, 1971, during Senate debate on Law 853. Massimo Annesi, *L'Intervento Straodinario nel Mezzogiorno nel Quinquennio 1971–1975* (Rome: SVIMEZ, 1972), p. 358.

World War. The Mezzogiorno was a land that the industrial revolution, which had transformed northern Italy along with central and northern Europe, had passed by. Unification of the country, in 1861, had done nothing to equalize the industrial development of the two regions. Indeed, it had worked the other way. Removal of tariff walls and improvement of transportation had opened the South to northern manufactured goods and so destroyed much of that region's local, uncompetitive industry. Between 1901 and 1936, industrial employment rose by 50 percent in the North but declined, by 10 percent, in the South.[2] At the end of that period, per capita income was but half that of the North. Southern provinces that contained close to a quarter of the country's population had one-fourteenth of the workers in industries supplied by mechanical power. Then came the war. Fought over mile by mile, the South lost one-third of its industry, compared to 5–7 percent in the Po Valley, and more than half of its hydroelectric capacity. And even as an agricultural region, the Mezzogiorno, mountainous, eroded, and arid, has always suffered a shortage of tillable land.

During the first six decades of unification, emigration had been the safety valve. Some five million Italians left the country during that period, two-thirds of them from the South, most of them going to the United States and other countries of the Western Hemisphere. But after the First World War the American countries placed restrictions on that movement, and so did Mussolini. At the end of the Second World War the surplus population of the South was dammed up there, without opportunity in either industry or agriculture. The land seizures dramatized the explosive potential. So did the Communist inroads among the peasants.

The Preindustrialization Period   *(1950–56)*

The de Gasperi ten-year plan was centered on a segment of the economy that, in employment terms, was one not of growth but of steady

---

2. Kevin Allen and M. C. MacLennan, *Regional Problems and Policies in Italy and France* (London: George Allen and Unwin, 1970), p. 40. Similarly, between 1881 and 1901, industrial employment fell by one-third in the South, while rising by 6–7 percent in the North. Kevin Allen and Andrew Stevenson, *An Introduction to the Italian Economy* (London: Martin Robertson, 1974), chap. 6.

decline in every country—agriculture. Yet that was the only area where quick achievement could be hoped for. Agriculture was the only economic base the Mezzogiorno had, the only activity for which its labor force was trained, and for which marketing and distribution systems were established. And land was what the peasants were demanding.

It was clear that to expropriate the *latifondi* for the peasants could be only an initial step. For the peasants to make the land productive would require investment in irrigation, drainage, and agricultural credit and marketing services. And beyond that, southern Italy had enormous need for expenditures for public facilities of every kind—roads, schools, hospitals, railroads, power plants, telephone services. Part of the need was to repair war damage; part was to overcome deficiencies in public services and facilities that had existed ever since the country was born.

For a portion of the necessary funds, the government turned to the World Bank. Out of discussions about how the programs would be organized and the money expended came the idea for a new agency with a broad charter for development of the entire Mezzogiorno region—an idea inspired in part, it was said, by the success of the Tennessee Valley Authority. The government accepted the proposal, and in August 1950 a law was enacted creating the Cassa per il Mezzogiorno (Fund for the South).[3]

The Cassa was a new government agency with a high degree of autonomy, operating under the policy direction of a committee of ministers. Its domain—44 percent of the country's area, and 37 percent of the population—extended from the southern tip of the peninsula to a line within a few miles of Rome, plus the islands of Sicily and Sardinia. It was authorized to spend $1.6 billion to carry out a ten-year program.[4] This was intended to be in addition to the regular expenditures of the various ministries, which would continue to give the South its fair share of attention. The industries in the state holding sector,[5] which are a large segment

3. The World Bank made two modest loans to the Cassa in 1951 and 1953, totaling $20 million. Edward S. Mason and Robert E. Asher, *The World Bank Since Bretton Woods* (Brookings Institution, 1973), pp. 167, 264, 271, and 289. The broad developmental assistance that was hoped for proved to be outside the bank's pattern of operations.

4. In 1952 another $450 million was made available and the plan extended for two additional years.

5. The state holding sector consists of industries taken over by the government, mostly during the depression of the 1930s, and placed under the control of state holding groups. The most important are the Istituto per la Ricostruzione Industriale

of the Italian economy, were specifically required to place a disproportionate share—60 percent—of their new projects in the Mezzogiorno, in order to bring the South's share of their total investment to 40 percent in fifteen years.[6] By a separate law, 20 percent of government procurement contracts were directed to be placed in the South.

To stake the prestige of the new democratic government on the solution of the Mezzogiorno's problems was an act not only of "humane obligation" and "political vision" but of "moral courage," the first president of the cabinet committee later wrote.[7] Launched amid widespread skepticism, he recalled, the effort ran counter to the general view in the North that the poverty of the South was the region's own fault, the product of southern "indolence." It encountered also some more sophisticated objections: that the organs of public administration lacked the capacity to carry out a broad program of regional development; that the effort would increase disappointment and discontent "measurelessly, or at best, in the measure by which the immensity of the needs would necessarily exceed the limitations of the resources"; and that deficiencies in technical and professional leadership would make it impossible for the region to profitably absorb the expenditures. Northerners were not yet convinced of the interdependence of northern and southern prosperity; the authoritative economic studies that made the case for interdependence in "vivid" and "combative" terms came only later, after economists became involved in the Cassa's work. But the government in power saw elements of political strength also, intuitively if not by calculation: northern industry was demonstrating a powerful capacity to expand; it would be seeking markets and there were "millions and millions of potential consumers in the

---

(IRI), a diversified group that includes steel and automobile, and the Ente Nazionale Idrocarburi (ENI), a group centered on petrochemical products, including synthetic textiles. The state-held industries are distinct from the nationalized ones, such as electricity and rail transport. Allen and Stevenson, *Introduction to the Italian Economy*.

6. In a separate 1950 law the parliament authorized $320 million to be spent over a ten-year period (increased to $400 million and fifteen years in 1954) to bring the infrastructure of depressed areas in northern and central Italy (the Centro-Nord) to the national standard. A committee of ministers was to designate the depressed areas and approve the public works, with the work to be carried out by the regular ministries rather than a special agency. Ettore Massacesi, "Regional Economic Development in Italy," in U.S. Department of Commerce, Area Redevelopment Administration, *Area Redevelopment Policies in Britain and the Countries of the Common Market* (1965), pp. 303–04.

7. Pietro Campilli, "La 'Cassa' e lo Sviluppo del Mezzogiorno," in *Cassa per il Mezzogiorno: Dodici Anni 1950–1962* (Bari: Laterza, 1962), vol. 1, p. 7.

Mezzogiorno." So, spurred by the communist challenge—although the communists, for their part, belittled the Cassa as an inadequate response to the problem—the government accepted the political risk.[8]

The act creating the Cassa spoke only of agriculture and tourism, mentioning manufacturing solely in relation to the processing of agricultural products. Of the $1.6 billion authorized in the original law and spent according to the ten-year plan, nearly half—$790 million—went for land reclamation and improvement, and another $452 million for land reform. Water supply and drainage accounted for $178 million, roads for $145 million, and projects to promote tourism, $48 million.[9] But even before the act was passed, far-sighted people had been arguing that no matter how drastic the land reform and how strenuous the efforts to reclaim swamps and arid land for cultivation, agriculture could not possibly absorb more than a tiny fraction of the Mezzogiorno's surplus population. The rest could be employed only if southern Italy were brought into the modern industrial world along with the country's northern half.

Some present-day critics of Italian regional policy contend accordingly that the early 1950s were the crucial lost years. When Italian industry was expanding at an extraordinary rate to meet the deferred demand for peacetime goods, they argue, was the critical time for governmental intervention to bring about dispersal. By the time the boom was over, industry was solidified in its Milan-Turin-Genoa "industrial triangle," and the amount of "mobile" investment that could be directed to the Mezzogiorno was greatly diminished. Yet, had the government foreseen that an "economic miracle" was in the making, it might have been all the more loath to interfere with the entreprenurial decisions that were bringing the miracle about. Like other European governments then, Italy was principally concerned about its balance of payments and, consequently, the competitiveness of its industry in world markets.[10] And the northern industrialists, powerful within the ruling Christian Democratic party, had no desire to disperse their factories. So the government waited, and hoped that expenditures for agriculture and for infrastructure would

8. On balance, Allen and Stevenson conclude, the communists gained more politically from their attacks on the program than the Christian Democrats, who controlled the government, gained by sponsoring it. *Introduction to the Italian Economy*, political appendix.

9. *La Cassa per il Mezzogiorno* (Cassa per il Mezzogiorno [1968]), p. 10. The $450 million added in 1952 was for land reform.

10. Allen and MacLennan, *Regional Problems and Policies*, p. 51.

somehow induce northern industries to expand into the South of their own volition.

Yet the economic facts of life became plainer year by year, and once the political decision had been made to commit the country to development of the impoverished South, economists and planners both inside and outside the government could press the view that there was only one way to make good on that commitment—through industrialization. One of the earliest and most influential of the critics, a Swiss economist, Friedrich Vöchting, began almost as soon as the Cassa was created to argue that the Mezzogiorno could not develop as an *agrikulturstaat*, like some European states of the nineteenth century. That could happen only if the total population were stable, he wrote in 1952.[11] But southern Italy was a region of rapid population growth. At best, the ten-year plan would create 5,000 additional permanent jobs in agriculture and 10,000 to 15,000 in hydroelectric plants, food processing plants, and so forth. At the end of the decade there would be 1.8 million unemployed—reduced somewhat, but not decisively, by emigration. The act may have been the best course "from the propagandistic-electoral point of view," as a "grand gesture" to the peasants, but essentially it was a "mirage," a palliative, offered by a government that was "compelled to navigate with the wind and content to live to the day." To defer industrialization through the entire decade of the 1950s would be to waste those years while the South remained a land of social struggle and poverty, the disparities between the "two Italies" widened, and all the resources lavished in the ten-year plan would be "like water poured in a hole."

Vöchting's thesis was supported elsewhere, particularly in the publications of the Association for the Industrial Development of the South (SVIMEZ),[12] which had been formed in 1946. Meanwhile, early experience was demonstrating the validity of his arguments. Land reform, while socially and economically desirable in itself, was having no effect on urban unemployment and hardly even a noticeable effect on underemployment in the countryside. By the end of the 1950s, only about 4 percent of the South's 2 million peasants had received land—and many of those, of course, had been fully employed already as farm workers on the estates that were expropriated. The public works expenditures

11. Friedrich Vöchting, "Sulla questione meridionale: industrializzazione o pre-industrializzazione?" Banca Nazionale del Lavoro, *Moneta e Credito*, vol. 5 (1952), pp. 84–92.
12. Associazione per lo Sviluppo Industriale del Mezzogiorno.

turned out to have almost a negligible effect on the South's economic base; supplies, materials, and equipment were brought in from the North.

The supporters of industrialization of the Mezzogiorno found their necessary ally in Ezio Vanoni, budget minister and advocate of national economic planning on the French model. In his ten-year plan for the Italian economy, presented to parliament in 1955, he fully incorporated the critics' thinking. If attaining full employment and righting the adverse balance of trade had to be two of the main goals of Italian planning, equalizing per capita income between the North and South had to be a third. And that goal posed the familiar alternatives: to eliminate the regional disparities, either workers could be moved north, or industry moved south. The planners had no difficulty in making their choice, like the British earlier and for the same reasons: the southern workers should remain in place. The plan's aims could be accomplished if 40 percent of new industrial investment was in the South. Per capita income would be raised in that region at a rate twice as rapid as that in the rest of the country—8 percent compared to 4 percent.[13]

The plan as such was not adopted, and Italy's initial venture into national planning was abandoned. But during debate on the proposal, sentiment crystallized in favor of the plan's governing principles, particularly those relating to the South. The government and the parliament shifted their emphasis decisively from agricultural to industrial development, and in 1957 they added to the Cassa's mandate a new program of industrial development that compared well in breadth and in level of assistance with those of other European countries.[14]

Industrialization of the South   (*1957–64*)

The 1957 legislation introduced a series of incentives for private investment in industry in the Mezzogiorno. The major provisions were:[15]

13. Vera Cao-Pinna, "Regional Policy in Italy," in Niles M. Hansen, ed., *Public Policy and Regional Economic Development: The Experience of Nine Western Countries* (Ballinger, forthcoming). For this "spatial dimension" of the national plan, Vanoni relied on research by SVIMEZ that he had promoted.

14. Three regional credit institutions had been created in 1953 to provide direct loans for southern industry. Their interest rate was high, however (5.5 percent), and by 1957 they had financed only 806 projects, at a value of $160 million. Vera Lutz, *Italy: A Study in Economic Development* (Oxford University Press, 1962), pp. 183–85.

15. The provisions of the 1957 and 1959 legislation are condensed from Allen and MacLennan, *Regional Problems and Policies*, pp. 54–61.

Tax incentives. Industrial investment there was wholly or partially exempted from six forms of taxation, of which the most important were a ten-year exemption from income taxation (normally 28–36 percent), exemption from customs duties on building materials and machinery (then averaging 15 percent), and 50 percent exemption from the turnover tax on machinery and equipment produced in the country (normally about 3.3 percent).

Grants. Capital grants were made available to new or expanding small industries (with fixed assets under $10 million). Grants for buildings varied, up to 25 percent, according to a formula that gave preference to modern industry, labor-intensive projects, and projects located in designated growth centers. Machinery and equipment grants, up to 10 percent, were left to administrative discretion, but presumably the same criteria were applied. In the growth centers, larger enterprises could qualify for grants covering the first $10 million of a project's costs.

Loan subsidies. The Cassa was authorized to pay subsidies to bring down the interest rate on loans for industrial projects. The rate was subsequently set at 4 percent for industries with fixed investments up to $10 million and 5 percent for larger ones. The 4 percent loans could also provide for repayment moratoriums up to two years on interest and five years on principal. These loans plus grants could amount to 85 percent of total investment.[16]

Risk capital. Institutions were established to purchase minority shareholdings in new enterprises.

In 1959 an institute was created to provide technical assistance to southern entrepreneurs, and a special loan program was enacted providing credit to small and medium-sized businesses at 3 percent interest, up to a limit of $2.4 million for new plants and $800,000 for conversion or expansion projects.[17] From time to time this system of incentives has been modified or embellished, but it is still essentially the system that remains in force.

16. These benefits were estimated in one study to add 6–9 percentage points, based on total capital investment, to the profit before taxes of a southern firm that received maximum assistance. The tax subsidies made the differential between southern and northern firms after taxes even greater. Study by Gardner Ackley and Lamberto Dini, cited by Lutz, *Italy*, p. 120.

17. The discussion here, as elsewhere in this chapter, is confined to the national programs available to all qualifying areas. Sicily and Sardinia, having been granted semiautonomous status (along with three northern border provinces) to counter separatist sentiment after the war, were able to enact supplementary measures through their regional governments. These were not, however, on a scale that provided a significant differential over the assistance available in the peninsular South.

If the Italians followed the British and the French in adopting capital grants and loan and tax incentives, they preceded both countries—and others as well—in developing the concept of growth centers. The statute of 1957 authorized the formation of local consortia that would nominate communities to serve as growth centers, plan the development of *agglomerati* (industrial parks) in the centers, and manage the *agglomerati*, all subject to the supervision and approval of the Cassa. The consortia were to be composed of both local public officials and representatives of private business and labor groups in order to mobilize all the leadership resources of the community. The Cassa's expenditures on infrastructure were to be concentrated in the *agglomerati*, and the financial incentives for investors discriminated in their favor.

In addition, the 1957 law authorized the Cassa to organize vocational educational centers, or subsidize existing centers, to teach industrial skills. (This extended powers that had been given it in 1954 in relation to agricultural training.) Finally, the new law added three years to the twelve-year plan, extending it to 1965, and authorized sufficient funds to enable the Cassa to nearly double its spending rate, from around $160 million to $300 million a year.[18]

By the end of the 1950s, then, the structure that was to induce industrial expansion in the Mezzogiorno was in place. The government and the parliament had given broad authority to the Cassa, their chosen agency. They had created credit and technical assistance organizations. They had authorized local consortia to prepare industrial sites and developmental plans, and some thirty-five were in the process of formation.

Above all, they had made a decisive political commitment, with the support of all parties in the parliament, and of national business and labor organizations. What opposition existed in the North on grounds of regional self-interest—"why tax us to subsidize them?"—was neutralized,

18. A companion measure to the 1957 legislation for the South extended some aid to depressed areas of the Centro-Nord. Small businesses and handicraft enterprises were exempted from income taxation for ten years, and in mountain communities, tourism enterprises were exempted as well. The fund for public works in the Centro-Nord was increased to $660 million and extended to 1965, but capital grants and loan-interest subsidies were not authorized as in the South. Subsequently, more than 2,000 communities in the Centro-Nord (under 20,000 population in the mountains and under 10,000 elsewhere) were classified as depressed. Massacesi, "Regional Economic Development," p. 304, and Organisation for Economic Co-operation and Development, "Salient Features of Regional Development Policy in Italy," report of a conference held in October 1968 (Paris: OECD, 1970; processed), pp. 130–31.

at least, by other arguments. Businessmen saw the prospect of a vast new market in a revived and growing South, opened to northern goods by high-speed highways. They would produce the equipment for southern industry. In short, government money spent in the South was sure to flow back northward through one channel or another. Labor leaders might fear that more jobs in the South could mean fewer in the North. But labor had an interest, too, in keeping southern workers in the South, out of competition for northern jobs. Economic studies, notably those of SVIMEZ, had been supporting the strong political consensus with theoretical analyses of the relationship between southern and national economic growth—or southern and national economic stagnation, as the case might be. So long as growth in the North was not actually restrained to benefit the South and employment directly transferred, the North was willing to accept the ideal that all regions should share fairly in the national prosperity.

The response to the new measures was prompt, and measurable. The Mezzogiorno's share of total private investment turned sharply upward, rising from 16 percent in 1957 and 18 percent in 1959 to 24 percent in 1962. From 1959, when the 1957 legislation became fully operative, to 1962, industrial investment in the South rose at an annual rate of 27 percent, almost three times as rapidly as in the 1951–57 period and more than twice as fast as investment in the North. The annual level of assistance under the Cassa's incentive program rose by 1962 to over $750 million in loans and $28 million in grants—although the funds available for grants during this period were not sufficient to assist all eligible applicants.[19]

Growth in investment in the South by the state holding sector of Italian industry was even more impressive. The 1957 legislation had reaffirmed the 1950 requirement that 40 percent of total investment and 60 percent of investment in new projects be located in the Mezzogiorno. But, since existing projects, 80 percent of which were in the North, required considerable new investment for modernization and expansion, it turned out to be necessary, in order to place 40 percent of *all* investment in the South, to locate well over 60 percent of investment in *new*

19. Massacesi, "Regional Economic Development," pp. 266 and 284–85, and Allen and Stevenson, *Introduction to the Italian Economy*, chap. 6. The 1957 legislation was delayed in taking effect by political events—an election and a subsequent delay in forming a stable government.

projects there. This period coincided also with a time of sharp expansion of the state-held enterprises, and their investment in the Mezzogiorno rose from $46 million in 1957 and $76 million in 1959 to $400 million in 1962 and $450 million in 1964. The 1964 figure for public industrial investment slightly exceeded the corresponding private figure.[20]

All this was encouraging, and if it led to a self-sustaining takeoff of southern industry, the region's problem of population surplus would be on its way to solution. But, from the standpoint of immediate results, the effect on morale was more significant than the effect on income and unemployment figures. Per capita income was rising, but the disparity between South and North was not lessening; it may even have been widening. In any case, income per capita in the South remained less than half the northern level.[21] In the period 1960–66, the rate of net emigration from the South, both to the North of Italy and to other countries, averaged 150,000 a year. Largely barred now from the Americas, the population surplus found an important new outlet in neighboring countries of Europe. Switzerland was the principal receiving country at the beginning, but after it imposed a quota on its foreign workers in 1964, West Germany became the leading recipient of Italian emigrants. Gross migration to Western European countries for employment exceeded 200,000 a year in the first half of the 1960s, totaling 329,500 in the peak year of 1961.[22]

Problems of Coordination and Concentration   *(1957–64)*

As industrialization of the South gathered momentum, under the 1957 law, so did criticism of the entire effort. Despite the existence of a fifteen-year plan, the work of the many government ministries engaged in the Mezzogiorno was poorly coordinated, both in the planning and in the

20. Massacesi, "Regional Economic Development," p. 283, and Allen and MacLennan, *Regional Problems and Policies*, p. 105. State-held corporations account for about one-quarter of Italian industrial production. The IRI has been the fourth largest industrial group in Europe.

21. Allen and MacLennan, *Regional Problems and Policies*, pp. 22–23.

22. Ibid., p. 20, and Muriel Grindrod, *Italy* (Praeger, 1968), p. 171. Much of the work in the European countries was seasonal and the emigrant workers might return home frequently, accounting for the large difference between gross and net figures. Overseas emigration from all of Italy in the mid-1960s amounted to about 40,000 a year.

execution. The assistance given the South was spread among too many growth centers, said some critics, while others argued that it was not spread widely enough, since nearly half the population lived in places receiving no help at all. All the critics could agree that the program, in relation to the magnitude of the problem, was underfunded.

To begin with, the Cassa and the interministerial committee that set its policies had proved inadequate as agents of coordination. Each member of the committee was concerned first of all with his own ministry's work, based on its own plans, its own budget, and its own responsibilities to the parliament. The ministries' programs were authorized by separate laws, each of which had its own formulas for distribution of public benefits, and their planning cycles were not necessarily synchronized with that of the Cassa. Sometimes their planning involved the participation of outside groups, as well as local governments. The committee did not have the means to upset long-established practices and combine all of these manifold and varied plans and programs into a single comprehensive and coordinated scheme for southern development. And the committee members, like bureaucrats everywhere, were not disposed in any event to surrender their independence to the Cassa or to their chairman, who was a minister without portfolio assigned to Mezzogiorno affairs. So they reacted in a spirit of competition and self-defense that "often isolated" the Cassa, reducing it to the status of just one more agency among many.[23]

At the same time, the fears that had been expressed at the beginning that a special agency and special fund for the Mezzogiorno would result in the diversion of regular funds from the South to the North appeared to be borne out. The South was falling below its pro rata share of the government's regular expenditures for public works and for transport. Ministries had various explanations: local authorities in the South lacked administrative capacity to develop suitable projects to qualify for national aid, or if they did qualify, they were unable to make use of assistance as rapidly as northern communities. Whatever the reason, during the period 1956–62 the Mezzogiorno received 33 percent of public works actually carried out, exclusive of the Cassa, and 26 percent of the spending of the Ministry of Transport, compared to 37 percent to which its population would have entitled it. While regular public works spending was 24 percent higher in the South in 1962 compared with the early

23. Massacesi, "Regional Economic Development," pp. 241–42.

1950s, it was twice as high in the North. (The South received more than half, on the other hand, of the expenditures by the Ministry of Agriculture.)[24]

The failure to achieve governmentwide coordination was reflected in legislation in 1962 that extended the Cassa more deeply into social and transportation programs related to industrialization. Responsibilities for construction or financing of housing, harbors, airports, hospitals, and nursery schools and kindergartens in areas of industrialization were assigned to the Cassa rather than to the regular ministries concerned with those functions nationally.

At the heart of the coordination problem was the question of how investment should be distributed geographically within the Mezzogiorno to achieve the maximum result. Responding to the original law inviting local groups to organize consortia to designate growth centers and acquire and develop industrial sites, some two score consortia had taken form. Only a dozen of their chosen growth centers had sufficient population base and existing transportation facilities and other basic infrastructure to show promise of any major development, but the Cassa met this by establishing two categories of centers. The dozen large ones (a population of more than 200,000, with at least one-third of that in a central city) were designated as growth "areas." There would be located the large enterprises producing for the world market. But the smaller proposed centers were not excluded from benefits; they would be accepted as growth "nuclei," where smaller enterprises would be developed to serve the local market. Most of the nuclei were under 75,000 in population. In practice, the distinction turned out to be not much more than one of name. In each case the Cassa was authorized to grant up to 85 percent of the cost of investment in the public facilities necessary to develop sites for industry. The Cassa might move slowly in recognizing the more unpromising of the proposed nuclei and in approving their plans, or it might insist that the plans be modified, but it did not find it politically possible to reject any of them outright. By 1963, twelve areas and twenty-three nuclei had been recognized, embracing 24 percent of the land area of the Mezzogiorno and 45 percent of its population, and by 1970 a half-dozen more of each had been added. Every province had at least one

24. Ibid., pp. 244–45 and 248. The southern share of ordinary public works fell below 30 percent in 1964 and 1965. Allen and MacLennan, *Regional Problems and Policies*, p. 80.

Figure 4-1. *Industrial Development Areas and Nuclei in Italy's
Mezzogiorno, 1970*

Rome

Bari

Naples

Palermo

- - - Northern limits
of Cassa intervention

Industrial development
areas or nuclei

Sources: *La Cassa per il Mezzogiorno* (Cassa per il Mezzogiorno [1968]), p. 35; and
Kevin Allen and M. C. MacLennan, *Regional Problems and Policies in Italy and France*
(London: George Allen and Unwin, 1970), p. 69.

growth center, and virtually every community that had experienced any
postwar industrial growth at all was included. The resulting pattern is
shown in Figure 4-1.[25]

This brought an outcry that the principle of concentration of industrial investment was being violated, and the investment funds would be

25. The 1963 figures are from Massacesi, "Regional Economic Development,"
p. 279. Cao-Pinna, "Regional Policy in Italy," gives the 1970 figures as 18 areas and
27 nuclei, covering 25 percent of the land area of the South and 55 percent of its
1961 population (grown to 61 percent at the time of the 1971 census).

spread too thin for maximum effect. But the smaller places had their defenders, too. These critics called for even more liberal policies. If 45 percent of the people lived in places designated for growth, they argued, an even greater number must be living in places scheduled for continued poverty and further decline. This included the inhabitants of most of the hilltop towns that made up the Mezzogiorno's *osso*, the mountainous spine that extended down the middle of the peninsula. Were those towns to be abandoned, their citizens compelled to move to the growth centers in the crowded flatlands along the coast? If so, the already severe problems of housing and public services in those centers would be exacerbated.

The government was not prepared to abandon either the principle of concentration or the people of the *osso*. The chairman of the interministerial committee saw the solution as one of concentrating resources but shifting that concentration from the larger areas to the smaller as soon as the former became self-sustaining. In the meantime, he recommended, a greater share of the country's total investment should be shifted from the North to the South.[26] Under his plan, private investment in the North would be discouraged by denying to northern industry certain credit and tax incentives then available to industry nationwide and by the introduction of disincentives, presumably patterned after the controls in effect in Britain and France; such controls had been suggested but hotly opposed, and defeated, during consideration of the 1957 legislation. And public investment would be shifted by requiring the state-held industries to put not just 60 percent but all of their new investment in the South. That, however, would do little more than confirm the policy that the state enterprises, in order to conform to existing law, had already adopted.

More Funds, More Power, More Planning   *(1965–70)*

A thorough reconsideration of Italy's regional policy in all its aspects was made inevitable by the expiration of the Cassa's charter in 1965. The whole question of how the resources of all concerned—the Cassa, the regular ministries, the state-held enterprises, the credit institutions, and

26. The 1963 report of the committee of ministers for the Mezzogiorno, quoted in Massacesi, "Regional Economic Development," p. 267.

the consortia—could be mobilized in a common effort would then be reviewed. As it happened, however, the review of the Mezzogiorno was to coincide with a broader reconsideration of the question of how development of the Italian economy as a whole should be guided and coordinated. A center-left government of Christian Democrats and Socialists had been formed, and the new leadership was determined to begin anew where Vanoni had left off a decade earlier and introduce national economic planning on the French model. And unlike the French, who had come late to the idea of regionalizing their national plan, the Italians had decided to regionalize theirs from the outset. So a regional planning process was initiated to relate regional development to national economic growth within a single coordinated scheme. The first national plan, covering the period 1966–70, set ambitious goals for the industrialization of the Mezzogiorno; the Cassa was given new authority and increased funds covering the same period, and incentives for private investment were liberalized to support the achievement of the planning objectives.

LIBERALIZATION OF THE INCENTIVES

The legislation of 1965, supplemented by further enactments in 1968, made the incentive system that had been designed originally for small and medium-sized enterprises far more appealing to large and technologically advanced industries—on which, it was by that time clear, the economic growth of the South depended. (The main features of the new system are summarized in Table 4-1, page 166).[27]

The 1965 law set a ceiling of 20 percent on capital grants for industrial investment, covering the costs both of buildings and of machinery and equipment up to $10 million. This new ceiling particularly favored enterprises with heavy investment in equipment, since the old limits had been 10 percent on machinery and equipment and 25 percent on buildings. In addition, investment above $10 million could be subsidized for the first time, at up to 10 percent on investment between $10 million and $20 million, and on investment above $20 million at 50 percent of the grant awarded for the first $20 million. The maximum grant for a single project could therefore be as high as $4.5 million. Moreover, whatever the amount of the grant thus computed, it would be raised by 50 percent on

27. Allen and MacLennan, *Regional Problems and Policies*, pp. 85–94, report in detail the provisions of the 1965 legislation.

the cost of machinery produced in the South. The maximum share of the
investment that could be covered by grants and loans combined was
raised from 85 percent to 90 percent.

The formula for determining what proportion of a project's costs,
below the ceiling, would actually be subsidized was revised and applied
to loans as well as grants. The principal change was to substitute a criterion of size for the previous one of investment per employee. The new
criterion discriminated in favor of larger enterprises in the case of loans;
those larger than a specified size, which varied with each industrial group,
received the maximum allowance, while at the other end of the scale,
investments under $50,000 for new enterprises or $17,000 for expansions
were excluded altogether. For grants, however, the criteria were reversed
to give the larger grants to the smaller enterprises, which, it was assumed,
would be less able to carry a burden of debt. Another factor in the formula—location—was liberalized to permit the maximum grant to be paid
on projects located outside as well as inside the *agglomerati* (but inside
an area or nucleus) upon a showing that the enterprise needed to be in
the location chosen. Beyond that, the new law confirmed the policy of
concentrating investment in growth centers; expenditures in the *osso*,
which had few suitable potential sites for industry in any case, would be
largely confined to improving basic public services, including the education and skill training needed to equip people to move to jobs in the
growth centers.

Some tax concessions and transport subsidies for southern industry
were also liberalized. Steps were taken to strengthen the enforcement
of the procurement set-aside required by the earlier legislation, and the
amount of the set-aside was raised from 20 percent to 30 percent. Low-
interest loans, and grants at a somewhat lower scale than those offered
to industry, were available for construction of hotels and other tourism
projects, and subsidies were also offered to research organizations.

To cover the liberalized incentives, the Cassa—whose life was re-
newed for fifteen years—was allocated $3.1 billion for the period 1965–
69, which enabled it to project a spending rate more than double that of
its first fifteen years. But the step-up in expenditures in the crucial sector
—industry—was from under $20 million to $260 million a year, or from
10 percent to 42 percent of the total budget. The agricultural sector,
which had been receiving more than half of the Cassa's budget up to that
time, was appropriated only 21 percent (although that represented a

maintenance of existing spending levels in absolute terms). The proportion spent for general infrastructure was also to decline.[28]

A further concession to large enterprises in 1968 went a long way
toward removing the remaining discrimination in favor of smaller plants.
Under the revised law, a project costing over $20 million was made
eligible for a grant of 12 percent of its entire investment and a loan, with
interest at 5–6 percent, covering up to 50 percent. Certain conditions had
to be fulfilled—that the plant provide considerable employment, that
it induce other investment, and that it be located in an *agglomerato*,
among other requirements—but these conditions were "so vague, and the
bargaining power of a company investing 12 milliard lire so great" that
most big projects would undoubtedly be found to qualify.[29]

A second major benefit granted in 1968 to all industrial establishments
in the South relieved them of their social security tax obligation for the
next five years, in an amount equal to 10 percent of wages paid on existing
employment and 20 percent on expanded employment. The subsidy,
amounting to about $150 million a year,[30] would serve to offset the effects
of action, to be initiated in 1969, to eliminate certain wage differentials
that had provided an advantage to southern employers.[31]

Once again, Italy chose not to reenforce its incentive program with a
system of disincentives to discourage industrial investment in the existing
centers of industrial concentration, as Britain and France had done. The
proposition was rejected, after extensive debate, in 1965. To discourage

28. *La Cassa per il Mezzogiorno*, p. 21. The $3.1 billion is made up of $2,645,000,000
provided in 1965 plus $420 million appropriated in 1967. Before the end of the period,
late in 1968, the funds were further increased.

29. Allen and MacLennan, *Regional Problems and Policies*, p. 86.

30. OECD, "Salient Features," p. 108.

31. The program for depressed areas of the Centro-Nord was also broadened,
again less generously than for the South. Among the criteria for designation of
depressed areas were impoverishment, low productivity, inadequate industrialization, and a high rate of out-migration. Mountain areas were included automatically,
with a few exceptions, and the smaller lowland communities designated under
earlier programs were combined into larger "zones." The new boundaries, proposed
by regional planning committees and approved by the ministerial committee, contained 66 percent of the land area of the Centro-Nord and 24 percent of its population at the end of 1966. Development plans were prepared by the regional committees, as in the South. The only incentive offered to industrialists, however,
beyond the tax incentive made available to small businesses and tourism enterprises
under earlier law, was a loan program with a subsidized interest rate as low as 4 percent (compared to 3 percent in the South) on loans of up to 10 years (compared to
15 in the South) in amounts up to $1.6 million (the limits were much higher in the
South). No capital grants were offered.

expansion of industry in the North, the prevailing argument ran, might simply drive industry out of Italy altogether, into other countries of the European Economic Community.[32]

NATIONAL AND REGIONAL PLANNING

In launching its economic planning experiment, the Italian government tried at the outset to introduce the decentralized pattern that had evolved in France only slowly. Temporary regional committees were appointed in 1964—composed of representatives of the larger local authorities, employers and labor, other local bodies such as the industrial development consortia, and independent experts—and charged with recommending regional targets for incorporation in the national economic plan. The targets were to be supported by an analysis of economic resources, social conditions, developmental problems, and possible lines of action. Specific proposals were to be worked out in cooperation with responsible public agencies.[33] On this basis, regional development schemes were prepared.

Meanwhile, the central planners in Rome were developing the aggregate objectives for the national economy—targets for employment, production, investment, and so on, with breakdowns by economic sector. Taking account of the regional development schemes, the aggregates were divided into targets for the four major subdivisions of the country —the Northeast, the Northwest, Central Italy, and the Mezzogiorno— with the most precise goals for the last of these. Out of this process, then, came the comprehensive economic development plan for the underdeveloped South that advocates of the region had long been demanding. The national plan provided the framework for the spending programs of individual ministries, and the regional development plans were to be revised in the light of the national determinations and made consistent with them.

After their initial effort, the temporary committees were disbanded and their responsibilities assumed by new regional governments that

32. Allen and MacLennan, *Regional Problems and Policies,* pp. 99–100.
33. Report presented by Giovanni Landriscina, in OECD, "Salient Features," pp. 11–13. In the five regions that had regional governments under the early postwar legislation, those governments were made responsible for the development schemes.

came into being with the election of their first officials in 1969. Creation of the new governments had been mandated by the postwar constitution, which designed Italy as a federal state, but a succession of national center-right governments reluctant to share their powers with regional governments (some of which would inevitably be under Communist or Communist-Socialist control) had deferred for two decades the enactment of the necessary enabling legislation. The Socialists, as a condition for entering the new center-left governing coalition, however, had demanded formation of the regional governments. For the second plan, and thereafter, these governments were to prepare and revise the regional development schemes and, within the limits of their constitutional authority, administer them. An unrestricted fund for regional development was created for the use of the regional governments in carrying out the measures defined in their plans. But a government commissioner resident in the region, corresponding to the French prefect, retained under the constitution a general supervisory power over all governmental bodies and activities within the region, including the authority to approve or veto original legislation.[34]

The basic planning decision for the Mezzogiorno for the period of the first plan (1966–70) was the allocation of 40 percent of the net national growth in nonagricultural jobs to that region. Even were that accomplished, a heavy out-migration from the region would still be necessary. The large natural increase in the southern labor force and the prospective continued release of labor from agriculture made a continued manpower surplus inevitable, as Table 4-1 shows.

To achieve the employment goal would require not only a sharp rise in the proportion of new industrial investment in the South but a reversal of recent downward trends. While 33 percent of the country's new nonagricultural jobs had been located in the South in the 1954–60 period, the figure had fallen to 16 percent in 1960–64. The state-controlled industries were already locating virtually all their new projects in the South, so to achieve the proclaimed goal of 40 percent would call for a drastic change in the current trend in the private sector. The plan might

34. Ibid., p. 9. The primary responsibilities of the regions are in the fields of agriculture and fishing, regional transportation systems and other regional public facilities, health, and welfare. Financial control by the national government, as well as the general authority of the regional commissioner, seem to assure that the degree of autonomy will be limited.

Table 4-1. *Job Needs, Job Creation, and Migration Projected for the Italian Mezzogiorno, 1966–70*

Item		Number
Nonagricultural jobs needed:		
To absorb increase in labor force and reduce unemployment[a]	770,000	
To absorb labor released from agriculture	350,000	
Total nonagricultural jobs needed		1,120,000
Needs to be met by:		
Creation of nonagricultural jobs in the Mezzogiorno	570,000	
Migration to northern Italy	350,000	
Migration to foreign countries	200,000	
Total, new jobs and migration		1,120,000

Source: Analysis of first Italian plan by Kevin Allen and M. C. MacLennan, *Regional Problems and Policies in Italy and France* (London: George Allen and Unwin, 1970), pp. 102–03. A figure of 590,110 as the plan's target for nonagricultural jobs is used in the report of a Chamber of Deputies committee on the 1971 Mezzogiorno bill. *Informazioni SVIMEZ* (Rome), vol. 24, no. 19 (Oct. 15, 1971), p. 869.
a. To bring regional unemployment down to the national level of 2.8–2.9 percent.

reflect a "laudable sentiment," observed Allen and MacLennan, but "sentiment is not enough. Good plans should not be based upon hope alone or pander to economically impossible wishes."[35]

NEGOTIATED PLANNING WITH INDUSTRY

The plan had scarcely been approved when it became plain that the critics would prove right. Reports coming in to the CIPE—the Interministerial Committee for Economic Programming[36]—showed little response by private enterprise to the new incentives. Forecasts for 1967 and 1968 showed, indeed, that the process of industrialization of the South was coming to a "halt."[37] The contention of the communist opposition that planning in a capitalist society must inevitably prove to be a useless paper exercise seemed on its way to being confirmed.

But if a capitalist government—even with socialist participation—

35. *Regional Problems and Policies*, p. 104.
36. Il comitato interministeriale per la programmazione economica. This is the committee responsible for the national plan.
37. Report presented by Giorgio Ruffolo of the Ministry of Budget and Economic Programming, in OECD, "Salient Features," p. 31.

could not compel industry to follow a governmental plan, it could consult and bargain. If existing incentives were insufficient, it could find out just what incentives the private companies required. In 1968 the CIPE directed a subcommittee to initiate a series of consultations with management and labor designed to influence major investment decisions. The consultation came to be known as *contrattazione programmata*, or "negotiated planning." With the sectoral and geographic guidelines of the plan as the starting point, government officers asked private firms what conditions would be required to fulfill the plan. What specific infrastructure investments were needed, and when? What financing was required? Did the companies require programs for the training of manpower? Was technical assistance needed? The meetings gave the government the chance not only to ask questions but to inform the companies of sites available in the South and the services and facilities provided.

In its discussions the government sought in particular to develop "block investments," which would group interrelated projects of separate firms. One scheme, for example, was for a complex of metalworking plants in Apulia province, based on the huge southern mill of the state-controlled steel company at Taranto; a plan for such an "interrelated industry complex" had been completed in 1965 by an Italian consulting firm, proposing eight principal heavy and medium engineering plants and twenty-three supplying units.[38] The negotiated planning with individual concerns or groups of companies led to firm commitments by the government to provide the specified public facilities and services on specific dates, and to equally firm commitments and schedules from the investors. The process served as a kind of substitute, also, for direct controls on industrial expansion in congested areas; if investment there could be curtailed by negotiation instead of prohibition and coercion, so much the better.

The prize achievement of negotiated planning in its first year was the agreement that Alfa-Romeo, a state-held concern, would locate a large automobile assembly plant (Alfa Sud) near Naples. Then the rival Fiat company, a private concern that, according to planning officials, had at first refused to decentralize to the South, followed suit with two smaller plants in the Mezzogiorno. As late as 1961, Fiat had built a large facility at Turin, a decision made without publicity or consultation with the

38. The plan, commissioned by the European Economic Community, is described in Allen and MacLennan, *Regional Problems and Policies*, pp. 318–27.

government. "If we had had a system of negotiated planning then," said an official of the planning ministry, "that plant would have been built in the South rather than at Turin; and if we didn't have this system now, the two new plants would have been built in the North."

Awarding subsidies on a negotiated basis created, of course, a serious problem of equity. The negotiations were conducted by the government in power, with no built-in safeguard against political favoritism. Quite apart from politics, it would be difficult to determine on purely technical grounds the equitable level of assistance for each particular case within the broad range of discretion the law allowed, even with the objective criteria developed by the Cassa. A further damper on public confidence in the process was the maintenance of secrecy on the details of the negotiated agreements—except as it was broken by occasional journalistic exposés.

Reappraisal—and New Directions   (*1971*)

As was predicted, the high aspirations of the 1966–70 plan were not achieved. Instead of receiving 40 percent of the growth in nonagricultural jobs, the Mezzogiorno got 27 percent.[39] The gain of 294,000 nonagricultural jobs was only about half of the planned increment. The exodus from agriculture, on the other hand, was substantially higher than anticipated (438,000 compared to 350,000); total employment actually fell by 144,000, therefore, and the unemployment level was held below 5 percent only by the out-migration of over a million workers, 622,000 to the North and 386,000 to foreign countries (almost double the number of out-migrants contemplated in the plan). Disparities between South and North in at least some respects increased; the South's gross product rose only 5.2 percent a year, compared to 5.8 percent for the nation.[40]

The flow of workers and their families to the northern cities during the period brought to 2,160,000 the number of persons who had migrated from the Mezzogiorno to the cities of the North in two decades. But the cities had made no preparations for such an influx. The migrants jammed

39. Majority report of the Chamber of Deputies committee on the bill to finance the Cassa per il Mezzogiorno in the quinquennium 1971–75, *Informazioni SVIMEZ* (Rome), vol. 24, no. 19 (Oct. 15, 1971), p. 869.
40. Figures cited during the 1971 legislative debate in ibid. Further summary data of trends during the 1960s are included below, pp. 177–78.

into what housing was available; rents shot up, and newspapers carried accounts of workers sleeping in their automobiles on the outskirts of Turin and Milan, and of sharing their beds in shifts. Schools were over-crowded. So were hospitals. The mayor of Milan estimated that each new immigrant cost the city $10,000. Acceptance and assimilation of the newcomers was slow, for rural southerners, despite the common language, were essentially alien to the urban northern culture. The migrants resented their exclusion, the inevitable discrimination, and the occasional outright hostility. They demanded better housing, rent and price control, and an end to discrimination, and they formed radical labor unions and direct action groups and took their protests to the streets. In this atmosphere, extremists of both the left and the right made headway, and industrial disputes became political as well as economic.

The crisis year was 1969. Trouble began in the South, at Battipaglia, when demonstrators protesting unemployment set fire to the city hall and the police headquarters and two lives were lost. A wave of demonstrations and strikes followed throughout the country, culminating in general strikes in July in Milan, Turin, Rome, and other cities. Major wage contract renegotiations scheduled for that year turned into political confrontations. The government fell. By the time the unrest quieted, and governmental and political stability was restored, 300 million man-hours and $750 million of production had been lost in strikes.

Throughout the crisis, Italy's leaders watched the ominous growth of antidemocratic elements of the kind that in similar circumstances half a century before had crushed Italian democracy altogether. At times in 1969 the neofascists and the communists came close to open warfare in Italian communities, north as well as south, and both seemed to grow in power and influence. When the crisis was surmounted, the margin of survival for democratic statesmen had been uncomfortably narrow. But at least the fundamental weakness of the country's social and economic structure had been illuminated by the turmoil. To solve the Mezzogiorno problem was now seen as a national, not just a regional, imperative; in the South, Premier Mariano Rumor and other spokesmen for the government and for the democratic parties had sought to ease tension with promises of a speedup in the creation of new jobs, and in the North they had made a corresponding promise to end the inundation of the northern cities with southern migrants.

The experience was fresh as the government approached the time for another renewal of the Cassa's mandate in 1971. In a mood of urgency and determination, it reassessed its approach to the whole problem of the industrialization of the South, took account of the experience of other European countries as well as its own, and emerged with a new structure for planning and administration and some new and revised policies and programs. In the parliament the opposition parties attacked the center-left coalition government for its past failures and proposed even stronger measures, with the result that the legislation finally adopted represented a toughening of the government's original proposals.

THE FUNDAMENTAL PROBLEM OF THE COUNTRY

In presenting its bill, the government termed the Mezzogiorno "the fundamental problem of the country," the one that would condition the whole "process of economic and social development in the coming years."[41] The senate committee to which the bill was referred wrote that view into the bill as its opening sentence: "The development of the southern regions constitutes the fundamental objective of the national economic plan."

If the Mezzogiorno were indeed the country's foremost problem, then it followed that the responsibility for regional policy and programming had to be elevated to the top of the government's organization structure. Accordingly, the ministerial committee for the Mezzogiorno was abolished and its functions transferred to the CIPE, the central economic planning committee, itself. That committee would be responsible for mobilizing the efforts of the Cassa, the regular ministries, and the state-controlled industries behind the total effort.

CENTRAL-REGIONAL RELATIONSHIPS

The role of the new regions occupied considerable attention in the parliamentary debate. At the initiative of the southern regional governments, an amendment was adopted in the senate creating a committee made up of the presidents of the southern governments, or their deputies, to advise the CIPE on decisions concerning the Mezzogiorno. The regions were given responsibility for supervising the industrial develop-

41. Report presented by the minister for the Mezzogiorno, in concert with other ministers, Feb. 4, 1971, in Annesi, *L'Intervento Straordinario*, p. 109.

ment consortia, with a continuance of national financial support, but the authority of the Cassa to initiate large undertakings—called "special projects"—was preserved and even expanded.

The special projects authority would be the means of making good on the government's side of the bargains struck with industry in negotiating sessions, particularly in the multicompany "block investments" that might be worked out. While the more routine, piecemeal projects represented in the consortia would be devolved to the regions, more and more funds—it was contemplated—would be channeled into broad and comprehensive activities interregional as well as intersectoral in their scope. These would become the main preoccupation of the Cassa, which would become more of a direct operating agency than before.

The government's report defined special projects as including

major basic infrastructure (high-speed transportation, desalinization plants, ports, communication lines, etc.); . . . major social infrastructure (hospital and university complexes, etc.); . . . major basic infrastructure related to the location of . . . industrial activity (access roads, rail links, service facilities); discovery and utilization of natural resources (projects to develop water for multiple domestic, agricultural, and industrial uses); specific infrastructure needed for the industrial agglomerations; provision of services important to industry; metropolitan area public works (systems of urban transport, area public works for industry or for new towns; centers of research and development, management centers, distribution centers, and so on).[42]

The requirement that the regular ministries allocate a fair share (defined as 40 percent) of their public works expenditures to the South was retained in the 1971 law; to make it enforceable, a provision was added that any unused portion of the 40 percent reserve at the end of any year be transferred to the Cassa's special projects fund.

FROM CONCENTRATION TO DIFFUSION

A government struggling to overcome the disparities between the North and the South of Italy found, in 1971, that it could no longer disregard the disparities that were developing within the Mezzogiorno. While the bigger coastal cities of the South were suffering "already serious congestion," the government advised the parliament, extensive internal areas capable of development had sunk into "degradation."[43]

42. Ibid., p. 111.
43. Ibid., pp. 109 and 114.

Their ability even to maintain public services was being lost. A shift in the incentive system was therefore essential to bring about a "greater diffusion" of the industrialization process. The parliament added even more specific language: it directed the CIPE to assure "the maximum penetration of the industrialization process into the territories adjoining the zones of concentration" and "to secure the location of industrial plants in zones showing the most intense depopulation features, in order to create conditions of demographic and productive equilibrium."[44]

The preference for growth centers that had been at the heart of Italian incentive policy since its inception was therefore modified—but only in the case of small factories. A new category of small plants was established, those with investment in fixed assets under $2.5 million (a limit of $600,000 in the government's bill was raised by the senate), and for this category the preference for location in the *agglomerati* was reversed. New and powerful incentives were offered small industries that located in the areas of greatest depopulation. Subsequently, some 2,500 communities, most of them in the mountainous *osso*, were made eligible. The object was to bring about the establishment of small growth centers within commuting range of almost every southern home. The Cassa's technocrats protested that infrastructure could not be established on so dispersed a scale, but the political imperatives were overriding.

This preference for location in zones of depopulation was not extended to larger enterprises, however, and they would presumably continue to be located, with rare exceptions, in the old growth centers. Major cities such as Naples and Bari would, of course, be the centers of tertiary activity.

THE MOST POWERFUL INCENTIVES IN EUROPE

As Italy's incentive system had been revised in 1965 and 1968 to stimulate the location in the South of large enterprises, so was it revised this time to give extraordinarily high subsidies to small industrial plants, particularly those locating in the zones of depopulation. The capital grant for a plant under $2.5 million was fixed at 45 percent—more than double the maximum previously given to any factory—if it located in one of the 2,500 declining communities. Moreover, the grant could be raised to 50 percent if expenditures were necessary for small infrastructure or for

44. Article 8, Law 853, 1971.

training of labor. Elsewhere, the grant for small plants was set at 35 percent. To these amounts was added 10 percentage points, available to industries of all sizes, for any portion of the investment spent for machinery or equipment produced in the South or for antipollution equipment produced anywhere. The interest rate on loans for small enterprises was required by the statute to be one-third less than the rate for larger undertakings.

The maximum grant was not raised for medium-sized and large plants, remaining at 20 percent and 12 percent, respectively, but new minimums were set. The amount of the grant, within the limits, was left to negotiation for plants costing over $8 million. For the intermediate category, enterprises were still classified by size and sector and also by two new factors designed to give preference to industries supplying, or using the output of, large plants.[45] The old criterion awarding higher benefits to plants located in growth centers was retained for the loans but not for the grants.

The loan ceiling was reduced to 50 percent from the previous 70 percent for small and medium-sized enterprises, but inventories were made eligible for plants of every size, up to a limit set in relation to fixed investment. In separate legislation designed particularly to encourage labor-intensive industries, the proportion of the employers' social security contribution borne by the national treasury in the case of new jobs created by expansion in the South was raised from 20 percent to 30 percent of wages paid, and the concession extended to 1980. This would represent a saving of about 18 percent in labor costs for a new plant. The subsidy paid since 1969 on existing wages was to expire, however, at the end of 1973.[46]

The resulting system of incentives, part of "the most comprehensive and powerful set of regional development measures in Europe,"[47] is summarized in Table 4-2. To finance the capital grants and loan interest

45. Decree of May 6, 1972, published in *Gazzetta Ufficiale*, no. 137, May 27, 1972, reprinted in Massimo Annesi, *Nuove Tendenze dell' Intervento Pubblico nel Mezzogiorno* (Rome: SVIMEZ, 1973), pp. 170–85.

46. "News from the Mezzogiorno," *IASM Notizie* (Rome), December 1973, p. 13. As part of a general tax reform measure that took effect Jan. 1, 1974, the full exemption of new industrial enterprises from the corporation tax (normally 25 percent of income) for a 10-year period was reduced to a 50 percent exemption. Full exemption for 10 years from the local tax on income (normally 15 percent) was continued.

47. Allen and Stevenson, *Introduction to the Italian Economy*, chap. 6.

Table 4-2. *Incentives to Industry Locating in Italy's Mezzogiorno, Under 1965 and 1971 Legislation*

Incentive	Under 1965 legislation, as modified in 1968	Under 1971 legislation, as modified in 1972 and 1973
Capital grants	Fixed investment of: $50,000–$10 million: 2–20% $10 million–$20 million: up to 20% of first $10 million and up to 10% of second $10 million Over $20 million: up to 12% of total (50% added to that portion of any grant used for purchase of southern-produced equipment)	Small project:[a] 45–50% in areas of greatest depopulation, 35% elsewhere Medium project:[b] 15–20% Large project:[c] 7–12% (10 percentage points added to that portion used for purchase of antipollution and southern-produced equipment)
Low-interest loans	Fixed investment of: Up to $10 million: 15–70% Over $10 million: up to 50%	Small project:[a] 35% Medium project:[b] 35–50% Large project:[c] 30–50% (percentage of fixed assets plus inventories up to 40% o fixed assets)
Method for determining amount of grant or loan within statutory limits	Formula based on (1) location (higher amounts if located in growth center); (2) sector (higher amounts to modern, growing industries); (3) size (higher amounts to plants over a specified size, which varies by industrial group)	Small project:[a] fixed by law Medium project:[b] for loans, formula applying criteria of location (higher amounts if located in growth center) and type of enterprise (embodying many factors); for grants, formula covering type of enterprise only Large project:[c] negotiated planning
Tax incentives	Ten-year exemption from corporate income tax; reduction of social security contributions; reduction of or exemption from company tax, some turnover taxes, registration and mortgage fees, electric power excise, and some local taxes	Same as under 1965 legislation, except: social security tax relief liberalized for new employment but scheduled to expire in 1973 for existing employment; corporate income tax concession reduced
Transportation subsidies	Reduction in rates on some shipments, including finished products	Same as under 1965 legislation
Procurement preference	30% of government purchases and contracts reserved for South	Same as under 1965 legislation

Principal sources: Allen and MacLennan, *Regional Problems and Policies*, pp. 85–94; Law 853, 1971, and implementing decrees and directives, reprinted in Massimo Annesi, *Nuove Tendenze dell' Intervento Pubblico nel Mezzogiorno* (Rome: SVIMEZ, 1973), pp. 170–85.

a. Fixed investment up to $2.5 million.
b. Fixed investment of $2.5 million–$8 million.
c. Fixed investment over $8 million.

subsidies, as well as its special projects and the rest of its programs, the Cassa was granted $5 billion for the period 1971–75 and authorized to make commitments during the period to spend another $6 billion in later years. The funds would permit a spending rate 60 percent higher than the one initially projected for the previous five-year period, and a commitment rate that would be substantially higher than the spending.

The state-controlled corporations were also put under heavier obligation. At the government's initiative, the proportion of investment on new projects that must be located in the South was raised from 60 percent to 80 percent. This was mainly a symbolic gesture since the state enterprises had already surpassed that level. But the senate wrote into the bill a more stringent requirement—that 60 percent of *all* investment in each two-year period be located in the South. Well over 60 percent of existing investment in communications, transportation, and many other public enterprises was in the North, and normal expansion would require something close to the same proportion of new investment on existing projects. The state-controlled enterprises thus faced the problem of either curtailing the investment in the North required for proper service or generating enough new projects in the South—perhaps by further diversification—to make up the required 60 percent, and complaints were soon being voiced by public managers about the arbitrariness of the law. "The instrument is a bit blunt, a bit blind," was one description.

AT LAST, THE ADOPTION OF DISINCENTIVES

The events of 1969 had shaken the prevailing view in the North that unchecked growth there, with an accompanying in-migration of Italians from the South, was in the northern interest, and that made possible, in 1971, the introduction finally of a system of disincentives. The government's initial proposal was for a penalty tax imposed on employers of 100 or more who expanded their employment in congested areas, in the amount of $1,600 for each employee added. Challenged in the senate by those who wanted a more stringent prohibition, the government yielded to an alternative approach. Industrial construction or expansion projects costing more than $11 million would be submitted to the CIPE for review. If, within 90 days, the CIPE found that the project would increase the level of congestion in an area, require excessive importation of labor, or otherwise violate the national economic plan, the company would be penalized in the amount of 25 percent of its investment costs if it proceeded with the project. The same liability would apply to any company proceeding without notifying the CIPE.[48]

This stopped short of authorizing the government to prohibit construction of factories in the Turin or Milan metropolitan complexes, in the way that the British and French governments were authorized to prohibit building projects in the London and Paris regions. But another clause in the law would presumably accomplish the same end by indirection: "State administrations, even if peripheral public entities, Regions, Provinces, Municipalities and minor territorial entities cannot release authorizations and licenses of their respective jurisdiction when a negative appraisal by the CIPE is expressed." Officials responsible for the *contrattazione programmata* expressed doubt that the new law would result in blocking many more projects than were being blocked already in the negotiated planning process, but it would result in more projects coming in for review. In addition, it gave a parliamentary mandate, and explicit statutory sanction, to the objectives being pursued.

Into the Third Decade

As the legislation of 1971 was being written, and as it was put into effect, knowledgeable Italians spoke of the problem of the Mezzogiorno as one that would preoccupy the country not for the next few years but for decades. No more the optimism of the early days, when the Cassa was given initially only a ten-year life and many of its backers fully expected that the Mezzogiorno, given a program of agricultural development and a modern infrastructure, would begin within that period to climb toward the economic level of the North. Since then the Cassa had committed over $15 billion to stimulate investment projects of over $24 billion, built 35 dams to store 2 billion cubic meters of water, reconditioned 20,000 miles of roads and highways, built or enlarged 21 seaports, reclaimed more than 2 million acres of land and irrigated nearly a million, financed 84,000 hotel rooms, 300 vocational training schools, 133 agricultural institutes and schools, and 71 hospitals,[49] and raised the level of extraordinary spending in the South—that is, over and above the normal

48. Article 14, Law 853, 1971.
49. Figures from *La Cassa per il Mezzogiorno* (Cassa per il Mezzogiorno, 1972).

expenditures of the regular departments—to over 1 percent of the gross national product. Yet the disparities between Italy's two economies had not notably diminished.

During the decade 1961–71 the gross regional income of the South rose at a slightly slower rate than in the North, 4.7 percent compared to 5.0 percent. On a per capita basis, this favored the South, 4.5 percent to 3.8 percent, because population growth in the South lagged even more. During the decade the population of the Mezzogiorno rose by a bare 1.2 percent, that of the North by 9.9 percent; even though the rate of natural increase in the South was more than double that of the North, the continued—indeed the accelerated—flow of migrants northward absorbed most of the South's natural increase. Consequently, the gross income per capita in the Mezzogiorno rose during the decade from 50.4 percent to 53.8 percent of the level in the North.

Only about a half of the 1,037,000 workers released from the South's agriculture in the 1960s (which amounted to 36 percent of the agricultural work force at the beginning of the period) could be absorbed in nonagricultural jobs in the region; out-migration, unemployment, and withdrawal from the labor force accounted for the rest.[50] The growth in manufacturing jobs was disappointing; total manufacturing employment grew by only 25,000, or less than 3 percent, during the decade. For almost every factory job created by the state-owned industries and the Cassa's incentive programs, in other words, another disappeared.[51]

But the aggregate figures on employment do not tell the whole story, for they make no adjustments for the marginally employed. Using the Italian statistical concept of "total labor units," derived from the sum of the full-time workers plus one-third of those classified as "marginal workers," the southern economy comes much closer to holding its own. In these terms the loss of agricultural labor units was 713,000 (or 31 percent of the 1960 total), and the gain in nonagricultural units was 667,000, for a deficit of only 46,000. And, here, manufacturing made a more sub-

50. The percentage of the male population in the labor force fell from 56 percent to 50 percent between 1961 and 1971, and the percentage of females from 20 percent to 15 percent. Net out-migration from the South was 2,318,000, about half to the North and half to foreign countries. The total out-migration was almost one-third higher than the net outflow of 1,767,000 in the 1951–61 period and was the highest of any decade in the country's history. Allen and Stevenson, *Introduction to the Italian Economy*, chap. 6.

51. The figures in this and the next two paragraphs are from ibid., table 6.7.

stantial contribution. Total labor units in manufacturing rose by 105,000, or 12 percent, and full-time employment by 164,000, or 20 percent. But these rates of gain were less than those of the North—16 percent and 22 percent, respectively. No matter what figures are used, the South got far less than its share of the growth in manufacturing employment: 4 percent of the gain in total workers, 11 percent in total labor units, and 16 percent in full-time employment—all far from the 40 percent figure set in the national plan at the mid-point of the decade.

Nevertheless, the figures reflected the continuing transformation of the Mezzogiorno from a preindustrial to a modern economy and society. The movement from subsistence and marginal agriculture to industry was one measure. Another was the shift in the components of the "total labor unit" figure: during the decade, the number of full-time employees in all occupations in the region grew by 194,000, or 4 percent; the decline in total employment was due entirely to the reduction in the number of marginal workers by 721,000—a remarkable 43 percent.

Beyond this was a qualitative difference between the new jobs and the old. The 1970 employment totals had a greater percentage of jobs in modern, technologically advanced industries that could hold their own in competition with plants anywhere in the world. The jobs being lost were for the most part in obsolete plants that were competitive only in the local market, that were bound to disappear as soon as the "protective tariff" of inadequate internal communications was removed.[52] The fine new *autostrade*, after all, were two-way roads. While they linked the new southern factories to northern markets, they also made it possible for Milanese ice cream to be sold in Calabria and even in Sicily, driving the local product off the market. And the state-held industries, it was also alleged, pirated labor from local firms to further contribute toward forcing them gradually out of business.

But all this can be seen as a necessary aspect of transition. By looking on the first two decades of the Mezzogiorno effort as a period of preparation, the optimists find ground for arguing that the basis for an industrial takeoff has been laid. Since 1950 the South of Italy has been brought at least partway into the modern industrial world. It now has, for the first

52. The results of the qualitative shift in employment are reflected in the rise in productivity—real output per labor unit—by 164 percent between 1951 and 1970 in the industrial sector of the economy, 178 percent in agriculture, 84 percent in the tertiary sector, and 19 percent in public administration. Ibid., chap. 6.

time, systems of transportation, communication, credit, vocational education, and other essential elements of infrastructure that put the South on a par—or nearly so—with the rest of the country, and of Europe. Agriculture has been modernized. Health and education standards have been raised dramatically. Those changes had to be accomplished first, in any case. No country anywhere in the developed world has made so heroic an effort to develop its underdeveloped areas, as measured by the proportion of its national wealth and income that have been devoted to the cause.

Moreover, as Allen and MacLennan have well argued, it is not quite accurate or fair to judge the progress of the Mezzogiorno against the standard of the North. The North, after all, was the site of the "Italian miracle," a spurt of phenomenal industrial growth that made the Italian economy for a time among the fastest-growing in the world. A region such as the Mezzogiorno, without an industrial base or tradition, could hardly be expected to keep pace, let alone make gains. If the Mezzogiorno is looked on as part of the underdeveloped world of the Mediterranean basin—sharing that world's common handicaps of an arid climate, a lack of natural resources, and a preindustrial social structure—then the record of the first two postwar decades takes on a different cast. The Mezzogiorno stands at the top in that competition, with a growth rate higher than that of any other European country in the basin.[53] On the other hand, there is much for the pessimists to point to. Before the hoped-for takeoff can be realized, as they see it, some formidable obstacles must be overcome. The major ones can perhaps be summarized under two headings—the problem of entrepreneurship and problems of devolution and direction.

The Problem of Entrepreneurship

A government can build an industrial infrastructure and provide incentives for private companies to use it—if it has the political will, and Italy has shown no lack of that. But to attain self-sustaining growth these must come into combination with a third element—entrepreneurship. And in Italy as elsewhere, governments have found the creation of entrepreneurship to be, in the short run at least, beyond their power.

53. Allen and MacLennan, *Regional Problems and Policies*, p. 111.

As early as 1958, Friedrich Vöchting had observed:

A large number of the young men and women of the South, who hold themselves intellectually capable of higher tasks, believe that they can find appropriate fields of activity only in the North of Italy. This stream of migrants . . . with little exaggeration, could be called the "intellectual hemorrhage of the South. . . ." At any rate, because of this thinning out of the intellectual groups, it is difficult to perceive from which social stratum a true class of leaders could emerge. This . . . is directly connected with another important phenomenon: the insufficient technical education of the Southern middle class and the aversion—at least until a very short time ago—of this class to a career in the techno-productive sector, an aversion which is both cause and effect of the scarcity of technical institutes and professional schools in these areas.

The . . . lack of men with the spirit of entrepreneurs, capable of courageous initiative in the business world, often constitutes the greatest negative element in the play of forces causing industrialization; it is, indeed, a much more serious obstacle to the economic development of the Mezzogiorno than the insufficient supply of capital or the deficiency of the credit institutions distributing this insufficient supply.[54]

Economists and administrators in the 1970s commonly cited the shortage of entrepreneurs as the factor above all others that made the Mezzogiorno problem so intractable. To create an industrial society out of a two-class, landowner-peasant culture presented difficulties of quite a different order from those faced by Britain, for example, in trying to stem the decline of cities like Glasgow and Newcastle that were among the oldest industrial centers of the world.

The southern peasant has shown no lack of adaptability, when industrial employment is available. Output per man in southern industry in 1970 was only 71 percent of the northern level (up from 64 percent in 1951), but the difference is attributed primarily to the structure of southern industry. Industrialists and government analysts testify that modern plants opened in Mezzogiorno towns wholly lacking in industrial tradition have proved as efficient after the initial break-in period as factories with comparable equipment in the North.[55] And while the available labor training facilities fell far short of meeting the demand for qualified skilled labor, a network of new vocational training centers had been established in the South—some of the schools located in the industrial parks themselves—with training courses fashioned to the needs of new or expanding industries.

54. "Sulla questione meridionale," p. 198, quoted by Massacesi, "Regional Economic Development," p. 262.
55. See OECD, "Salient Features," p. 128, for official comment on the data.

Location was an inherent disadvantage, for some industries. A spokesman for the state-held petroleum-chemical corporation estimated that a southern plant might cost 7–11 percent more to operate than one located in the North, simply because of the greater distance to European markets. By the same token the state-held steel company, on the basis of economic factors alone, would have located its principal new mill at or near Genoa rather than Taranto. But for both private and public entrepreneurs the incentive system was designed to offset the locational disadvantages, and most analysts appeared to be agreed that, on a strict cost calculation, the subsidies authorized in the 1965–71 legislation were more than adequate to do so.

Moreover, the establishment of basic industries such as steel, chemicals, and automobiles in the South would presumably remove any disadvantages of a southern location that would otherwise exist for firms supplying the basic industries or utilizing the materials they produced. But it was here that the Mezzogiorno policy had been most frustrated. The dream that around the state-owned plants (which accounted for about one-third of all southern industrial investment in the 1960s) would spring into being scores of medium-sized and small industries had simply not been realized. The huge state enterprises stood almost alone, derided as "cathedrals in the desert." "The only plants in Apulia with links to Italsider [the Taranto steel mill]," said an observer in that province with some exaggeration, "are the one that makes uniforms for the workers and the one that makes their beer." The story in Campania was more encouraging; some satellite plants had been established with links to the Alfa Sud automobile factory near Naples.

For the most part, the entrepreneurs who had been relied on to establish satellite plants, it turned out, did not exist. Only the largest enterprises, as experience in other countries has also shown, are truly mobile. They are the concerns that establish branch factories. A small or medium-sized enterprise, if located in Milan or Turin, does not close down there in order to locate elsewhere, nor does it have the capacity or inclination to supervise branch operations in far-off places. If small industry were to grow in southern Italy, it had to be through southern entrepreneurship—and this was the missing factor.

Many critics, especially those of the left, placed a heavy share of the blame on the state-controlled industries themselves: The public corporations were essentially disinterested. They had built in the South because they were forced by law to do so, but beyond that they had no more sense of social purpose than any private corporation. They could have become dynamic centers of stimulation, promotion, and technical assistance in the creation of a new class of southern entrepreneurs, it was argued, but the northern experts sent to the Mezzogiorno as managers lived apart from the southern population, sometimes in compounds built by the companies. It was even difficult for small southern enterprises to buy from the state-held plants, because the latter's marketing headquarters were in the North. The supply channels of the state-controlled enterprises were also established in the North, and plant managers in the South found it safer and easier to use them than to try to create new ones in their own region. The line of promotion for the southern managers was back to the North, and the criterion for promotion was the profitability of their operations. Any resources devoted to such unrelated activities as assisting southern entrepreneurship could only detract from that. Finally, the criticism ran, if small and medium-sized supplying and using industries did not spring up under private ownership around the basic plants, the state-controlled concerns should extend their own operations into the supplying and using sectors.

Such criticism did not serve to change the outlook of the state-held enterprises. They emphasized that the requirements of international competition, as well as the requirements of political survival, compelled them to operate with the same concern for efficiency that guided their private counterparts. The suggestion that they expand their operations widely outside the basic industries they dismissed as being beyond their accepted missions, and as politically impossible in any case. Their occasional adventures into small business operations had proved administratively difficult and the results unencouraging; the state-holding groups, too, have a limited supply of managerial talent.

The state-held industries could also point to growing evidence that they were having effect on the industrial world outside their plants, if only an indirect and long-term one. For the first time, a generation of southerners was growing up in an industrial setting; sons of peasants knew that their own futures lay outside of agriculture, and they were preparing themselves accordingly. As industrial skills spread among the populace, industrial entrepreneurship would follow, as it had elsewhere. There were signs of this already. Northern technicians in the state-held plants might not be assigned by their employers to become technical assistance missionaries but there was nothing to prevent them from moonlighting as advisers—and some did. Northern managers and specialists completing their southern tours of duty were increasingly being replaced by the southerners they had trained; these men had closer links with the Mezzogiorno's nascent entrepreneurial community, were more likely to see opportunities that the latter could exploit, and were more highly motivated to promote them. Some of these men had even taken the gamble of leaving their secure careers and becoming entrepreneurs themselves.

Meanwhile, the incentive system had been altered, particularly in the 1971 law, to favor the smaller, labor-intensive enterprises on which southern development was seen now to depend. Through its credit institutions, as well as through the technical assistance institutes that it financed, the state was engaged directly in assisting and encouraging individual entrepreneurs. In the early 1970s, supporters of the Mezzogiorno effort were discouraged by the slow rate of change in the South's economy, but most of them believed that social and economic forces had been set in motion that, over a span of perhaps two generations, could work the South's salvation. The question was whether frustration and unrest—exacerbated, if not created, by the upset of the old social and economic equilibriums—could be contained that long.

Problems of Direction and Devolution

Despite the difficulties and frustrations, the always-high level of political support for the Italian Mezzogiorno effort has shown no decline. Indeed, the trend has been the other way, especially since the strikes and violence of 1969. Those events had demonstrated the indivisibility of the country's welfare. "The mayor of Milan is now our ally," observed a southerner. "I couldn't have said that just a few years ago."

Yet Italy has had exceptional difficulty, among the nations of Europe, in translating political determination into administrative zeal and effectiveness. For most of the postwar period, Italy's governments have been unstable, short-lived, and weak. Even though the country has had an unbroken succession of premiers from the Christian Democratic party since the war, that party has been riven with factionalism and most of the time it has governed in coalition with other parties. Moreover, the Italian civil service has the reputation of being among the weakest in Europe, rigid and restricted in its recruitment processes and excessively bureaucratic in its procedures. The latter handicap was circumvented to some degree by making a new agency, the Cassa, and the state holding sector the principal agents of change in southern Italy. But many other agencies, both central and local, had to play a part, and the problems of coordination and of expeditious administration have not been solved.

The secretary general of the planning ministry, Dr. G. Ruffolo, blamed the weakness of the Mezzogiorno effort on its administration:

> The fact that the powers of the laws for the Mezzogiorno have not been used in a fully effective manner is due in large measure to the fact that the general and specific objectives of the law have never been translated into precise directions for the operation of the diverse components of public administration. In fact, the policy for the Mezzogiorno has been carried out as a sectoral undertaking pursued through individual projects. In practice, the public decisional apparatus (legislative–executive–public administrative) has occupied itself intensively in recent years only on the occasions when the laws for renewing the financing of the Cassa were under consideration. There is no practical procedure for the examination of the operations of the diverse administrations with regard to the numerous direct obligations they derive from the same laws for the Mezzogiorno. The response of their actions to the goals that the laws intended them to pursue has never been examined.[56]

This has had a bearing, particularly, on the negotiated planning process, Dr. Ruffolo went on. While responsibility for the negotiation and approval of agreements with industry was clearly centralized in the CIPE, that body "could not itself activate through the various public agencies the initiatives and the procedures necessary to organize a continuous rapport between the central authority and the companies and to manage the various facets and instruments of the agreement," including those within the competence of the ordinary ministries, the local authorities, and the special state agencies. The process had served as an instrument of pressure on individual firms—"a solicitation at a high political level"—and a means for negotiation of incentives. But as for the provision of infrastructure, the national CIPE, like the local consortia, "could not bring together numerous agencies to do their jobs either in time or in a coordinated way."

Dr. Ruffolo's solution was to develop and utilize the national plan as the instrument of discipline and coordination; it would rationalize, and relate, the separate operations of public agencies, so that reforms could

56. G. Ruffolo, *Rapporto Sull' Esperienza di Programmazione del Segretario Generale della Programmazione Economica* (1973).

proceed together across the whole range of governmental activity, and so that public and private effort could be synchronized as well. But his proposals came at a time when the planning process itself had been somewhat discredited by the failure of the first plan to achieve its goals—not only in those aspects pertaining to the Mezzogiorno but in other respects as well. Indeed, a "second national plan," originally intended to cover the period beginning in 1971, did not get beyond the draft stage, and the national planning experiment was still in suspension in 1974. In any case, the weaknesses of the planning process, and of administrative control and coordination, could only be corrected by a government that was itself in a secure position and strongly led. And none of a succession of governments in the early 1970s had the necessary security and strength.

As a reflection of governmental weakness, some critics pointed to the administration of one of the crucial innovations of the 1971 law—the authorization of controls on industrial expansion in congested areas. Months passed before a decision was reached on the areas to be defined as congested, where proposed new plants would be subject to a formal "negative appraisal." When the decision was taken, it represented the narrowest definition of the boundaries. The disincentives would not be applied in the entire Milan-Turin-Genoa "industrial triangle" nor even the major part of it. Only the agglomerations of Milan and Turin were included; even the intermediate section of the seventy-five-mile industrializing corridor linking the two cities was excluded. One official observed that while Italy had a southern growth policy, it still had no national growth policy, one that embraced clear objectives regarding population distribution within the North. Nevertheless, in August 1973, more than two years after the authorizing legislation was enacted, the Italian government issued its first rejection: Alfa-Romeo, the state-held automobile manufacturer, was denied permission to build on the outskirts of Milan a new factory that promised 11,000 jobs, pending the outcome of negotiations for further expansion of the company in the South.

Problems of coordination were immeasurably complicated, during this period, by the establishment of the new regional governments and the need to define a host of relationships between regional and central authorities. The regional governments, moreover, had a tendency toward instability no less than that of the central government; some were coalition governments, and at least one province had seen a succession of four governments in the span of a few months. Central authorities, as well as southern observers, complained that the regional governments—especially in the Mezzogiorno—were so engrossed in struggles over power and patronage that their developmental responsibilities were being lost sight of. Some regional politicians were indifferent or even hostile to industrialization; they preferred the old order, and they feared the political power of the trade unions that industry would bring. The regional plans, which were to become elements of the national plan and guide the developmental work of the regional authorities, had been contracted out to research institutes and consultants and, even when adopted, carried little authority. For their part, the regions complained that they could not organize competent planning and development agencies because of civil service regulations, carried over from the central to the regional governments, that restricted professional recruitment to persons trained in public law and so prevented the lateral entry of planners, economists, and other specialists into key jobs in the regions. Moreover, the funds made available by the central government were still coming into the regions earmarked for specific categorical programs and projects rather than being assigned to the noncategorical fund that had been authorized for regional development—as an Italian equivalent of revenue sharing.

Again the reformers have been disappointed, but again they find elements of promise. Italy had at least established the structure of regional leadership that each of the large centralized European states had felt the need for, at a time when France had not yet created its regional bodies and Britain was still in the stage of debating whether and how to design a regional governmental level. Already, the first of the key instruments of economic development at the regional level is in place, for the industrial development consortia that had managed a hundred separate industrial parks are now consolidated into a single one for each region. Detailed decisions regarding the development of industrial sites that formerly had to go to Rome for approval can now be made in the regional capitals, certainly more expeditiously and perhaps more wisely as well. Development planning and land-use planning can be better linked. Regional officials have visions of what could be done if they had more tools at their disposal; some are already agitating for participation in the management of the state-controlled enterprises located within their boundaries, in order to reorient their buying and marketing practices; for control of the public credit institutions serving small and medium-sized business; and for participation in the negotiated planning with industry. With these resources and powers, they argue, the regions could become dynamic centers of leadership, innovation, and technical assistance. But the agencies of the central government, including the state holding sector, can be expected to defend their privileges. Dr. Ruffolo noted "a total lack of reorganization" of central agencies in response to the creation of the regions and the devolution of authority that was then mandated.[57]

Like every other federal state, Italy is experiencing the endless tug-of-war between central and regional authorities, which can eventuate in either "creative tension" or unproductive conflict, or both, differing from region to region and from year to year. As for the effects of this struggle on development, if the regional governments, particularly those of the South, turn out to lack the competence to lead and innovate, their assured role in developmental programs is still so limited that they are not likely to detract much from the total effort. If they prove able, on the other hand, their role can grow, and they can provide an element of local leadership and vitality that the Mezzogiorno program has been lacking. From the viewpoint of its developmental programs alone, then, Italy may have little to lose and much to gain from its long-delayed leap into federalism.

57. Ibid.

CHAPTER FIVE

The Netherlands: Protecting the Green Heart

The unequal distribution . . . of population over the country is a crucial problem of the physical development of the Netherlands. . . . Metropolitan sprawl and congestion in other countries may be regarded as a warning illustration of uncontrolled urbanization. . . . A sound decentralization is not necessarily detrimental to the great urban centers.—The West . . . and the Rest of the Netherlands, 1956[1]

THE NETHERLANDS is the most densely populated country in Europe; its population of 13.5 million, about one-tenth greater than that of Pennsylvania, is crowded into a land area less than one-third the size of that state. Yet even so small a country is divided into distinct regions. Almost half of the people live in three western provinces covering only 20 percent of the land, and most of that half—or about one-third of the total population—live in an urban complex known as Randstad Holland, or the Holland Rimcity, a horseshoe-shaped conurbation embracing the nation's four largest cities, Amsterdam, The Hague, Rotterdam, and Utrecht, and many intermediate cities and villages, separated in most cases by carefully protected open space. In the Randstad lie the national capital, the country's great ports, most of its industry, its cultural centers, and the headquarters of its major corporations. The rest of the country is still a mainly rural landscape, dotted with smaller industrial cities.

As the Netherlands emerged from the devastation of the Second World War, it also entered its period of "conversion," from a predominantly agrarian to a modern industrial economy. The Randstad, with its existing industry and infrastructure, including its ports, was the natural center for the new spurt of industrial growth. So the country found itself dichotomized—composed of a thriving, industrializing metropolis and a hinterland whose economy was growing little if at all and whose

1. The Netherlands, National Physical Planning Office and Central Planning Bureau.

rural areas, like rural areas everywhere, were in decline. The consequences were inevitable: a southward and westward rural-urban migration flow, and pockets of unemployment in the East ranging up to 25 percent of the labor force—twelve times the national average.

The government responded with a dual approach, much like that of Britain in the 1930s. On the one hand, it subsidized migration, to help the workers go where the jobs were. On the other, it initiated a program for its depressed areas, to try to create jobs where the idle workers lived.

Creation of Jobs, Movement of People   (1949-58)

Dutch regional policy began with an official study of the plight of Emmen, an isolated peat-producing town near the German border that had been left stranded, with the highest unemployment rate in the country, when the technological advance in industrial processes killed much of the market for peat.[2] The study, initiated in 1949 and carried out jointly by the national and local governments, laid out a program to convert Emmen into a town attractive to modern industry. The parliament in 1951 authorized $1.5 million, largely financed by Marshall Plan assistance from the United States, to help local authorities provide the city with a suitable industrial infrastructure—improved road communications, adequate public utilities, and industrial sites with factory buildings that would be available for rent or sale.

The Emmen plan immediately became a model for programs to revive other depressed areas—or development areas. Eight met the criteria of high structural unemployment that could not be solved by migration alone, and a potential for industrial development that could be realized at reasonable cost. Funds were appropriated to carry out development plans, including not only the creation of industrial parks with utilities and industrial buildings, but also the training or retraining of workers

2. This section is based primarily on L. H. Klaassen, "Regional Policy in the Benelux Countries," in U.S. Department of Commerce, Area Redevelopment Administration, *Area Redevelopment Policies in Britain and the Countries of the Common Market* (1965), pp. 37-39 and 46-49; and F. W. Dirker, "Regional Industrialisation Policy in the Netherlands," in Organisation for Economic Co-operation and Development, "Salient Features of Regional Development Policies in the Benelux Countries," report of a conference held in April 1968 (Paris: OECD, 1969; processed), pp. 37-38.

and the provision of worker housing. The expenditures would be concentrated in growth centers, called "nuclei."

But it was at once apparent that merely to prepare a nucleus to receive new industry did not assure that industry would come. So in 1953 a system of incentives was instituted that has remained the basis of Dutch regional policy ever since. Grants were made available to industrial firms to cover 25 percent of the cost of new factory buildings in the nuclei (up to a limit of 70 cents per square foot), on the condition that one unemployed person from the depressed area must be hired for each 500 square feet of floor space. To be eligible, a plant must employ at least ten workers.

Meanwhile, assistance was authorized to help unemployed workers move to areas of labor shortage, including the expanding cities of the Randstad. Full compensation was authorized for moving expenses, plus a resettlement allowance based on the size of the family. Unmarried workers were excluded from the benefits. Subsidies were also paid to encourage emigration to foreign countries.

By the end of the decade a total of 16,000 new jobs had been created in the subsidized factories. The average increase in manufacturing employment between 1950 and 1960 in the nine development areas was 46 percent. In the absence of regional policy, a 1962 study showed, the average increase would have been only 30 percent;[3] a third of the increment, in other words, could be credited to governmental action. Two of the areas saw gains more than three times what would have been expected under normal circumstances, four others experienced better than normal gains, and three had growth rates smaller than those projected. The study found that the excess growth in the development areas was not at the expense of neighboring centers but was instead a net gain for their entire regions.

A Crucial National Problem: Population Distribution (*1956–57*)

The dualism of the initial set of policies—the impartial willingness either to move capital east or workers west, whichever would most suc-

---

3. The averages for the nine areas (unweighted) were calculated by N. Vanhove in a study summarized in Klaassen, "Regional Policy," pp. 46–49. Vanhove used a complex formula to measure the tendency toward decentralization in particular industrial groups, and then compared the projected movement with the actual.

cessfully bring together the unemployed workers and the new jobs—reflects the original conception of the problems of depressed areas as local in nature. The measures, like the early measures in Britain, were seen as elements of social policy—aimed to ease the plight of the unemployed in a few distressed localities—rather than as aspects of a population distribution policy. But within a few years the conceptual base for Dutch regional policy was transformed, as the question of how population was to be clustered in settlements across the land came to be recognized as a national problem—indeed a "crucial" national problem, in the words of a 1956 government report.[4] This transformation was primarily the contribution of physical planners, who have played a role probably greater in the Netherlands than in any other European country in the formulation of national development policy.

As in other countries, physical planning has been decentralized in the Netherlands, but in so small and densely settled a country the notion that the scores of independent city plans should be consolidated, through the provinces, into some kind of national physical plan was perhaps bound to develop. In any case, that idea gained support in the late 1930s, and in 1941 a National Physical Planning Office was established. Its mission was to make broad determinations as to the best use of the country's land—identifying areas of scenic beauty and prime agricultural land that should be protected from urban encroachment, dividing the urban areas between residential and industrial uses, and so on.[5] After the war, with the sharp rise in the rate of population growth and the concentration of that increase in the West, the planners had to cope with an increasingly severe pressure of population on land space in that crowded area. On top of that, the national policies in the 1950s actually encouraged, through subsidies, the movement of additional people from the depressed areas to the West.

In 1956 the National Physical Planning Office, in conjunction with the Central Planning Bureau (the economic planning body), published a report reminiscent of Gravier's *Paris and the French Desert*. In the next quarter-century, predicted *The West . . . and the Rest of the Netherlands*, 500,000 persons would migrate from the North, East, and South to the western provinces. The Randstad, already embracing 4 million people, would grow to 5.5 million by 1980 and probably to 6 million

4. *The West . . . and the Rest,* p. 5.
5. The Netherlands, Ministry of Housing and Physical Planning, *Physical Planning in the Netherlands* (1972), p. 1.

afterward. From the standpoint of the West as well as the rest of the country, that was undesirable.

In the West "the sprawling cities might swell to a greater size than desirable and merge into one another in different places." Problems of water management, traffic, and public administration would grow. The costs of services would rise out of proportion to the population increase. The threat of floods to areas below sea level presented a constant danger. Some of the best land needed for recreation, agriculture, and horticulture, and for industries that by their nature had to be in the conurbation, would be used up. "Metropolitan sprawl and congestion in other countries may be regarded as a warning illustration of uncontrolled urbanization. . . . A country like France actually suffers from a hypertrophical growth of her central agglomeration." Meanwhile, the disparities in income and living standards between the West and the rest of the country would be accentuated. For all these reasons the unequal distribution of economic opportunities over the country, and the unequal distribution of population that resulted, were "a crucial problem of the physical development of the Netherlands."

Advocating "a sound decentralization," the report proposed as a first target the creation of enough jobs in the other regions to forestall the expected flow of 500,000 migrants to the West. If that succeeded, the government should then attempt to bring about a net flow the other way. As a last resort, a "prohibitive policy for the West" might have to be considered. In any case, a national growth policy should be adopted, and "firmly maintained." Otherwise, "the balance of the nation will be increasingly upset. The experience of other countries gives ample evidence of that."

The West itself concurred. A working committee representing the national government, the three western provinces, and the cities of Amsterdam, The Hague, and Rotterdam, assigned to develop a plan for the West, concluded in 1957 that "the necessity of decentralization" was even more "in the foreground" than before. It raised the estimate of the number of migrants who would come to the West by 1980 from a half million to 700,000. Looking beyond 1980, the group said the national objective must be "a satisfying population dispersion over the whole country." The three provinces and the three cities gave their support to that objective.[6]

6. *The West of the Land*, report of a joint committee representing national, provincial, and local governments (1957).

Defining the National Growth Policy (*1958-60*)

In the three years following these reports, the government defined and adopted a policy explicitly aimed at "promotion of a better spread of population and sources of employment throughout the country," and modified accordingly its measures for regional development.

The most obvious step, for a government committed to decentralization, was to eliminate the conspicuous element of the existing program that worked the other way—the subsidy for the relocation of unemployed workers from the development areas to the West. In 1959, in a comprehensive revision of the industrial development incentive system, subsidies for relocation were restricted to workers in the depressed areas moving to the designated development nuclei.

In other respects the new legislation strengthened the incentive system. Instead of limited development areas, broad "problem areas" were defined, embracing those parts of the country that were predominantly agricultural or, for other reasons, were sources of labor surplus and out-migration. There were four such areas, covering four entire provinces (three in the North and one in the Southwest) and parts of four others (including a northeastern rural section of North Holland, the province containing Amsterdam). Only South Holland and Utrecht provinces in the West and Gelderland province in the East contained no problem territory. Close to half the area of the country was included. A total of forty-seven developmental nuclei were designated. Three of them lay outside the problem areas but were included to serve sections within those areas tributary to them. For government public works and aid to municipal works in the problem areas, $9 million a year was authorized.[7]

The capital grants were extended to cover expenditures for land as well as buildings. Industrial firms were granted 50 percent of the cost of land purchased in the nuclei, provided that one-fifth of the acreage was used immediately for industrial buildings. The grant for new factories was shifted from a percentage of cost to a flat rate—$1 per square foot for the first 10,000, $1.25 for the next 10,000, $1.50 for the next 20,000, and $2 for all above 40,000. And the subsidies were extended to expansion of existing plants as well as construction of new ones; here the grant was $1 per square foot, regardless of size. The payments were con-

7. H. C. de Meijer, "Means to Implement the Regional Development Policy," in OECD, "Salient Features," p. 44.

ditional on employment of one man per 1,000 square feet in new installations, and one per 500 square feet in expansions.[8]

Meanwhile, an interministerial group was preparing a definitive statement of the government's population distribution policy. Its *Report on Physical Planning in the Netherlands*[9] gave official status to the general objectives and some of the specific recommendations of the 1956 and 1957 studies.

If population concentration in the Randstad were not held back, said the report, by 1980 the open character of the conurbation would be "threatened from two sides." First, the cities making up the ring would grow together, destroying the buffer strips of green space that separated them. Second, the thousand square miles of lakes, canals, cattle, and picturesque farming villages that made up the "open heart," or "green heart," of the urban ring would be overrun with suburban development. To preserve the open pattern of the Randstad, local plans should direct the growth of the western cities outward—Amsterdam to the north, Rotterdam to the south, Utrecht to the east, and so on—rather than into the Randstad's center. And national policy would seek to avert the projected migration to the West, now estimated at 400,000 persons in the years to 1980. A "harmonious distribution of population" would both lighten the pressure on the West and solve the problems of the North, South, and East. Diverting industrial expansion to the other regions would enable better use of the limited western space for activities that had to be there.

In language similar to that surrounding the French concept of the "urban hierarchy," the report outlined a "system of settlements" for the problem areas. At the top would be centers of at least 100,000 population, if not 200,000 or more, which would (like *métropoles d'équilibre*) be brought to the level of the Randstad cities in urban amenities—"a wide variety of shops . . . all kinds of possibilities for social contact and recreation . . . seats of important organizations and institutions, institutes of higher learning, theater companies, orchestras, etc." Such centers would be attractive to highly trained personnel, and the labor market would be large enough to provide adequate manpower resources to the employer

8. Klaassen, "Regional Policy," pp. 43-44. The rates of subsidy were lowered in 1962 due to budgetary limits but later restored to approximately the original levels.

9. National Physical Planning Office, *Report on Physical Planning in the Netherlands* (condensed ed., 1961), quotations from pp. 15, 16, 35, and 51.

and a wide range of choice to the worker. To try to develop all forty-seven of the nuclei designated the year before would "split up the available resources"; expenditure therefore would be concentrated at the outset on "those centres which are likely to be most successful." Eighteen were subsequently designated as primary centers. Development could be expected to spread to the twenty-nine other, secondary centers later.

With these positive measures, said the report, the "prohibitive" policies adopted in Britain and France to directly control the growth of areas of concentration should not be needed. Congestion was more serious in those countries; the Netherlands was in an earlier stage of urban concentration and, the government contended, "it is still possible . . . to make a successful attempt at preventing the development of situations such as exist in the English and French cities."

If its admonitions to industry and other private organizations to decentralize were to be heeded, the government recognized that it must take the lead in dispersing some of its own activities. A committee headed by a former prime minister was established late in 1960 to plan the dispersal to the interior of agencies of the central government that did not have to be located in The Hague.

A National Land-Use and Population-Distribution Plan (1966)

To translate the policy laid out in the *Report on Physical Planning* into a concrete plan, another interministerial committee was convened, under leadership of the National Physical Planning Office. Its plan was adopted in 1966, published under a title as straightforward as that of its predecessor, *Second Report on Physical Planning in the Netherlands.*[10]

Called a "structural" plan, the scheme is comparable in status and impact to the "strategic" plans prepared by the regional planning teams in Great Britain. It describes the general settlement pattern of an area and demarks broad zones for urban, industrial, agricultural, recreational, or other use but does not provide legal constraint on the use of any parcel of land. That remains the function of regional and municipal land-use plans. But the national plan is intended to lead to more definite regional plans, with which municipal plans would have to be made consistent.

10. *Second Report on Physical Planning in the Netherlands* (Government Printing Office of the Netherlands, 1966).

Moreover, in the Netherlands as in Britain, the national government reserves the right to intervene in, and override, the regional planning decisions. It has the means to require, then, that land-use planning at all levels conform to the structural plan, and the plan's principles become binding on the whole planning process to the degree that the national authorities are willing and able to use their reserved powers to that end.

The *Second Report* was prepared at a time when the Netherlands, like other European countries, was anticipating enormous population gains: by the year 2000, officials estimated, room had to be found for nearly 8 million more people—a two-thirds increase—on the country's crowded land. Moreover, more space could be required per inhabitant, as people moved from congested city centers to more spacious neighborhoods. In all, the land required for urban purposes would triple. Without a dispersal policy and rigorous controls, obviously, the existing cities would merge into "a single, colossal urban complex in the southern half of the Netherlands."[11] The "green heart" of the Randstad would be destroyed and areas of the greatest value for recreation, agriculture, and horticulture would be paved over.

The 20 million Dutchmen of the year 2000 had first to be distributed, then, in a planned pattern of dispersal. Weighing the need to reduce population pressure in the Randstad and other areas against the capacity of the less developed areas to grow, the planners came forward with a scheme to divert 1,750,000 people from the crowded areas (the West and, by then, the South) into the less developed regions of the country. That would amount to one-eighth of the 13 million people seen as the prospective population of the West and South in the absence of new and strong preventive measures, as Table 5-1 shows.

The regions that would receive the diverted millions would require industrial and service centers sufficiently large to set in motion a vigorous self-generated expansion—"draft horses," as they were called. In the North the region's largest city, Groningen, was chosen as the principal new metropolis, linked to expanded port facilities on the Eems estuary. In the East three neighboring textile cities in the Twente region near the German border would be developed as a single urban complex. Two new urban centers of about 100,000 each would be built on the IJsselmeer polders. "Concentrated deconcentration" was the slogan. The scheme

11. The Netherlands, Ministry of Housing and Physical Planning, *The "Rand-stad": The Urbanized Zone of the Netherlands* (1970), p. 22.

Table 5-1. *Population Distribution Plan for the Netherlands, 1965–2000*
In millions

		Population			
		2000			
				Diversion required	
Region	1965 actual	Projected under existing policies	Target	In	Out
North[a]	1.3	2.25	3.00	0.75	...
East[b]	2.2	4.00	4.25	0.25	...
West[c]	5.7 ⎱ 8.3	8.50 ⎱ 13.25	11.50	...	1.75
South[d]	2.6 ⎰	4.75 ⎰			
Southwest[e]	0.3	0.50	0.75	0.25	...
Southern IJsselmeer polders[f]	...	negligible	0.50	0.50	...
Netherlands	12.1	20.00	20.00	1.75	1.75

Source: *Second Report on Physical Planning* (condensed ed., Government Printing Office of the Netherlands, 1966), pt. 1, p. 13.
    a. Groningen, Friesland, and Drenthe provinces.
    b. Overijssel and Gelderland provinces.
    c. Noord-Holland, Zuid-Holland, and Utrecht provinces.
    d. Noord-Brabant and Limburg provinces.
    e. Zeeland province.
    f. Land reclaimed from the IJsselmeer not yet assigned to provinces. In the absence of policies to speed settlement, the projected population there for the year 2000 was only about 50,000.

sought to avoid, on the one hand, massive agglomerations like those of other European countries, with their high-cost infrastructure including mass transit and motorway systems, and, on the other, a scatteration of small towns that would invade needed recreation space. As the middle course, it envisioned a network of communities of medium size grouped in most instances in "city regions" within the urban zones. Each community would be compact in design and separated from its neighbors by areas of open space. Thus protected, old cities and towns would retain their social and cultural identities even though functioning as part of an integrated urban complex.

Between the urban zones, as Figure 5-1 shows, would be broad areas reserved for agriculture and for recreation. The green heart of the Randstad would be extended southeastward, through the Lower Rhine, Waal, and Maas river valleys, to separate two parallel extensions of the Randstad's urban complex. The finest of the remaining moors and woodland would be designated as national parks, not all in public ownership

Figure 5-1. *Structural Land-Use Plan of the Netherlands, 1966*

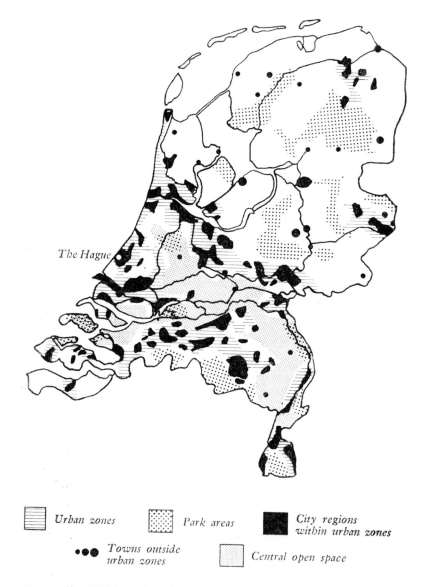

The Hague

▤ Urban zones	▦ Park areas	■ City regions within urban zones
●●● Towns outside urban zones	□ Central open space	

Source: *Second Report on Physical Planning in the Netherlands* (Government Printing Office of the Netherlands, 1966), pt. 1.

but all barred from urban development as the population flowed outward from the West and South.

Accompanying the land-use plan in the *Second Report* were functional plans setting out national development schemes for transportation, recreation, water management, and so on, as a guide to public investment. These functional plans were subsequently refined and others developed. In addition to public works, said the report, a strengthening of regional industrialization policy would be required for fulfillment of the plan.

The Plan in Execution (*1966–71*)

The strengthening of the regional industrialization policy came in a series of actions between 1966 and 1971, which fashioned the system still in effect in 1974. First came a liberalization of the inducements to industry to locate in the problem areas—renamed "stimulation areas." Then, as the cost of the program mounted and in order to permit a concentration of effort, the territory eligible for aid was cut back sharply. Problem areas nearest to the Randstad, which were benefiting most from the spontaneous decentralization of the West's industries, were denied further assistance. The areas left eligible for benefits, shown in Figure 5-2, were the original northern area, including three entire provinces and part of a fourth; South Limburg, a coal mining district in the extreme Southeast, which because of imminent mine closings had been brought into the incentive system as a "redeployment area" in 1966; and the new town of Lelystad, which the plan contemplated would become the center of the IJsselmeer polders, with a population of 100,000 by the year 2000. A score of previously eligible development nuclei were stripped of their status, permitting a concentration of resources in the remaining thirty-two that would need the greatest help in attaining their population goals.

The revisions of the incentive system were designed particularly to increase its appeal to the technologically advanced, capital-intensive industries that appeared to the Dutch, as to the Italians, to have the power to attract ancillary enterprise to a lagging region. For the first time a subsidy was offered toward the cost of machinery and equipment, as well as land and buildings. The new scheme, introduced in 1967 as an alternative to the existing formula but a couple of years later substituted for it, authorized a flat grant of 25 percent of investment in the fixed assets of

Figure 5-2. *Areas of Incentives and Disincentives for Growth in the Netherlands, 1974*

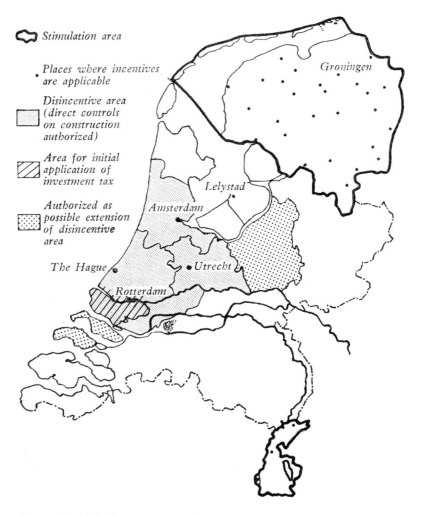

Source: The Netherlands, Ministry of Economic Affairs, *Guide to the Establishing of Industrial Operations* (Amsterdam: International Business Contacts, 1973), p. 48; and Article 2, Selective Investment Regulation Act, 1974.

new industrial enterprises, including land, buildings, and equipment. For expansion of existing plants involving new expenditure of at least $180,000 the grant was set at 15 percent. To assure that weak and risky enterprises would not be encouraged, the investor was required to supply at least 40 percent of his total capital. The condition that a minimum number of workers be hired, which had been in the Dutch incentive system since the beginning, was eliminated.[12] The subsidies were automatic and non-selective, as in Britain, up to a maximum grant of $1.1 million for new factories and $650,000 for expansions. Beyond that, discretionary power was vested in the minister of economic affairs.

For the first time, new service enterprises were made eligible for the same grants offered new manufacturing projects, provided they employed at least seventy-five persons and were "of more than regional importance." Some new incentive measures also were adopted: the government was authorized to purchase equity in plants unable otherwise to raise enough capital; a loan guarantee program was instituted, and an interest payment subsidy, up to 3 percent annually for fifteen years, was authorized. Direct government lending was not included among the types of assistance, because private sources of financing were considered adequate. Finally, accelerated depreciation, applying to one-third of the cost of buildings, was authorized; this was the one incentive made available not just in the stimulation areas but in all of the provinces outside the West.[13]

Once again, the possibility of imposing restrictions on industrial expansion in the West was considered, and once more it was rejected. "The main objection," said a government spokesman, was "the infringement it would mean on the present freedom of the entrepreneur to choose his own location and to bear the full responsibility for, and the full risks of, his choice."[14]

The subsidy to encourage migration, used until 1959 to help unemployed workers relocate in the West, was now made available to facilitate a reverse flow of workers from the Randstad to the development nuclei.

Meanwhile, $60 million was authorized for the period 1965–68 to provide the development nuclei with their industrial infrastructure, and

12. This exception did not apply in Lelystad, where the subsidy was limited to $3,600 per male employee hired, up to the maximum of 25 percent of investment.
13. Lelystad was not made eligible for the new benefits for service enterprises or the new incentives.
14. de Meijer, "Means to Implement the Regional Development Policy," p. 50.

another $20 million was authorized for 1966–70 for South Limburg. The provinces, in consultation with the municipalities in the nuclei and with the Ministry of Economic Affairs, drew up their priority lists for each year's public investment program; an interministerial committee reviewed the recommendations and prepared a recommended program for the minister's approval. On the average, the national share of the public works expenditures was about 60 percent. During the 1959–69 decade, more than $200 million in public works was put in place through this program, in addition to the extra funds made available through the regular departments, mainly for highways, in the amount of $3 million–$4 million a year.

By the end of the decade the Dutch dispersal policy was showing significant results. Indeed, as Figure 5-3 shows, the flow of migration within the Netherlands to the western provinces had been reversed as early as 1961. In every year since 1961 the net flow out of the West had continued, usually at an accelerating rate. In 1965, 1966, and each year from 1969 through 1972, the net out-migration had been more than 10,000 persons; in 1971 and 1972, it approximated 20,000.[15]

With the pressure of migration removed, the rate of population growth of the West had markedly slowed down. The region as a whole, which contained 48 percent of the country's population in 1950, had received 44 percent of the national growth in the 1950s but only 38 percent in the 1960s and 32 percent in 1971–72. In the most congested areas, growth actually came to a halt. The largest agglomerations—Amsterdam, Rotterdam, The Hague—stopped growing first, in the first half of the 1960s. In the last half of the decade the metropolitan regions embracing those centers had reached their population peaks, and the Randstad as an entirety showed a decline after 1968.[16] The agglomeration of The Hague was experiencing a job loss of 4,000 to 5,000 a year, or about 1.5 percent of total employment annually, in 1971–74, according to municipal officials.

How much of this was the result of national policy measures was, of course, not known. Many industries had been showing a decentralizing tendency before any national programs were instituted—although local,

15. The net loss of the West from internal migration was made up in most years, however, by a net inflow of migrants from other countries so that the combined migration figures—both internal and external—showed an almost even balance for the period 1960–72.

16. *The "Randstad,"* p. 13 and app. 1.

Figure 5-3. *Internal Migration to and from North and West Regions of the Netherlands, 1948–72*

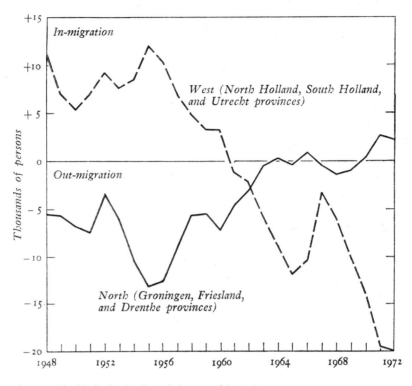

Source: The Netherlands, Central Bureau of Statistics.

if not national, planning policies that restricted the use of land for industry had a bearing on that. But spontaneous decentralization from the West had been almost wholly to the regions closest to the Randstad, not to the stimulation areas. The latter, as areas of out-migration and decline, relatively far from markets, with a limited labor supply, were the type of locations that mobile industry had traditionally avoided. In the absence of policy, they would hardly have become areas of net attraction. Yet, in the 1960s, the flow of out-migration from the largest of the problem areas—the three northern provinces, to which the government had devoted the most attention—was stemmed and in the 1970s it was actually reversed. Figure 5-3 shows the trend line: in the period 1963–67, migration between the North and the rest of the Netherlands came into approximate balance for the first time, and the years of 1971 and 1972 saw a net inflow to the North from the rest of the country. As the result, the North was receiving close to its proportional share of the country's population increase; with 12 percent of the nation's people in 1950, it had registered only 4 percent of the increase in the decade of the 1950s but 9 percent in the 1960s and 11 percent in 1971–72.[17] Unemployment in the North was still higher than the national average, but by 1970 it had fallen to 2.3 percent.

A study by A. J. Hendriks concluded that governmental action—industrial incentives, infrastructure development, and other stimulating measures—accounted for 5,094 of 10,309 new industrial and service jobs in 1960–67 in the largest northern center, the Groningen agglomeration, for half or more of the growth in 1960–67 in three other of the larger centers, and between a third and a half of the growth in a dozen of the smaller places.[18] The direct employment in 700 factories that received government assistance between 1959 and 1967 in all stimulation areas, outside as well as within the northern region, was 35,000.[19] Between 1967 and 1972, another 230 new establishments received $140 million in grants to bring about $1 billion in investment that would eventually create about 22,500 jobs.

Growth Controls on the Randstad   *(1971–)*

But the record was still not good enough, either in terms of achieving the objectives of the plan or in terms of the exigencies of Dutch politics. Though migration from the North had been stopped, no significant flow of population into the North had been generated. Though the West was getting less than its share of the national growth, it was still growing. The political aims of the underdeveloped regions were not being fulfilled. In

17. The North also experienced a reversal in the balance of external migration. For the first time in the postwar period, the region enjoyed a net gain in the years 1961–66 and again in 1969–71.

18. "Regional Policy in the Netherlands," in Niles M. Hansen, ed., *Public Policy and Regional Economic Development: The Experience of Nine Western Countries* (Ballinger, forthcoming). Hendriks' conclusions are based on empirical research by Vanhove designed to separate the effects of government programs from those of other factors influencing employment growth.

19. de Meijer, "Means to Implement the Regional Development Policy," p. 50.

1971 they saw their chance. In the negotiations that led to formation of a five-party, right-of-center coalition cabinet under Prime Minister B. W. Biesheuvel, eastern politicians obtained a pledge that the new government would move to impose restraints on investment in the West. The primary instrument of restraint, it was agreed, would be a "selective investment tax."

After "intensive deliberations," the cabinet came forward the following year with its proposals to redeem the pledge.[20] In accordance with the agreement the government proposed a levy on construction of commercial buildings (with certain exceptions, such as retail stores) in the three western provinces (see Figure 5-2)[21] at a rate unprecedented in Europe—40 percent of the cost of the fixed assets. That rate was selected as being high enough to impel those planning investment in the West to reconsider their projects but not so high as to be prohibitive for those who had a valid reason to be there. The government would, however, be able to make lower rates applicable in particular districts or for particular types of buildings. For industrial plants not housed in buildings—oil and chemical refineries, for example—a rate of 5 percent was proposed as roughly equal to the burden on buildings. The government also asked for authority to require licenses in cases where it was evident that the tax alone would not provide a sufficient deterrent—on office buildings, for example, or enterprises at deep water ports. Described as a "middle course," the policy was designed to allow projects that were "clearly useful" to go forward while yet imposing enough restraint to preserve the livability of the Randstad area.

In presenting its proposal, the government once more enumerated the costs and burdens imposed on the country by the high concentration of its population in the West: In that region, the difficulty of assuring decent public services, the intensification of traffic congestion, the spreading of urbanization into the "already scarce open space and the even scarcer natural areas and recreation lands," the threat to land needed for economic activities that by their nature were tied to the West, the im-

20. See Proceedings of the Staten-General, Zitting 1972-12045, Oct. 10, 1972, pp. 6-9.
21. The northern section of North Holland province, which had been classed in the 1950s as a problem area, and an island in South Holland province were excluded. The statute authorized the government to extend the controls to the rest of South Holland and parts of two additional provinces; this was under consideration in 1974.

pact of industrial and urban pollution "no matter how stringent" the regulations designed to control it; in the northern provinces and South Limburg, failure to reach the takeoff point of sustained economic growth. Concentration of new investment in the West had adverse economic consequences on both the regional and the national scale. Labor was drawn into industrial construction at the expense of home building. The chronic labor shortage in the West produced inflationary local wage settlements that were then generalized over the whole country; the so-called 400 guilder wave that spread across the nation at the end of 1970, for instance, originated in the tight labor market in the port of Rotterdam. High concentration meant higher infrastructure costs, which had to be borne by the whole economy. The saving that an individual industry calculated to justify its location in the West was not necessarily reflected in a corresponding saving to the society as a whole.

The cabinet had hoped that the increasing costs of congestion borne by industry itself, coupled with the incentives to investment in the stimulation areas, would have provoked a flow of new projects out of the West to other provinces. But "this hope has so far not been realized. Meanwhile, the burdens of congestion grow ever heavier." Hence, the government would be irresponsible if it continued to rely solely on the incentive system for the realization of national policy.

At the same time that it proposed restraints on private construction, the government finally came to grips with the question of decentralization of government offices on which successive administrations had been temporizing for more than a decade. It announced that 16,000 jobs would be relocated from The Hague within twelve years, 6,500 of them in the next four to five years. Of the 16,000, half would go to Groningen, another 2,000 to two other northern growth centers, 5,000 to Heerlen in southern Limburg. The number was calculated as approximately equal to the expected increase above the 40,000 headquarters-type jobs then located at the seat of government.

The immediate political reaction was wholly favorable. In the parliament a commission representing eleven parties supported the principle of the proposed selective investment tax and supplemental licensing system to control the Randstad's growth. The parties in the government's conservative-moderate coalition stuck by their original agreement, while the opposition socialist parties—always more responsive to the depressed areas and more inclined toward governmental planning—

could only offer technical criticisms and chide the government for its slowness in seeing the light. Only two small parties dissented. A general election in November 1972 brought an end to the Biesheuvel administration but when the new cabinet took office 168 days later—this time under a socialist prime minister, Joop M. den Uyl—it reaffirmed support of the legislation. In the face of a rising opposition within the western provinces the government had to accept a modification of the measure, but it was able to push it through to passage.

The opposition came, naturally enough, from the business and industrial community and allied labor groups in the West and from the affected municipalities, particularly The Hague. To the surprise of some, many western businessmen in their anxiety to avert the new tax burden actually came to advocate a more extensive system of direct controls— which the government had rejected on the theory that restraint through taxation was more compatible with the free enterprise philosophy. The "selective" tax was in fact not selective at all, the opponents argued; it would add to the cost of doing business for every firm that, for whatever valid reasons, had to be located in the Randstad. (The official estimate was that the 40 percent levy would reduce the profit of a typical firm by one-half of one percentage point—e.g., from 12 to 11.5 percent.) Those firms would be at a disadvantage in international competition. Investment would be driven over the country's southern boundary; "Belgium will get the industry and we'll get the smoke." Taking this view, the Economic and Social Council—an official advisory body representing business, labor, and other groups—had recommended at the outset that the tax be held to not more than 20 percent and greater reliance be placed on controls.

The argument that investment would be driven out of the country did not influence the government initially, for its proposal was made at a time when the country had been suffering the highest rate of inflation in Europe and it appeared necessary to dampen the investment boom somehow. The measure proposed would fortuitously serve that objective and the policy of population dispersal at the same time. The government's economists estimated that the 40 percent tax would cut new construction in the West by 15 percent, and that half of that invesment would be diverted to other points in the Netherlands, leaving a net loss of 5–10 percent that the government found acceptable or even desirable. But the economy slackened in 1973 and restraining measures that seemed necessary for economic reasons the previous year lost much of their appeal.

The loudest outcry against the government's proposals came from the mayor of The Hague. While The Hague's rival cities, Amsterdam and Rotterdam, would be hit only by the restraints on private business, The Hague was the target also of the decision to decentralize the government itself. That, from the government's point of view, was appropriate enough, for it was The Hague that epitomized the congestion problem of the Randstad. With proper planning controls, the growth of Amsterdam could be directed toward the north and that of Rotterdam toward the south, away from the "green heart." But The Hague was backed up against the sea and flanked on either side by coastal recreation areas and by land devoted intensively to the "glass culture" of hothouse gardening. So the agglomeration had nowhere to spread except into the open center of the conurbation.

That to the city appeared not only proper but desirable. What was the green heart anyway, asked an official spokesman for the mayor, besides a "literary term"? What was the use of "all that pasture"? A city should have many green areas of intensive use within its boundaries, as The Hague now has, but "what city needs a big, unused green hole?" If the total number of jobs within The Hague continued to decrease—and the agglomeration had been losing jobs ever since 1967, even in the absence of the proposed stringent new policies—the capital would become a city of old people, schools would stand empty, the housing stock would decay, the tax base would decline, and cultural institutions could no longer be supported. "Everybody agrees that government must deal with unemployment in the north and east of the country," said the mayor, "but this cannot be done by creating a similar problem in this important part of the Netherlands."[22] Even as the government was proceeding with plans to decentralize its administrative agencies, the city was contemplating the creation of a "job acquisition" organization to actively solicit "high-level," tertiary activities to replace them.

The provincial government of South Holland reflected The Hague's position. The province insisted that the proposed investment tax be made truly selective, with rates graduated from the maximum amount to zero according to the type and purpose of the building. The higher rates

22. Mayor V. G. M. Marijnen, "The Hague under the Scalpel," *International Union of Local Authorities Newsletter* (The Hague), December 1972.

would be reserved for strictly mobile enterprises, particularly factories, that could be located elsewhere. But, as a South Holland official put it, "hotels, like retail stores, can't move to Groningen—why penalize them?" Valuable tertiary establishments for which all countries are competing—corporate headquarters, research activities, international institutions—should be sought rather than discouraged; "why should Brussels get them all?"

The kinds of restraints that the Netherlands was considering, argued the opponents, could be imposed effectively only on an international scale. The other countries at the densely settled center of the European Community—France, Britain, Belgium, and West Germany, at least—had to act in concert with the Dutch. France and Britain, which were already controlling the growth of their congested areas, would presumably be ready to support action at the Community level; the key country was Belgium, and the Belgians—beneficiaries already of growth diverted out of France and Britain—were showing no interest in checking the expansion of their major cities. Since the European Community's cumbersome machinery requires the unanimous consent of its member countries, in effect, for major new policy departures, no one expected that body to move at any time soon into the field of urban growth control.

Confronted by these arguments, the government held to its basic goal but made major concessions to save the legislation as it moved through the parliament. The maximum tax rate was reduced from 40 percent to 25 percent on buildings and from 5 percent to 3 percent on open-air industrial investment. Hotels were added to the list of exempt categories, and an understanding was reached that a rate of half the maximum would be established for office buildings, warehouses, and certain other types of buildings. The 25 percent rate would be limited essentially to factories. The first $95,000 of investment would also be exempt. Certain municipalities within the controlled area were to be designated as "growth centers" —"reception municipalities" for the overflow from the large cities—and taxes there would be cut in half for a limited period. It was agreed that, as the Economic and Social Council had suggested, more reliance would be placed on direct controls to achieve a greater selectivity. With these concessions, the bill passed, but the effective date was left to the discretion of the government. The cabinet temporized for a time, as the country continued in an economic slump. Finally, in October 1974, it announced its intent to virtually abandon the unpopular tax in favor of direct controls. If the parliament approved, the licensing provisions would be applied to the entire controlled area, effective January 1, 1975, but the tax would apply only to Rotterdam and its surrounding port area at the mouth of the Rhine. The minimum size of projects to be controlled would also be raised, to $380,000 for buildings and $1.9 million for open-air industrial installations.

The parliament did approve the planned dispersal of government agencies, and in March 1974 the den Uyl cabinet ordered the first stage of the moves to begin. By 1978, a total of 8,300 jobs would be relocated, 6,200 of them to the North and 2,100 to South Limburg. The largest unit to be relocated was the headquarters of the national postal, telegraph, and telephone service, which with certain associated activities of that ministry employed 5,300 persons in The Hague. These would be moved to Groningen and Leeuwarden, in the North, with the headquarters in the former city. The reaction from the mayor and aldermen of The Hague was immediate and vociferous, and a major controversy appeared in prospect.

At Issue: The Future of the Green Heart

In the early 1970s some of the demographic and political circumstances that had made possible the forceful population dispersal policy supported by successive governments for more than a decade seemed to be weakening. The dominant influence was evidently the sudden slackening of population growth, which the Netherlands has experienced along with every other country of northern Europe. The population of 20 million that was forecast in 1966 for the year 2000 has already been scaled down to 17 million and in the next round of planning will probably be between 15 million and 16 million. A third report on physical planning, in preparation in 1974, was bound to modify drastically the quantitative dispersal goals established by its predecessor. The structural plans for the northern provinces designed to accommodate the equivalent of a new city of 100,000 population each two years were also in the process of revision; the municipality of Leeuwarden, for instance, once expected to grow from 85,000 to 250,000, now has a prospect of well under half the larger number.

Many northerners, moreover, are pleased enough with the new outlook—perhaps persuaded in part by the very arguments about pollution and other evils of congestion that the government was using to support its case for decentralization of the Randstad. Northern opinion appears to be shifting, according to national officials, from an indiscriminate support of industrial development to a desire for a selective growth that will screen out "environment-hostile" industry. If it becomes clear that this is indeed the dominant opinion of the North it suggests at least a modification of regional policy: enterprise kept out of the Randstad for reasons of congestion could be simply allowed to go where it would choose to go in the absence of incentives—to the growth centers in the nearer provinces, the half-way zone, where the greatest potential for expansion lies.

A third major factor weakening Dutch policy is the birth of determined political resistance within the Randstad, which coincided with the reversal of the migration flow. The West had gone along with national policy in what it conceived to be its own interest, but when it began to experience an absolute decline in jobs and population in its major centers, its conception of its interest changed. The demand of The Hague that it not be condemned by central planning to a slow economic and cultural death won an increasingly sympathetic reception. And people began to ask seriously whether with "concentrated deconcentration" the Randstad cities as a group could maintain their place among the great centers of European culture. "The fear that the Netherlands will ultimately remain at a too low urbanization level, especially in the social and cultural sense, would appear to be not entirely unfounded," said the director of the National Physical Planning Office itself.[23]

At the center of the argument was the green heart of Randstad Holland; was it an oasis, a refuge from the urban hubbub to be preserved at all costs, or was it "a big unused, green hole" to be appropriately filled with brick and concrete? Public opinion had supported solidly the former view, and so every government for two decades, whatever its party makeup, had reaffirmed its allegiance to the goal of preserving the open character of that area. But could that position be maintained indefinitely if to maintain it required onerous taxes and tight controls? And could the objective be attained in any case—even with restraints on economic growth? To a degree, the green heart was already being filled; its popula-

23. Th. Quené, address at Waginengen, March 8, 1968.

tion grew by 27 percent in the 1960s, by one calculation. "Towns in the green heart that were to be held to 5,000 are already double that," lamented a provincial planner.

The pressure was inexorable. Even if, as predicted, the country's total population stabilized, that did not solve the problem. Households within the Randstad long accustomed to life in urban flats now wanted their own private open space, in suburban tracts. Slum clearance speeded the outward movement. Cities and towns within the green heart were making their plans for development; the salaries of the mayors, for one thing, were based on population. Provincial and national authorities, through their structural plans, could try to channel that development, but the law that defined the right of the provincial authorities to block projects inconsistent with the structural plans had a loophole,[24] and even when the right was clear, the political realities dictated that the provincial and national planners choose carefully the occasions on which to exercise their power, in order to limit the number and strength of those who would discredit planning altogether. The political weight of agriculture, once important in defending "all that pasture," had declined. So the planners were fighting what some referred to as a "rear-guard action," a "losing battle."

Yet the outcome of the struggle was far from settled. One more comprehensive study of the appropriate use of those controverted green acres was launched in 1973 by the Ministry of Housing and Physical Planning. A more intensive development of the area for public recreational use, converting agricultural land to lakes and picnic grounds, would indeed help to preserve it from those who reasonably asked what good to city dwellers were hundreds of square miles of privately owned farms. In the third report on physical planning, the government would have to either reaffirm or modify the seminal doctrines that had made the preservation of the green heart the central objective of Dutch population distribution policy.

In any case, the concept of population distribution planning as a national responsibility appeared secure. In a land so crowded, no voice was heard to suggest that the growth of cities and the use of the national

24. The planning legislation provides that any project under way at the time a plan is adopted must be allowed to continue. Thus municipal officials could grant building permits under their local plans, and by the time those plans could be reviewed by the provincial planners for consistency with the structural plans and revisions worked out, the projects could not be stopped.

living space were matters for laissez faire. Center-right and center-left coalitions had agreed so far on the role of government, as well as on the basic philosophy of dispersal, and so they had been able to express that philosophy in the most explicit plans for the spatial ordering of growth on a national scale found anywhere in Europe—and probably in the world—as well as in increasingly powerful program measures. New questions were being raised in the debate on population distribution policy, but they went to the substance of the policy, not to the process. Whatever the distribution pattern of the Dutch population that eventuates in the coming decades, it seems certain that it will be planned.

CHAPTER SIX

Sweden: Allocating a Scarce Resource—People

Regional development policy should aim at creating new or promoting exist-
ing conditions for growth in a number of regional centres with a development
potential in different parts of the country. In order to make this feasible, the
powerful growth of the three metropolitan regions should be somewhat
curbed and part of the expansion be allocated to these regional centres.
—Swedish Government Policy Statement, 1969[1]

As IN ALMOST every other advanced country, the long-time trend toward urbanization gathered speed in Sweden in the war and postwar
decades. The rapid growth of a modern industrial economy drained
population out of the rural areas into the cities, with the largest metropolitan areas registering the greatest gains.

The county of Stockholm, which held only 7 percent of the country's
people in 1870, grew to 13 percent by 1930 but then expanded rapidly to
17 percent by 1950 and to nearly 20 percent of the country's 8 million
people by 1970. The country's other two major metropolitan centers,
Göteborg and Malmö (which is part of the Copenhagen, Denmark,
metropolitan region) grew almost as rapidly. Together, the three metropolitan areas absorbed nearly three-quarters of the country's population
growth between 1930 and 1970. Another nine urban centers accounted
for almost all the rest. Between 1960 and 1965, the aggregate population
outside these dozen largest cities actually declined.[2]

In Sweden, urbanization meant in particular a north-south drift. All
but one of the dozen growing centers (and that one a relatively small
one) were in the country's southern third. The counties covering the
northern and west central two-thirds of the elongated country—known
traditionally as Norrland or as the "forest counties"—suffered the heavi-

1. As reported in Ministry of Labor and Housing and Ministry of Physical
Planning and Local Government, *Planning Sweden* (1973), p. 58.
2. Folke Kristensson, "People, Firms and Regions" (Economic Research Institute,
Stockholm School of Economics, 1967; processed), pp. 1:3–4.

est out-migration as forestry and agriculture declined. Soon a cry of protest arose from that depleted region: migration was depriving the forest counties of the most productive element of their population and converting them into a demographic backwater—their communities composed disproportionately of the old and the handicapped, lacking the resources to support public services at the standard that was being established for the rest of the country.

As elsewhere, the politicians responded to the plea from the areas of out-migration. The government initiated studies, and in 1964 the parliament adopted a comprehensive "active location policy" to stem the southward flow of population. That course was necessary, the government concluded, for four reasons: First, for economic reasons—to assure full utilization of the capital and manpower resources of the country. Second, for reasons of equity—to retain a population base in northern communities sufficient to support a satisfactory level of social and cultural services in all areas. Third, for welfare reasons—to protect the security of individual families by slowing down structural change. Fourth, for reasons of national defense. Later, a fifth justification was added—protection of the environment by avoiding population concentration.

Perhaps more than any other Western European country, Sweden had been actually facilitating internal migration. As a feature of its "positive labor market policy," which had attracted much favorable attention abroad, it had been paying relocation allowances to workers who moved from unemployment areas to communities where jobs existed. Under the active location policy this program would continue, but the emphasis would shift to "taking the work to the workers"—the same shift that had been made by the British thirty years before and by the Dutch in the 1950s.

The means were to be twofold: a system of subsidies to promote industrialization of the North of Sweden, and a system of planning that would determine an optimum settlement pattern for the whole country. The subsidy system was patterned after devices adopted earlier by other European countries. The planning system reflected earlier European experience as well, but Sweden ultimately went further than any other Western country toward defining the role and position of every city in a national urban hierarchy and assigning to each a quantitative target for population growth.

The System of Subsidies for Northern Industry   *(1963–)*

Even while studies leading to a permanent program were in progress, the first temporary steps were taken in 1963. One was a decision to include the construction of industrial buildings among the types of municipal work-relief projects that the central government would assist. Parliament authorized about $10 million a year for each of two years to provide one-third (or in some cases as much as half) of the cost of erecting buidings for sale or rent on easy terms to private firms. Communities in a defined "aid area"—the northern and west-central two-thirds of the country—were eligible.

A second measure was the authorization of the release of "reserve funds" for investment in the aid area. These funds, designed originally and used earlier as a means of stimulating investment in times of recession, are set aside by businesses from their profits and are exempted from taxation if used when the government determines that economic stimulus is necessary.

These two approaches were superseded in 1965 by the permanent program, which authorized grants and loans to companies investing in the aid area. Parliament authorized $15 million in grants and $25 million in loans annually for the five-year period from 1965 to 1970. Construction or conversion of buildings was eligible for grants, which generally covered 35 percent of the cost but could run up to 50 percent. Loans were available both for buildings and for machinery and equipment, and exemption from interest could be granted for a maximum of three years and exemption from amortization for five. Grants and loans combined could not exceed two-thirds of total investment. While the assistance was intended primarily for the aid area, it could also be used in other places where exceptional unemployment existed or was anticipated. Tourism as well as manufacturing enterprises were eligible for assistance.

In the development of this policy, a major debate centered on the question of growth centers. The more prosperous cities of the region were spaced along the shores of the Gulf of Bothnia, and they had been and were growing as small industrial centers without benefit of government aid. It was plain that if they were made eligible for benefits along with the interior communities of the North, they would experience most of the growth. Existing firms there would be ready with their expansion plans, and new firms seeking locations in the North would in most cases choose sites on or near the water.

But, argued one group, it was the interior communities—those of the hilly and wooded farming areas, where the term *depopulation* could justly be applied—that had provided the impetus for the whole assistance effort. It was they the policies should be designed to help. Accordingly, government assistance should be concentrated in the interior in the hope of creating a network of expanding centers there, and the relatively flourishing coastal cities should be excluded from the benefits, or limited to a minor share.

The opposing view was that few centers in the interior would be attractive to industry even with the most generous government assistance. If Norrland were to be saved, it would be through the encouragement not of its least suitable but of its most suitable industrial locations—in other words, those cities that had already shown capacity to attract investment and grow. The National Labor Market Board had estimated in the 1950s that a city must serve a population of at least 30,000 in order to provide "many service facilities that are important to people's choice of a place to live and manufacturing firms' choice of a place to operate."[3] Such a city could be expected to have a college preparatory high school, well-differentiated vocational training, a hospital, and a daily newspaper, and to be well served by rail and highway transportation. There were only twenty communities of that size in the aid area, most of them on the coast. Here, it was argued, was where the effort should be concentrated, and therefore the coastal centers and the interior rural area should be eligible alike for benefits.

The government adopted the second view. It extended the assistance on equal terms to the whole of the northern aid area. And, as predicted, most of the new investment went to the existing growth centers. About 75 percent of the 17,000 new jobs that by 1967 had been, or were being, created in the aid area through the four years of government action were in the twenty largest communities. Their growth was attracting surplus workers from the declining interior. So, it turned out, the new programs were actually hastening, rather than retarding, the depopulation of the interior, and the social problems that had given rise initially to the new policies were intensified, not ameliorated.

3. "The National Labor Market Board: Classification into Regions," 1961, quoted in ibid., p. 1:6.

In the official view, however, the experience of the early years confirmed the wisdom of the original decision. Time had shown, said a government spokesman in 1967, that "there are a very small number of places —even using high subsidies—which are attractive to industry, or attractive to the individuals, since the important question for industry must be to locate an undertaking in a place with good recruitment possibilities." The goal of taking work to the workers simply could not be met for those workers who lived in unattractive places. They would have to move. Rural-urban migration therefore could not be stopped. Indeed, in the interests of national economic growth it should be encouraged, and that included some continued north-south movement. The problems created in the sparsely populated areas would simply have to be met through social welfare programs, such as work relief and sheltered workshops, "for people who because of age and other handicaps cannot move."[4] For the young and able-bodied, the subsidies for relocation were continued. In fact, in 1967–68 the government was spending more on measures to promote mobility than on assistance to industry—$50 million compared to $40 million.[5]

In 1970, however, the government reversed itself. It created an "inner aid area," comprising the more depressed inland segment of the general aid area (as shown on Figure 6-1), and established a series of differentiated benefits in the hope of bringing more work to the workers there. Most important of these was an employment grant for new jobs created. For increased employment in manufacturing, $1,250 per additional job was granted for each of the first two years and half that amount for the third. Effective in 1973, the grants were raised to $1,750 for the first and second years and $875 for the third. In 1972, payments amounted to more than $3 million, covering 2,700 persons. When the inner aid area was established, projects there were generally given the maximum grant of 50 percent (the limit was raised in 1973 to 65 percent) of investment in buildings, compared to 35 percent for the rest of the aid area. The government also decided to experiment once more with constructing factory buildings on a speculative basis. Two small ones, with space for 150 jobs

4. C. Canarp, division head, National Labor Market Board, in Organisation for Economic Co-operation and Development, "Salient features of regional development policies in the Scandinavian Countries" (Paris: OECD, 1968; processed), p. 133. Proceedings of a meeting in June 1967.

5. Ibid., p. 145. In the first half of the 1960s, more than 10,000 workers a year were assisted to relocate.

Figure 6-1. *Aid Areas under the Regional Development Policy in Sweden, 1973*[a]

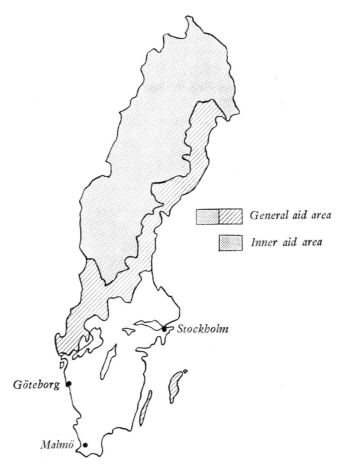

General aid area

Inner aid area

Stockholm

Göteborg

Malmö

Source: Sweden, Ministry of Labor and Housing and Ministry of Physical Planning and Local Government, *Planning Sweden* (1973), p. 75.

a. The lines are the same as in 1970, except that a small portion of the inner aid area at its southern end was added in 1973.

each, were to be erected; if they succeeded, others were to be under-taken.

In 1973 a broader range of enterprises was made eligible for assistance in both parts of the aid area. Besides manufacturing and tourism, enter-prises engaged in certain forms of wholesaling to business and such enterprises as marketing and technical consulting firms that worked for business were made eligible.

Industries relocating in the aid area could also be reimbursed for the costs of moving machinery and equipment. For that purpose, about $4 million had been spent by the end of 1972. Training allowances, usually amounting to $1.25 an hour for each trainee for six months, have also been paid since 1970. By 1972, almost $30 million had been expended for training 18,000 employees, of whom 15,000 were in the aid area.

Finally, to offset the disadvantages of location, transportation subsidies have been enacted for articles manufactured or processed in the aid area, varying from 15 percent to 35 percent of the normal charge, depending on distance. Interestingly, the original proposal to apply the reduction to transportation of articles in both directions was revised at the behest of manufacturers in the aid area to cover only goods which they shipped out. Articles shipped in, which might compete with their own products, were excluded. But in 1973, raw materials and semimanufactured goods necessary to the manufacturing process were included in the transportation subsidy.

The System of Planning   *(1964–69)*

When the government in 1964 determined that the time had come for a conscious population distribution policy, it assigned responsibility for planning to established institutions at both the national and the regional level. In the capital the Ministry of Labor and Housing (Inrikesdepartementet) was given the job, in the regions the twenty-four county (or provincial) governors—national government appointees whose status and duties correspond to those of prefects in France. But at each level new mechanisms were created. The Ministry of Labor and Housing was provided a national advisory committee, a research organization (the Expert Group on Regional Studies), and a planning secretariat to coordinate the development planning of the counties. Each provincial governor was provided a planning unit and a planning council to aid in the preparation of a developmental plan containing "definite proposals and a program for action."

To begin the first cycle of planning—"county planning 1967"—the central government provided the counties with population projections based on common demographic assumptions. These distributed an anticipated national increase during the 1965–80 period of 930,000, or 12 percent. To reflect recent trends more than three-quarters of the increase went to the three major metropolitan areas—more than half, or 471,000, to Stockholm. For six northern counties, absolute declines were shown, totaling 83,000 and ranging up to 16 percent for the wholly inland county of Jämtland.

With these figures as a point of departure, the counties were to do two things. First, from their own knowledge of employment trends and prospects they were to revise the forecasts, taking into account the expansion or contraction plans of particular industries. Second, they were to establish population targets, which would take into account the planning objectives of their individual communes—in other words, they were to propose alternative population levels if they did not like what the revised forecasts showed. Both the forecasts and the targets were to be broken down by communes, and the targets would be used to determine the allocation of resources for infrastructure, particularly for housing.

The results of this process were as might have been expected. Twenty of the twenty-four counties thought the population projections received from Stockholm were unduly pessimistic and revised the forecasts upward by as much as 18 percent. In particular, they raised the forecasts for industrial employment. Whereas the central ministries anticipated a decline in manufacturing jobs in the country as a whole by 1980—a continuation of the existing trend, which reflected a slow aggregate population growth and a steady decrease in the proportion of total national employment that would be in manufacturing—the counties collectively forecast an increase. When it came to determining their targets, not a single county was satisfied with the population level that had been projected for it, and only six were satisfied with their own optimistic revised forecasts. Only one of those six wanted a level lower than its own forecast. That was Uppsala, which desired to slow down the movement of population into its southern communes from neighboring Stockholm. In all, the county targets called for an increase of 59,000 in industrial employment and for half a million more people than the demographers estimated would be in Sweden in 1980. And this in itself often represented a drastic scaling down of the communes' targets. "People are a scarce resource," remarked one official. "There just aren't enough of them to go around."

Faced with this dilemma, the minister of labor and housing in his report to parliament in 1969 had to emphasize that the targets set by the counties could not be accepted as binding. He expressed sympathy with the rejection by the forest counties of the population declines that had been forecast for them. Yet even with the use of all the government's powers—industrial subsidies, infrastructure development, allocation of housing construction—it would plainly not be possible to industrialize the North at the pace the targets called for. That being the case, it was urgent for the northern counties to set priorities among their communes. Some of the governors had stated priorities explicitly but others had only implied them. The minister now called on all of them to come forward with a precise "grading" of all their communities. In the interior areas it would be necessary to concentrate "growth promoting measures" on a relatively small number of carefully selected growth points, which would act as service centers for the sparse population. For these priority areas, the county targets would be accepted as the basis for planning.[6]

If the targets for the northern priority areas were to be accepted, then population had to be diverted from somewhere else. That should be, obviously, the areas that had been growing most rapidly at the expense of the declining North—the big cities. So the government accepted the policy objective of restraining the growth of Stockholm, Göteborg, and Malmö, and this objective was confirmed by the parliament. But again, because the means at the government's disposal were insufficient to assure that that end would be accomplished, the three areas were instructed to prepare their plans on the basis of the population forecasts. For the non-metropolitan counties outside the North, the ambitious targets were rejected; those counties were also told to plan on the basis of their population forecasts.

Subsequently, these policies were reduced to specific figures, which were called a "population framework" for planning and approved as such by the parliament. The framework for each county was not a single figure but a narrow range, with the upper limit about 5 percent above the lower. The new framework eliminated the drastic population declines in the North that had been forecast earlier but, realistically, it still showed most of the country's 1970–80 growth (93 percent at one end of the

6. Rune Olsson, "Experiment in Provincial Planning in Sweden" (Jan. 7, 1969; processed), pp. 12–15. Sweden, Ministry of Labor and Housing, Ministry of Physical Planning and Local Government, "Regional Policy and Planning in Sweden" (August 1970; processed), pp. 61–65.

range and 58 percent at the other) going to the three major metropolitan centers.

Big City Alternatives, and the Restraint of Stockholm *(1969-)*

Since the government had acknowledged that it lacked adequate means to bring about the dispersal of population it had proclaimed as an objective, what then? How did it get the means? For their part, the counties made clear their view that too much was being expected of them in the setting and attainment of population distribution goals. Faced with the legislative mandate of 1964 instructing them to prepare "definite proposals and a program for action," they were explicit in casting that burden back on the central government. The counties and the communes could identify necessary public works expenditures and propose their concentration in growth centers, and they could prepare industrial sites and advertising brochures, but beyond that they saw little that they could do. What was needed, several of the governors and county planning councils contended forcefully during the 1967 exercise, was a stronger and more determined national policy. So they drafted definite proposals for action to be taken not by themselves but by the national authorities. Perhaps impressed by the experience of Great Britain and France, the hinterland counties argued for direct controls on the growth of the three major metropolitan areas. And they suggested an accelerated and concentrated program of investment in the major secondary centers of the country to build them up as true alternatives to Stockholm and the other major metropolitan areas.

The government was not ready for any such drastic step as the imposition of controls on industrial construction in its major centers, like those in effect in London and Paris, and when such a proposal was offered in parliament it was rejected. The basic argument was that expansion of manufacturing in the metropolitan areas did not appear to be the real problem. Rising costs of land and labor there had already been bringing about industrial decentralization—particularly from Stockholm—even before the introduction of government subsidies in 1965, and the subsidies were presumably having an additional impact.[7] Between 1962

---

7. In addition, the three metropolitan areas must bear the "full cost" of some infrastructure improvements that are subsidized for the aid areas. This adds to the cost differential of locating an enterprise in a metropolitan area.

and 1968 the number of industrial employees fell by 17,000 in the three major urban regions while it rose by 10,000 in Norrland and the more rural parts of central and southern Sweden.[8] The growth of Stockholm, and Göteborg and Malmö as well, lay in the service sector, just as was the case in large cities elsewhere in Europe. So the government contented itself, in regard to manufacturing, with introducing a voluntary system of control. A company contemplating an expansion project of over 5,500 square feet in any of the three metropolitan areas would be required to notify the government of its intention. The government would then discuss with the company the possibility of its locating its activity in the aid area or elsewhere outside the major centers and it would make information available as to alternative sites. But coercion was ruled out.

In searching for effective means to curtail the expansion of service activities in the private sector, the Swedish government found itself as baffled as the British and the French have been. In Stockholm, however, it had a large part of the service sector under its direct control—the agencies of the central government itself. And here the government moved boldly. A royal commission created in 1969 to identify those parts of the central government that could be relocated out of Stockholm came up with a preliminary and a later supplementary list designating more than fifty activities, employing 11,000 persons—or 25 percent of all central government employees in the capital. The parliament accepted the first list virtually unanimously. The movement was to begin in 1974 and to be completed by 1980, with more than half the affected employees relocated in the forest counties. But in regard to private enterprises in the service sector, such as banking and insurance, the government has taken no steps beyond expressing a wish that they would follow suit.

The adoption of the policy objective of curbing the capital's growth was not based on any widespread conviction that Stockholm was too big in and of itself. The action was not an end but a means; the end was the prevention of depopulation in Norrland, and that purpose was seen as unattainable without restraint on the growth of employment opportunities in the capital and the other two metropolitan complexes. True, to buttress their other arguments, proponents of population dispersal had made a case against big city congestion. Rapid population growth in the

8. Sweden, Ministry of Finance, *The Swedish Economy 1971–1975 and the General Outlook up to 1990: The 1970 Long-term Survey* (1971), p. 165.

metropolitan areas, said an official spokesman in 1972 in summarizing the government's rationale for its population distribution policy, "has led to waiting lists or delays in certain sectors, particularly in the health service and communications," and "environmental nuisances in the form of air pollution, noise and the like have become increasingly marked."[9] Commuting journeys of up to 75 minutes are cited as one of the inconveniences of Stockholm life. A study of the costs of future expansion in Göteborg concluded that for the first seven years at least the labor required for building houses and expanding services would be greater than the number of workers the new housing and services would accommodate.[10]

But complaints about the evils of big city congestion are not uttered with the same fervor or the same frequency as in London or Paris. The Stockholm metropolitan area, after all, contains only 1.4 million people, compared to London's 12 million and Paris' 9 million. It is, indeed, about the size of some of the secondary cities whose growth France has been trying to expedite to take the pressure off its capital. And the Swedish capital has a modern subway system and is experiencing no inordinate difficulty in maintaining city services. Göteborg and Malmö, the other metropolitan centers, have a combined population near that of Stockholm.

But if Stockholm's population is not great relative to other capitals, neither is Sweden's relative to other countries. So Stockholm contains almost the same proportion of its nation's population as do London and Paris—in Stockholm's case, about one in six. The three major Swedish centers together contain one-third of the country's population, and the proportion, at the time the decentralization policies were introduced, was rising. The expansion of the three centers over a long period, said the government's spokesman, "has limited the possibilities of achieving balanced development in other parts of Sweden."[11] This was the crux. Stockholm had attained the same dominance of national life as had London and Paris.

9. Sweden, Ministry of Labor and Housing, "Swedish Government Urban Policy and Relocation Policy," excerpts of speeches by government officials at an international working party meeting at Norrköping, May 31–June 1, 1972 (processed), p. 6.

10. Sweden, Ministry of Labor and Housing, Expert Group on Regional Studies, "Balanced Regional Development" (May 1970; processed), pp. 31–32.

11. Ministry of Labor and Housing, "Swedish Government Urban Policy," p. 6.

The difficulty was expressed perhaps more often in qualitative than in quantitative terms. Half of Sweden's university students were studying either in Stockholm or in nearby Uppsala. "Anyone who gets a university degree virtually has to move to Stockholm, whether he wants to or not," said a government adviser. "In many fields, there is no career opportunity at all anywhere else." The advocates of dispersal of government offices, in particular, seemed to emphasize the beneficial effects of the move on education and leadership resources in provincial towns more than they did its numerical effects. The key word was "balance" among the various regions, in the sense both of population growth and population composition. If the concept did not lend itself to precise definition, it was still understood clearly enough to form a sufficient basis for policy determination.

The second line of criticism from the provinces—that the government should concentrate on the development of the principal secondary growth centers—was wholly in accord with the thinking of the national administration's own planners. The original suggestion that cities in the North should be graded according to priority was expanded in the parliamentary resolution authorizing a second round of county planning—"county program 1970"—to call for definition of a complete urban hierarchy for the whole country with each city allotted its position and its role. At the top of the structure would be the three metropolitan centers whose growth was to be curtailed. The cities ranking next in size—named, appropriately, "big city alternatives"—would be encouraged to grow as rivals to the metropolises. Below them would be designated regional centers believed to have a possibility of increasing, or at least stabilizing, population. Finally would be communal centers, which could not expect significant growth but which could be sustained as service centers for their communes.[12]

The number of big city alternatives was determined, however, not by planning criteria but by the nature of the planning process that had been earlier established. Since the responsibility for planning rested basically on the counties, it was they who chose the big city alternatives, and no county of reasonable size with a normal quotient of ambition and self-respect could fail to find a potential alternative within its borders. The result, then, was one (and in a couple of cases two) proposed big

12. The number of communes in Sweden has been dramatically reduced in a series of steps over the past two decades, from 2,500 in 1950 to 278 in 1974.

city alternatives in each of the mainland counties, plus typically three to five regional centers.[13] Some counties that lacked a single center of sufficient size and promise to qualify as a genuine alternative to Stockholm formed their alternatives by designating two or more neighboring small cities in combination. In no position to overrule the counties, the government made a symbolic change of name, from big city alternative to "primary center," and went along. The decision to designate twenty-three primary centers disappointed some experts who felt that the objective would have had a better prospect of achievement if resources were spread among half as many centers or fewer. These could have ranged from just under 100,000 to 300,000 in population, whereas most of the primary centers actually designated are in the 50,000–100,000 bracket. However, proponents of the final solution could point to the earlier conclusion of the Labor Market Board that a population of 30,000 in a growth center was sufficient to sustain the range of services normally required for industrial expansion.

In any case, the decision was consistent with Sweden's developmental planning structure, in which the county was the basic unit. If a county was to plan and carry out a developmental program, it had to have a growth center on which to focus its attention. If twenty nonmetropolitan counties were the appropriate number for developmental planning, then twenty had to be the minimum number of primary centers. Those who were arguing for fewer primary centers should logically have been contending, instead, for fewer planning bodies.

And this is what they have been doing. Several royal commissions have been created over the past decade to consider the problem of regionalism. One commission, in the late 1960s, recommended consolidation of the twenty-four counties into fifteen, a number that was criticized as being too many for economic development while too few for other county functions. A Commission on Regional Organization was in 1974 considering various proposals for consolidating the counties into one-third to one-half the current number or, alternatively, creating a new regional level of government for economic planning and development. The commissions have further been concerned about whether the gov-

13. Only the island of Gotland, by far the smallest of Sweden's twenty-four counties with barely 50,000 population, failed to propose a big city alternative. Twenty-one counties, including the metropolitan county containing Malmö, proposed one each; two counties proposed two. Seventy regional centers were designated.

ernor's powers should be transferred to the county council, an elected body whose authority now extends only to health programs and some activities in the field of education.[14]

Meanwhile, there is nothing to require the government to treat all the primary centers as though they possessed equal prospect of development. The services available in each primary center are to be brought up to a certain minimum level, presumably; each is to get a branch of one of the five state universities, and each is to have a complete facility for technical education and a major hospital. But beyond such minimums, there is room for considerable discrimination in the emphasis that will actually be given to the individual primary centers. In the relocation of government offices, for example, thirteen of the primary centers were selected as recipients.

Balanced Growth: The Objective Attained

By the early 1970s the goal that many Swedes had been seeking for a decade and more had been achieved: For the first time in modern history, net migration into the Stockholm metropolitan area had been stopped. By 1972 there was a net outflow, and Stockholm and its environs suffered an absolute decline in population. That had happened but twice before since records had been kept—during the potato famine of 1868 and the influenza epidemic of 1918. Net migration into the Göteborg area had likewise been brought to a halt, in the 1970s, and migration to Malmö had at least been slowed.

No one could say how much of this result was attributable to the government's regional policy, for other factors were at work. Economic recession was one of them. For the first time in over forty years, in 1972, more foreigners left than entered Sweden, attracted by better employment prospects elsewhere, and the loss was chiefly recorded in the metropolitan areas. Yet in both 1971 and 1972 Stockholm, at least, showed a net loss in domestic interregional as well as international migration. And for this result, government policy had to be given a major share of credit.

14. In 1971 the composition of county administrative boards was changed from government officials to private citizens, half of them appointed by the government and half by the county council. In each county the board, of which the governor is chairman, shares his authority—as, for example, in making a collective recommendation on applications for industrial grants and loans.

Figure 6-2. *Geographic Distribution of Swedish Industrial Workers,*
1960, 1965, and 1970[a]

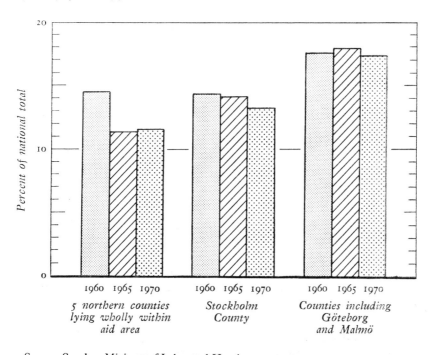

Source: Sweden, Ministry of Labor and Housing.
a. Economically active population in manufacturing and mining.

By the end of 1972, government assistance had been granted, in one
form or another, to 870 firms that had created 18,000 jobs, net, and
promised 12,000 more (about half of which, on the basis of experience,
would be ultimately provided). Of the new jobs, 70 percent were in the
aid area.

By 1970, when the subsidy program had been in effect for only five
years, a significant shift in regional employment trends was registered,
as shown in Figure 6-2. Between 1965 and 1970, the proportion of Sweden's total industrial (that is, manufacturing and mining) employment
located in the three major metropolitan areas, which had been stable for
the preceding five years, fell from 32.0 percent to 30.5 percent. Most
of the loss was in Stockholm. At the same time, the proportion in the
northern assisted counties, which had been declining, showed a slight

upturn. Government statisticians believe that this trend has continued in the years since 1970.

The expenditures, by European standards, have not been great. Since the beginning of the subsidy program, building grants have averaged between $10 million and $15 million a year, loans about $50 million. Including the $25 million spent during the 1963–65 period, total expenditures during the first decade of active location policy have been a little less than $500 million. The grants and loans have covered slightly over half of the nearly $1 billion in total investment that has been aided, which amounted to 6 percent of the country's aggregate investment in manufacturing during the period. For the 1973–78 period the figures will be higher—a proposed $22.5 million a year for grants, $77.5 million for loans, and $7.5 million for employment grants.

Success and Its Dilemmas

The reaction in Stockholm to the abrupt turnaround in the city's fortunes was such that government officials may have been inclined to claim less credit for their policies than they deserved. During the 1960s, Stockholm city and county officials had not actively resisted the decision of the central government to restrain the city's growth. They were making plans then to serve a population of perhaps 2.5 million by the year 2000—almost double the number in the capital area at that time— and, given a steady lowering of density, that meant an urban agglomeration spread over six times the area that Stockholm had occupied in 1950. That appeared to be quite enough for the city to attempt to handle, and a lessening of population pressure was welcome.

But a slowing of growth is one thing, and an absolute decline in population quite another. As the city suddenly realized that its historic surplus of in-migration had given way to out-migration, it raised an echo of the cry of Norrland a decade earlier. Unemployment was up. If the unemployment rate in Stockholm was still less than the national average and had risen only as part of a national cyclical increase, the fact remained that the capital had not had full employment since 1968. Stockholm was becoming a city of pensioners, it was argued, as its productive population left. Why should people be forced to move against their will from Stockholm—any more than from the North? If an economy balanced between blue-collar and white-collar occupations was good for the rest of the country, and that called for decentralization of government offices, then it was good for Stockholm, too—and that called for an increase in manufacturing.

The Stockholm labor unions, backed by the Social Democratic party of Stockholm county, demanded an end to government support for moving industrial enterprises out of Stockholm. The Social Democrats and public employee organizations also opposed plans for removal of government agencies from the capital. Early in 1973 the city organized a corporation with the task of encouraging the growth of enterprise, including manufacturing, in the capital. Like any long-time depressed area in any of a score of countries, the city began the production of brochures extolling its merits as a production and distribution center while its planners devoted themselves to the preparation of suitable industrial sites. The corporation was to give first attention to assisting established industries to grow, but beyond that lay the prospect of worldwide solicitation. "While the government is trying to get industries to go to Norrland," observed a central government official, "the city of Stockholm is not above sending information to industries in Norrland to try to induce them to come south." Officials of the Stockholm corporation insisted, however, that it was not created to pirate industry from other parts of Sweden, and had no intention of doing so.

All this was bound to have its effect on government policy. The objective of that policy had never been to stop entirely the growth of Stockholm and the other metropolitan areas, but only to slow it, in the interest of a "balanced" growth among the various regions. But now the growth of Stockholm had indeed been stopped, and balance, as measured by interregional migration to and from the capital, had been attained. To what extent, under these circumstances, should the policies of restraint be pursued? Would their continuance—the execution of the planned dispersal of government agencies, for example—create an imbalance in the other direction? Sweden's rate of population increase had fallen so low—a natural increase of 0.4 percent, or barely 30,000 a year—that any absolute gain in employment and population in one area could be achieved only at the expense of some other area's decline. If the pleas of Stockholm for a softening of policy were heeded, then, the prospect would appear to be a further depopulation of the North, and advocates of the northern cause were not persuaded that the capital had yet suffered enough injury to warrant a change in the policy that had been emphatically reaffirmed as late as 1969. But Stockholm's political leadership made clear that it would no longer quietly acquiesce in the continued shift of employment and population to the hinterland. The natural impulse of any national government is to respond to the legitimate demands of all of its regions. The dilemma in Sweden is how to respond when those legitimate demands have become mutually contradictory.

In presenting its program to the legislature in October 1972, the Social Democratic government tried directly and explicitly to satisfy both sides.[15] A major restatement of regional development policy recognized Stockholm's fears and sought to allay them while at the same time reiterating a determination to help the assisted regions. The 1969 decision to restrain the growth of the major metropolitan areas still stands, declared the government. But they should not be restrained to the point where they would cease to offer a sufficiently differentiated labor market. Nor was it desirable that manufacturing employment in the metropolises should continue to decline at a rate like that of, for example, Stockholm in recent years. The interests of the major areas and the rest of the country should not be thought of as being in conflict. Regional policy must concern itself with the welfare of all citizens, no matter where they might live. So while it was obviously a main task of regional policy to assist those areas suffering from employment problems, this should not be done in such a way as to create difficulties for the people who live and work in the big cities. To shrink public investment there or reduce housing construction was neither a possible nor an acceptable means to the end of reversing the population flow and strengthening the economic life of the rest of the country. Nor could the problems of the unemployed in the depressed areas be solved by denying them the opportunity to migrate when job and livelihood were not offered in their home regions.

This restatement of policy was not accompanied by any proposals to reduce the assistance being offered for relocation of industry in the North, or any reversal of the decision to decentralize government employment. But there was one area that offered some flexibility, and that was the consultative procedure that had been adopted to try to persuade manufacturers to relocate out of the metropolitan areas to other parts of

15. "Regional utveckling och hushallning med mark och vatten," Kungl. Maj: ts proposition 1972: 111, especially pp. 11–12.

Sweden. In 1972 that requirement was reduced to nothing more than a "nuisance," according to a Stockholm official who opposed the policy. It was considered so innocuous that the city was not even trying to get it eliminated.

The fact is, of course, that the consultative scheme had never amounted to much. After two years of operation, officials who administer the program could claim by 1973 only nine successes among four hundred applications processed. Eight firms planning expansions in Stockholm and one in Malmö had been induced to locate elsewhere. Of these, only two had gone to the aid area. Only fifty of the four hundred plants, it was explained, could be considered truly mobile. Sometimes, companies had simply gone too far with their plans, by the time they applied, to permit reversal. But the program in any case was voluntary. Even if the government had wanted to do so, it had no means by which to force the other forty-one mobile plants outside the metropolitan areas against the will of the companies concerned.

Fine Tuning of Population Distribution Policy?

The proposal to give the government direct power to control the location of private investment, which had been defeated in the parliament in 1969 and 1970, was revived in 1974 in a path-breaking report. A Swedish royal commission set up at the insistence of the Center party and the national labor federation recommended a system of licenses to govern the location of major new mobile enterprises of all kinds. The licensing procedure would be much the same as those in effect in Britain, France, and Italy, but its application would be nationwide rather than limited to congested areas, and its motivation and its objectives would be different. Alluding to the reversal in migration trends since 1969 and the consequent modification of governmental policy, the commission defined a more sophisticated objective for the proposed controls than one merely of restraining the growth of Sweden's major cities:

Connections in regional economic development appear more complicated and objectives in regional policy more diversified than previously. The emphasis in regional policy is in the process of being shifted from the 1960s' focus on the quantitative problems to a discussion on the qualitative dimensions of regional economic development. The motives for a general reduction of development in certain regions are not now as apparent as the need for a structural adaptation geared to an improvement of the balance between branches of the economy and occupations. The need for balance in the regional structure and in the structure and development of the individual regions is maturing into the primary target.[16]

Illustrating its concept, the commission pointed out that "there may be a need to prevent moves which involve the closing down of a production unit in one region and the establishment of an equivalent unit in another region, if this creates local employment problems" but does not give the company or the economy any considerable compensating gain in productivity. Similarly, the exact location of a manufacturing plant within a region should be subject to control to assure the best use of infrastructure and other community resources and of the available labor supply. The consultative system, the commission contended, had proved unsatisfactory because communication between the government and the investors was not established early enough to permit the introduction of planning considerations into the locational decision. That would be the defect, too, of the alternative method of control through a penalty tax (like that authorized in the Netherlands). A tax would not require consultation at all, the commission reasoned; moreover, the permit system had the advantage of imposing no "economic burden" on the company.

The licenses, as proposed by the commission, would be required for office and administrative buildings as well as factories, and not only for new construction but for acquisition or rental of existing facilities or even for a change in the utilization of premises in the absence of a change in ownership. Nonmobile establishments such as stores, hotels, restaurants, and local public buildings would be exempt. So would factories under 11,000, or office buildings under 5,500, square feet. The commission estimated that 700 to 800 applications a year would have to be acted on, somewhat fewer than half in the major urban regions.[17]

Whether the imposition of controls would be actively considered in the absence of an overriding motive for restraining the growth of Stockholm and the other major metropolitan centers remained to be seen. "The advocates of controls lost a part of their audience" when Stock-

---

16. Commission on Regional Political Control Measures, "Proposal for Regional Political Influence (Summary)" (1974; processed), p. 15.

17. Ibid., pp. 5–14.

holm's population went into decline, a former city official remarked in 1973. Whether that trend was an aberration or an indicator that novel and basic influences were at work remained the critical question. No one could be sure how much of Stockholm's population decline was due to the temporary factor of the economic slump and how much was due to structural change, including the changes induced by governmental policy. The country would have to wait for a period of boom to find the answer. If, at that time, the rapid growth of the capital and the other major metropolitan centers were resumed, it could be assumed that the advocates of direct controls would get back their audience, and the set of recommendations of the royal commission would be among those seriously considered. But if, in good times, the metropolitan centers continued their relative decline, what then? The royal commission anticipated that possibility and recommended the introduction of controls in either case.

The experience of Sweden, as well as that of the Netherlands, suggests that a democratic country's population distribution policy goes through two stages of development. In the first stage, the object is a relatively simple one—to curb the flow of people from rural areas and small cities to the major metropolitan areas. That goal has something approaching universality of political support, for it appears to be in the clear interest of both the depleted areas of population loss and the congested areas that have been gaining at an excessive pace. Relatively crude measures can be employed to reduce the migration flow, and they can be simply administered: incentives to encourage growth at the sending end of the migration stream, and controls (and other measures such as government decentralization) at the receiving end. There is no theoretical limit to the effectiveness of these measures: the incentives can be liberalized, and the controls tightened, until the forces making for centralization are fully neutralized. Sweden may be the first country to have reached that point, but several others are surely approaching it.

When the point of neutralization is reached, a country's population distribution policy enters its second stage. New policy questions have to be confronted: Should measures initially intended only to curb the growth of the major metropolitan areas continue to be pressed, and strengthened, after they have succeeded in achieving their initial purpose? In other words, should the object of policy be to reduce the rate of metropolitan growth all the way to zero and even below zero? When these questions are asked, the political context changes dramatically: the universality of support is gone; the metropolitan areas shift from support of the dispersal policies, or indifference, to outright and often vociferous opposition. Great metropolitan centers turn out to be no less sensitive to the consequences of population decline than are depressed rural areas, and the big cities are even better organized to protest their plight.

The indications from Sweden, expressed so strikingly in the government's policy statement of 1972, are that a government confronted by such opposing pressures will attempt to find a position that will satisfy both sides—while perhaps blandly asserting, as did the Swedish statement, that no true conflict exists. In other words, the new objective becomes one of stabilizing population flow so that no region loses—so that each region, metropolitan and rural alike, is able to retain its natural increase.

But for this purpose the old crude measures of regional policy are far from adequate. The new objective calls for a "fine tuning" of population distribution policy such as no country has yet achieved—or even attempted. In a nation such as Sweden, with close to a zero rate of population growth, to distribute the tiny natural increase in such a way that no region loses would be fine tuning indeed. It would require the tightest kind of governmental controls, administered with the utmost precision. This the Swedish royal commission understood clearly and faced squarely, and its proposal for the tightest system of location controls in the free world is the consequence.

There is an alternative course available to Sweden—and the countries in the same position—that would permit both the metropolitan areas and the hinterland counties to enjoy the economic growth they seek without the necessity for doing so at one another's expense. That is to expand the total population at a faster pace than the present low rate of natural increase through the importation of foreign workers. Such a course would not horrify the Stockholm expansionists who are promoting their city's industrial growth: "We had foreign labor in the 60s, and it worked fine," said one. But others in Sweden are loath either to follow the example of Germany and Switzerland in admitting large numbers of temporary "guest workers" or to open the country to free immigration and change the character of what has been a highly homogeneous society.[18] Better to "take the work to the workers" on a European scale, is the prevailing view; Sweden can avoid a host of social problems by simply exporting capital, managers, and technicians to employ the workers where they live. Since 1972, Sweden has been officially discouraging immigration by requiring employers to finance two hundred hours of Swedish language training for any workers they import. Unions must also agree to the importation. Consequently, immigration except from the other Nordic countries has virtually ceased.

For Swedish policy to respond fully to the concerns of Stockholm and to move from the stage of simple and crude dispersal measures to that of fine tuning would require wrenching political adjustments. All of the national parties have been fully committed to the existing policy of decentralization. The Center party, which made the most spectacular showing in the 1974 general election and would play the leading role in any alternative coalition to the Social Democrats, is perhaps the most committed of all. Its 1974 campaign was built around a call for "decentralization in every aspect" of national life. Yet these commitments were made before the long-time centralizing trend had been reversed and the consequences of actual decentralization had begun to be felt. The combined influence of all the primary centers and rural counties would still presumably be enough to outweigh that of the three metropolitan areas, if the former were united and the issue were settled by confrontation rather than by compromise. But the Swedish political tradition has been one of compromise, and the metropolitan areas are not likely to be ruthlessly ridden over in the future any more than they were in the Social Democrats' policy statement of 1972.

The question facing Sweden is whether a country that has made perhaps a more thorough commitment to population distribution planning than any other democratic nation in the world should maintain its commitment if its fulfillment would require an intricate, and unprecedented, system of controls over locational decisions. Sweden would become the

18. Immigrants represent about 8 percent of the Swedish population, which is a higher proportion than in Germany. They amount to 650,000, of whom 250,000 have become Swedish citizens. But one-third of the immigrants are Finnish, and others are from Norway and Denmark. The four Nordic countries allow free movement of people across their common boundaries. Nordics are considered "assimilable" in Sweden, in contrast to the southern Europeans who were admitted in the 1960s. All of the immigrant workers receive the same wages and benefits as native workers. *Economist* (London), April 13, 1974, pp. 34 and 39–40.

first country, if it follows its royal commission's advice, to carry its population distribution policy openly and boldly into the second stage, accepting all the administrative and political difficulties that decision would entail. But it is not alone among European countries in approaching, or having reached, the end of the initial stage. Sweden's dilemma—whether to undertake the fine tuning and tight controls that are necessary to allocate people among communities when people become a scarce resource—foreshadows the problem of all the advanced nations that are committed to population distribution planning as they join in approaching a zero rate of population growth.

CHAPTER SEVEN

Lessons for the United States

The objective of encouraging a more even population distribution is not considered to be a valid objective for a Federal program at this time.—Secretary of Commerce Frederick B. Dent and Director of the Office of Management and Budget Roy L. Ash, 1974[1]

AFTER 1970 AND 1971, the ringing declarations of those years on behalf of a national growth policy dropped out of the presidential rhetoric. The transition was marked in President Nixon's 1972 report on national growth, which reiterated the need for such a policy but made no proposals as to what the policy should be and put its emphasis, instead, on the difficulties that stood in the way of formulating one. By 1974 the administration had completed its reversal. Reporting to the Congress on behalf of the President, Secretary Dent and Director Ash took the position that growth policy was no longer a "valid objective for a Federal program," but was instead a matter for each of the fifty states: "If States desired more even population distribution, the States themselves could decide on policies and incentives for redistribution within the States."[2] Earlier, the President had recommended that the Economic Development Administration (EDA)—the agency created on the recommendation of his predecessor, Democratic President Lyndon B. Johnson, to administer programs of economic development in depressed areas throughout the country—be abolished and federal funds for area development be distributed among the states on a formula basis to be expended in accordance with federally approved state plans.

The Congress has not acquiesced in the dissolution of the EDA, and the laws calling for the establishment of a national growth policy are still on the statute books. Yet the Congress has shown no capacity

1. "Report to the Congress on the Proposal for an Economic Adjustment Program" (Feb. 1, 1974; processed), p. 19.
2. Ibid., p. 18.

or will to itself produce the policy that the administration, in spite of the clear language of the statutes, has declined to offer.[3] Responsibility for legislation relating to growth policy is still divided among several committees in each house, and the Congress has no mechanism for developing common objectives or a general strategy to guide the work of each. Two Democratic senators, Hubert H. Humphrey of Minnesota and Vance Hartke of Indiana, have introduced measures to create a joint committee of both houses to formulate a growth policy, and Representative Thomas L. Ashley, Ohio Democrat, has advanced a similar proposal in the House. But to establish such a body would require the active backing of the congressional leadership, and there was no sign in 1974 that such support would be forthcoming. So American policy is in suspension, as the Congress finds itself capable only of inviting the administration to take the initiative in defining a national growth policy while the administration denies that such a policy is even needed.

Yet while the Nixon administration withdrew from the political consensus that had formed in support of a policy of population dispersal in the United States, the other elements of the coalition of the early 1970s have shown no weakening of their commitment. The congressional backing remains bipartisan, and the Democratic party at its 1972 convention reiterated its demand for "a national urban growth policy to promote a balance of population among cities, suburbs, small towns and rural areas . . . a logical urban growth policy, instead of today's inadvertent, chaotic and haphazard one that doesn't work." (The Republican party, reflecting the administration's change of heart, did not repeat in its platform its 1968 declaration.) The National Governors' Conference continues its support. So it can be assumed that at some point, in the normal alternation of political control in the United States—or even in the absence of a change of party control, given the strong advocacy of a na-

---

3. The 1974 presidential report on national growth, required by statute to be submitted in February, made its appearance on December 16. It posed a series of questions but recommended no new national measures to influence population distribution. "There appears to be no great demand for massive programs to relocate businesses or induce large population shifts," the report said. "Most of the time, a competitive, private-decision economy that effectively utilizes its capacity to produce will provide a geographic and functional distribution of people, activities and resources that is more efficient and more desirable than alternative methods." The Domestic Council, Committee on Community Development, *Report on National Growth and Development 1974*, forwarded to the Congress by President Ford, pp. 19 and 3.

tional growth policy by many Republicans in the Congress and elsewhere outside the administration—the United States will again turn seriously to the question of whether it should adopt policies and programs for population dispersal and, if so, what they should be. In short, this country will decide whether to resume its course down the road the European states have traveled.

Britain, France, Italy, the Netherlands, and Sweden have all progressed in the same direction, though some moved sooner and some faster than others. All moved gradually from an initial narrow objective of relieving localized unemployment toward a broader goal of reducing interregional population flows and even, in some cases, toward planning the geographical distribution of jobs and population. Simultaneously, the program measures to achieve the ends grew and broadened. On the foundation of their initial cautious steps to provide local industrial parks and limited aid to investors through loans and tax concessions, these European countries have erected complex structures of mutually reinforcing measures, including comprehensive regional development planning, generous cash grants to investors, disincentives to the growth of major cities, and decentralization of government agencies, universities, and state-controlled industries.

The range of experience in the advanced industrial democracies extends, of course, beyond these five European countries. Among others offering incentives in the form of grants to industries agreeing to locate in development areas are West Germany, Ireland, Denmark, Norway, and Canada. Some of these countries, and Belgium, Finland, and Japan as well, offer subsidies in the form of tax concessions or low-interest credit. Japan has imposed controls on industrial development in the Tokyo and Osaka areas comparable to those in force in the London and Paris regions. Indeed, in treating the geographical distribution of economic activity and population as a matter for market forces, rather than national planning and national action, to determine, the United States stands alone among the advanced democratic countries of the world.

Imbalances in U.S. Population Growth and Distribution

That the United States has experienced the same kind of geographic imbalances that stirred the European nations to act is plain enough. Economic growth has been unevenly distributed in the United States too. Whole regions, such as Appalachia, have suffered resource depletion, and throughout rural America the manpower requirements of agriculture have steadily diminished. On both sides of the Atlantic, old cities based on declining industries have suffered localized depression. Workers seeking opportunity, particularly the young, have streamed into the cities, and the consequences have been the same as those in Europe—congestion in the metropolitan centers that received the migrants, and economic decline, community decay, and social malaise in the areas from which they came. Depressed areas in the United States, as in Western Europe, have high rates of unemployment and underemployment, low labor force participation rates, and hence low per capita output and low income, which can be raised only to the extent that capital moves into the areas of labor surplus or people move out. The consequences of geographical imbalance in economic opportunity are not essentially different on the two sides of the Atlantic. What is different is that, on the European side, governments have made the conscious choice to "take the work to the workers" as the preferred way to right the balance and have taken measures on the scale required to make that choice effective, while the United States government has not.

The slower response of America's political institutions may be attributable in part to the more complex patterns of urbanization and migration that have developed in the United States. In most of the European countries, and especially in France and Britain, a single metropolitan center has been the dominant magnet of attraction, and in each of the five countries included in this study the migration flow has been heavily in a single direction, whether north-south as in Britain and Sweden, east-west as in the Netherlands, or south-north as in Italy. In contrast, the migrant flow in the United States has been in many directions, to many centers. There has been no problem of building *métropoles d'équilibre*, as in France, for great regional capitals have long been flourishing to counter the magnets of New York and the eastern seaboard. Indeed, the liveliest metropolitan growth in recent decades has been experienced, for the most part, by centers farthest removed from the northeastern areas where major population concentrations first formed. In the 1960s, among the twenty-five largest metropolitan areas, seven of the eight with growth rates above 25 percent were in the South and West—Orange County (California), Houston, Dallas, Atlanta, Miami, San Diego, and Seattle (the eighth was Washington, D.C.). Meanwhile, the old great centers of the Northeast, from Boston through New York City and Philadelphia to Cleveland, Detroit, and Chicago, grew at rates well below the national average and one—Pittsburgh—suffered an absolute population decline. Similarly, among smaller metropolitan areas, every one that gained more than 50 percent in population in the decade was in the West or South, while the Northeast had more than its share of losers.[4]

The result, then, has been a net migration flow away from the old areas of population concentration to the more sparsely settled regions of the country. Pennsylvania lost 378,000 people in the 1960s through net migration, New York 101,000, Ohio 126,000, Illinois 43,000.[5] The twenty-one states comprising the Census Bureau's Northeast and North Central regions experienced a net loss of 428,000 persons through out-migration, while the South gained 593,000 and the West 2,855,000 (the excess of gains over losses is explained by net immigration of 3.0 million from outside the fifty states).

Thus, in its larger dimensions, the migration picture in the United States appears to be the opposite of that in Europe. There in every country the strongest and most densely settled regions—the Londons, Parises, Milans, and Randstads—were still gaining relatively at the time that regional policies were introduced. The already weak regions—the Scotlands, Brittanys, Mezzogiornos, and Norrlands—were losing further ground. In those circumstances the arguments for governmental intervention to right the balance seemed to policymakers to be irrefutable. But in the United States the interregional imbalance appears, since 1960, to have begun to right itself without any broad intervention by the national government for that explicit purpose. So the arguments for action have been less compelling. If in recent years New York City, or even the eastern seaboard megalopolis as a whole, had been gaining in national

4. The comparisons are for standard metropolitan statistical areas. Boundaries, and hence growth rates, differ for "daily urban systems" or "economic areas" (Orange County is part of the Los Angeles area, for instance) but the same pattern appears. Except for Washington, D.C., all of the twenty-four fastest-growing (rates above 21 percent) daily urban systems in the 1960s were in the South and West. Brian J. L. Berry, "Population Growth in the Daily Urban Systems of the United States, 1980–2000," in Sara Mills Mazie, ed., *Population Distribution and Policy*, vol. 5 of research reports prepared for the U.S. Commission on Population Growth and the American Future (1972), pp. 248–49.

5. Migration figures in this section are from U.S. Department of Commerce news release CB71-34, March 3, 1971.

economic dominance, as London and Paris had been, the U.S. response to the population concentration problem might have more nearly approached in strength and timing the British and the French responses.

Yet subcurrents within the larger migration trends in the United States have corresponded to the flow from weaker to stronger areas that precipitated the concern and action in the European countries. One important subcurrent has been the outflow of blacks from the South—scarcely diminished in the 1960s—that was concealed, in the total figures, by a reverse migration of whites. The decade saw a net out-migration from the region (excluding Maryland, the District of Columbia, and Delaware, which showed a net gain) of 1.5 million blacks, equivalent to about one-eighth of the 1960 population and only 62,000 fewer than in the previous decade. Six contiguous "black belt" states running from North Carolina to Louisiana lost more than 150,000 Negroes each during the decade, with a high of 279,000 net out-migrants—equal to 30 percent of its 1960 black population—from Mississippi. The outflow from these six states exceeded the natural increase, for an absolute decline of 72,000, or 1.2 percent, in the number of Negro inhabitants.

Besides the black communities of the South, there were in the 1960s large rural regions of predominantly white settlement where the out-migration flow was large enough to exceed the natural increase of population in the 1960s. Of the 173 economic areas into which the Department of Commerce divides the country, 33 experienced a population decline during the decade. Of these, two-thirds comprise a Great Plains belt from 200 to nearly 1,000 miles wide, stretching all the way from the Canadian to the Mexican border, with an extension eastward through the corn belt across most of Iowa and into adjacent counties of Illinois and northeastern Missouri (see Figure 7-1). Two states lying wholly within that belt, North and South Dakota, lost 94,000 and 92,000 people, respectively, through net migration in the decade, or the equivalent of about one-seventh of their 1960 populations. Iowa lost 183,000, Kansas 130,000, Nebraska 73,000, and Montana 58,000. Another region of population decline covered most of Appalachia, embracing almost all of West Virginia and extending from Pennsylvania to Tennessee. West Virginia's net out-migration during the decade was 265,000, the equivalent of one of every seven of its 1960 inhabitants; like the Dakotas, it experienced a decline in total population during the decade. Other declining areas were in the southern region of heavy black out-migration, the lower Rio

Figure 7-1. *Areas of Heavy Out-migration in the United States, 1960–70*[a]

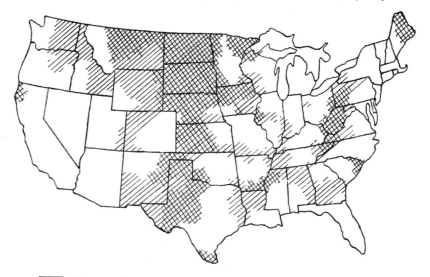

▨▨▨ *Net out-migration exceeded natural population increase*

▨▨▨ *Out-migration reduced the rate of population growth to less than half the national average*

Sources: Brian J. L. Berry, "Population Growth in the Daily Urban Systems of the United States, 1980–2000," in Sara Mills Mazie, ed., *Population Distribution and Policy*, vol. 5 of research reports prepared for the U.S. Commission on Population Growth and the American Future (1972), pp. 247–49; and letter to the author from Calvin L. Beale, August 1974. Based on economic areas as defined by the Office of Business Economics, Department of Commerce.

a. Alaska and Hawaii, which are not shown on the map, were not areas of heavy out-migration.

Grande valley of Texas, northern Maine, the mining and forest counties of northern Minnesota and Wisconsin, and northern California.

By the same token, if the Northeast as a whole was declining relatively, the seaboard megalopolis was still a powerful attraction. Its perimeters were a zone of heavy net in-migration. New Jersey had a net influx of 488,000 migrants in the decade, Connecticut had 214,000, the rest of New England 102,000, and Maryland 385,000. The Washington metropolitan area, southern anchor of the megalopolis, was the second fastest growing of the country's largest metropolitan areas.[6] Within the West

6. It was the fastest growing of the ten largest daily urban systems (since Orange County, which ranked first among metropolitan areas, is included in the Los Angeles daily urban system) and sixth among all of the 173 such systems shown in Figure 7-1.

and South, population was concentrating in a relatively few great urban complexes, notably in California, Florida, and Texas, states that together accounted for nearly one-third of the country's total population growth.

Thus, while the United States has not experienced the clear unidirectional flow that has made the conception of regional policy relatively simple in some European countries, it has nevertheless experienced movement on a comparable scale, set in motion by the same kinds of economic change. If the United States is likened not to a single European country but to the European Community as a whole, the similarities become more readily apparent. Western Europe has many growing centers and many areas of relative decline and heavy out-migration, which form a patchwork on the map (Figure 7-2). These form the basis for individual country policies, and in 1973 they also became the basis for a multinational policy when the nine-country European Community announced its intent to establish a fund for regional development that will supplement the resources of the individual members. As late as the 1960s, then, the United States had the same reason for regional policy as the European countries had: people had to migrate in large numbers from poorer and more rural regions to richer and more urbanized areas in order to find economic opportunity—by European logic, a movement that on any massive scale imposes excessive hardship on the migrants themselves, affects adversely the communities from which they come and those to which they go, and hence should be checked and reversed by national policy.

The Slackening of Population Pressures

As the 1960s ended, however, two momentous demographic shifts took place in the United States. First, early in 1971 the birth rate turned abruptly downward, and it has continued precipitately downward since. The number of births, which had averaged 3.9 million a year in the 1960s, fell to 3.1 million by 1973—the lowest number since 1945. The natural increase, which had averaged 2.1 million a year in the previous decade, dropped below 1.2 million in 1973. For the first time in history, the birth rate fell below the level necessary for a new generation to replace its parents. If this shift proved permanent, it would portend—as the popula-

Figure 7-2. *Principal Assisted Areas in the Countries of the European Community, 1972*

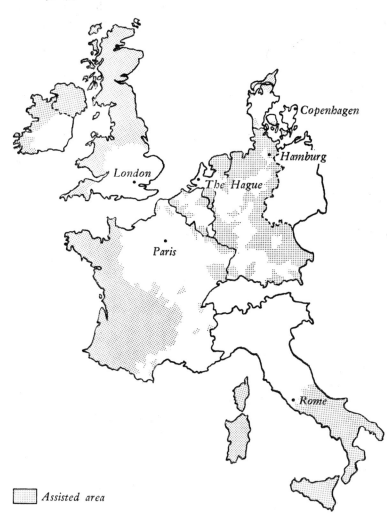

□ *Assisted area*

Source: Philippe de Castelbajac, *Les Aides à l'Expansion Industrielle Régionale dans Les Pays du Marché Commun*, Notes et Études Documentaires 3917 (Paris: La documentation française, Sept. 11, 1972), p. 17.

tion aged and the death rate consequently rose—a decreasing aggregate
population within fifty years or so.

Demographic experts warned that a trend that had turned suddenly
downward could just as suddenly turn up again. But, from every sign,
it was continuing in 1974, and some at least of what appeared to be the
causative factors—improved contraceptive technology, heightened concern for the pressure of population on environment, the rise in living
standards, urbanization, and the changing role and aspirations of women
—bid fair, in most cases, to remain. The European countries, where the
birth rate took its sharp drop several years earlier than in the United
States, have found the decline lasting, and the rates of natural increase
in some countries have remained steady at 0.2–0.3 percent a year, or even
lower, well below the United States 1973 rate of 0.6 percent. Indeed,
West Germany in 1972 experienced a natural decrease—an excess of
deaths over births.[7] So Americans who as late as 1970 had worried about
how an additional 100 million people could—or should—be distributed
within the United States by the year 2000 could now draw comfort
from the probability that the total increase might be barely half that
number, or even less, by the time the total population leveled off.

Second, the dispersal of population that the European countries had
been seeking to bring about through deliberate policy appeared to be
beginning to occur spontaneously in the United States. In the early 1970s
the movement of people away from the older population centers of the
country accelerated. The two census regions embracing the Northeast
and the North Central states experienced a net out-migration of 448,000
in the three-year period between 1970 and 1973, according to the Census
Bureau's provisional estimates[8]—an outflow greater than that of the
entire decade of the 1960s. The nation's heaviest population losers were
no longer the more rural states of the Great Plains, Appalachia, and the
South but the states at the opposite end of the density scale—those of
the northeastern megalopolis itself. New York's population was almost
stationary during the three-year period, its net out-migration of 1.5
percent offsetting all but 24,000 of its natural increase. Ohio, Illinois, and
Michigan each also lost through net out-migration 1 percent or more of

7. *Times* (London), Sept. 8, 1973.
8. Contained in U.S. Bureau of the Census, "Estimates of the Population of the
United States with Components of Change, 1970 to 1973," *Current Population Reports*, series P-25, no. 520 (July 1974), table 1, p. 19; the figures cover migration
from April 1, 1970 to July 1, 1973.

their 1970 population. Altogether, nearly 700,000 more persons left those four states than entered them in just three years. The St. Louis and Cleveland metropolitan areas joined Pittsburgh as large concentrations with an absolute population decline.[9] Almost all of the states of the South and West were net recipients of population, including some that lost heavily through out-migration in the 1960s, among them North Dakota, South Dakota, Iowa, Nebraska, Montana, and West Virginia. While the migration figures for 1970–73 were not broken down by race, Census Bureau officials and other demographers believe that a reverse North-South movement of blacks—made possible by improvements in economic opportunity for Negroes as the result of the advances in civil rights—seemed even to have brought the net interregional flow of blacks into balance in the early 1970s after the decades of mass migration northward.[10]

The historic migration flow from rural and small town America to metropolitan areas in the country as a whole appeared also to have been reversed. During the 1970–72 period the country's nonmetropolitan areas (that is, rural areas and cities up to 50,000 that are not suburbs of larger cities) grew in population at a rate faster than the metropolitan areas—3.1 percent against 2.2 percent.[11] Some of the nonmetropolitan growth occurred in counties adjacent to metropolitan areas, but when those counties are removed from the calculation, the rest of nonmetropolitan America grew at a rate of 2.8 percent—still faster than the cities and their suburbs. The rural regions of most spectacular turnaround from decline to growth in the 1960s and early 1970s have been the southern uplands—predominantly white counties of the Ozark and Ouachita mountains, the Cumberland plateau, and the southern Appalachians—relatively removed from metropolitan influence.

A major factor in the reversal of the ancient rural-metropolitan population flow has been the virtual cessation, finally, of the release of workers out of agriculture. Since 1940 the nation's farm population has fallen from more than 30 million to barely 9 million, and obviously it cannot

---

9. So did the officially defined New York City metropolitan area; however, that excludes Nassau and Suffolk counties in New York and includes no territory in Connecticut and only one county in New Jersey.

10. See B. Drummond Ayres, *New York Times*, June 18, 1974; and Peter Milius, *Washington Post*, July 24, 1974.

11. Calvin L. Beale, "Rural development: population and settlement prospects," *Journal of Soil and Water Conservation*, vol. 29 (1974), pp. 26–27.

drop much further. But farm employment is still decreasing by 15,000 to 20,000 a year, and even if it were stabilized that would only enable the nonmetropolitan areas to hold their own. That they are now gaining population at a faster rate than are the metropolitan areas reflects the fact that nonfarm jobs are increasing more rapidly in small town America than in the larger centers.

The rural trend has been particularly pronounced in manufacturing. In the period 1970–73, the proportion of the nation's factory employment located in nonmetropolitan areas rose from 25 percent to 27 percent, as those areas gained 356,000 jobs while the metropolitan areas suffered a net decline of 673,000. But the nonmetropolitan areas grew faster than the larger urban complexes in almost every other category of nonfarm employment as well, including construction, trade, and such typically high-level tertiary activities as those in the finance-insurance-real estate and transportation-communications-utilities classifications. For nonfarm, nonmanufacturing employment as a whole, the annual rate of increase in the nonmetropolitan areas was 3.9 percent, compared to 2.5 percent in the metropolitan areas. The nonmetropolitan areas had in 1970 only 22 percent of total employment in this broad category but received 31 percent of the net increase in the next three years. While the trend of manufacturing employment favored the nonmetropolitan areas in the 1960s as well as the early 1970s, this was not true of the tertiary categories. There the shift in favor of the nonmetropolitan areas occurred at the end of the decade.[12]

The end of rural-metropolitan migration was foreshadowed in the 1960s, when the net flow from the nation's nonmetropolitan areas fell to 2.2 million from the 5.5 million of the previous decade. The 2.2 million accounted for only 11 percent of total metropolitan growth, even in that decade. Migration from rural America had already become a relatively minor cause of the problems of the "unlivable, ungovernable" cities. In the early 1970s it apparently ceased to be a factor altogether, except perhaps in a few cities still growing rapidly in the South and West.

A three-year trend is perhaps too short to support a conclusion that the forces that have made for urbanization and centralization throughout the entire history of the nation have been wholly neutralized. The eco-

12. Figures compiled by Claude C. Haren, U.S. Department of Agriculture, 1973; they cover wage and salary employment, excluding the self-employed and private household workers.

nomic slowdown at the beginning of the 1970s, with its resultant rising unemployment rates in the industrial centers, may have contributed a temporary impetus to the shift in the direction of migration. Nevertheless, the trend continued at about the same pace when the economy recovered in 1972 and 1973. Calvin L. Beale, the U.S. Department of Agriculture's authority on rural demography, is one who believes that the new tendencies of the 1970s—so radically different from those of the country's whole previous history—have come to stay:

Essentially every current trend in residential preferences, business location decisions, land use effects of affluence, closure of comparative differences in facilities and amenities of rural and urban areas, and the end of major adjustments in extractive industries supports rural and small city growth . . . it is essential for policy-makers and the public in general to realize that the curve of rural and nonmetro population trends has inflected. The factors that impelled outmigration in the midcentury years have lost most of their force. A new perspective is needed.[13]

Yet if most metropolitan areas are approaching stability of population, that does not resolve the issue of whether population dispersal policies should be adopted. It only alters the context in which the issue is considered. Several questions remain.

First, within a more stable growth pattern, there will still be metropolitan areas of very rapid growth and nonmetropolitan areas of stagnation and decline. Should policies of limited geographical scope be adopted to influence the growth of these areas? In the South, for instance, new employment opportunities are being concentrated in the major metropolitan areas and in nonmetropolitan counties that are predominantly white in composition; the rural counties of the black belt are being largely bypassed.[14] If the objective of dispersal policy is to assist lagging areas to hold their natural population increase—or, in this case, to attract a share of the reverse movement of blacks from northern cities—then a policy that can be flexibly adjusted to include or exclude areas as circumstances change is still in order.

Second, even though population growth may be finally approaching an end, an increase of perhaps 50 million nevertheless will be registered before the end is reached—an increment almost equal to the total population of Britain or France. Since most Americans now live in big metro-

13. "Rural development," p. 27.
14. Niles M. Hansen, *The Future of Nonmetropolitan America* (Lexington Books, 1973), p. 164.

politan areas—those of over a million—most babies will be born there,
too, and unless the current and novel out-migration stream from those
areas is substantially augmented, most of the future population growth
still will be in the big concentrations, as in the past. Even for those
metropolitan areas that have stopped growing absolutely—and by 1980,
60 to 80, or one-fourth or more of the total, may have stabilized[15]—
should dispersal policies be pushed in order to accomplish further decentralization of the national population? In other words, should the
country seek not only to prevent further concentration but to undo some
of the concentration that has occurred over past decades in the absence
of national policy to prevent it?

The European countries have given an affirmative answer to that
question. They have maintained the momentum of their dispersal policies—indeed, they have accelerated them—in the years since their major
cities began to approach stable population levels. The British government has deliberately reduced by several million persons the population
of the London conurbation, with the full assent, until recently, of the
government of London. French, Dutch, and Swedish policies have been
successful in achieving net out-migration from their congested centers—
and absolute declines in The Hague and Stockholm—and those policies
have been in general maintained or even strengthened after the outward
movements were apparent.

Yet in Europe when the object has become redistribution of population
from the major cities—instead of merely halting the influx to those cities
—the policies have had a far lower level of political acceptability. The
mayors and other spokesmen for the major cities, who supported national
deconcentration policies when they offered a welcome relief from too-
rapid urban growth, reversed their attitude when the population pressure
first eased and then altogether disappeared. A slower rate of growth was
one thing, an actual loss of growth was quite another. And so, beginning
at the point when national policies began to take sharp effect, the leaders
of The Hague, Stockholm, and even London were moved to vigorously
contest those policies.

While the European countries have so far upheld their policies in the
face of a rising clamor from the affected urban centers, they do so in a

15. William Alonso, "The System of Intermetropolitan Population Flows," in
Mazie, ed., *Population Distribution and Policy*, p. 328. Twenty-five declined between 1970 and 1972, compared to twenty in the decade of the 1960s.

political setting more favorable than would exist, in the same circumstances, in the United States. The question in Europe is one of continuing to apply principles of dispersal that were well settled in a time of population pressure; in the United States the question would be the initial adoption of the principles at a time when pressures have been relaxed. European parliaments are made up of disciplined parties whose members reflect a national point of view established by the party as a whole; the U.S. Congress is made up of members whose loyalty is usually to territorial interests when those conflict with party policies—insofar as American parties even have policies—or the desires of the party leadership. Given the multiple points of veto in the American system of separated and divided powers and the extraordinary degree of consensus that is consequently necessary for major policy departures, it would be difficult even for a committed majority to impose population dispersal policies that would be vigorously opposed by a substantial bloc of territorial representatives from the major metropolitan regions of the country.

There is reason to predict, however, that the metropolitan bloc would not be a monolithic one. The Pearson-Ribicoff amendment of 1971[16] indicates the type of political bargain that can be struck: it represented a coalition of the zones of decline—the central cities and the rural areas—seeking to divert a share of industrial investment from the zone of expansion, the suburbs, and it passed the Senate by an overwhelming margin. Indeed, any future city-rural coalition against the suburbs would probably find considerable support from the suburbs themselves in those parts of the country where rapid growth has given rise to strong political movements aimed at slowing development.[17]

Nevertheless, on balance, the new context of population stability makes the need for policies of population dispersal less urgent and hence less likely—even though, intrinsically, they still may be desirable. Whereas in the past the interests of the major metropolitan areas and the rural areas in stemming excessive migration could be seen as coinciding, their interests when the question becomes one of creating a reverse migration flow will in all likelihood be seen as in some degree divergent.

16. See pp. 15–16, above.

17. Political antigrowth movements in Colorado, California, Florida, New York, and other states with fast-growing metropolitan complexes are reviewed in William K. Reilly, ed., *The Use of Land: A Citizens' Policy Guide to Urban Growth*, a Rockefeller Brothers Fund task force report (Crowell, 1973), especially chap. 1.

As in Sweden, people will become a scarce resource, and even the largest metropolitan areas can be expected to resist any suggestion that they give up all share in the nation's limited population growth, or become net contributors to other regions. Any realistic appraisal must recognize that that will reduce substantially, if not decisively, the possibility of enacting in the United States population distribution measures approaching in power and effectiveness the policies now being carried out in Europe.

Are State Growth Policies the Answer?

If growth policies are a good idea, can they simply be left to the states, as the Nixon administration proposed? The fifty states, the Dent-Ash report suggested, could decide on policies and incentives for redistribution of population within their boundaries. New York, California, and Illinois, as examples, could reduce pressures on their metropolitan centers by steering growth to areas of relatively sparse settlement within those states.[18]

That is true enough insofar as the problem is one only of intrastate imbalance. But when a major problem of interregional and interstate population imbalance exists (see Figure 7-1), that problem is by its nature quite beyond the competence of the states—even if they were suddenly to develop the will to act in new and unfamiliar fields. Where whole states are declining, or experiencing little growth—as in the 1960s, when eighteen relatively sparsely settled states lost by net out-migration a total of 2.3 million persons—redistribution within those states is a futile exercise. Only national action can channel a greater share of the national growth into the relatively underdeveloped states.

It may be countered that the declining states have the responsibility to provide the incentives that will attract industry and so check the population flow. Yet if these states were to begin to offer incentives at anywhere near the levels that are accepted throughout Europe as necessary for an effective population distribution policy—outright grants of 20 percent or so of the cost of new industrial projects—the burden on state treasuries would be not only heavy but glaringly inequitable. Moreover, the growing states might enter the competition as well, and their

18. "Report to the Congress," p. 18.

greater resources would enable them to be the automatic winners. Subsidy competition among the states would result in a haphazard, unplanned distribution of investment, which might or might not come close to any rational conception of the national interest. If there is a national interest, it seems hardly disputable, only the national government can define it. And unrestrained subsidy competition among the states is so potentially wasteful, even counterproductive, that it should not be encouraged—as in the Dent-Ash report—but positively discouraged.

The European experience seems particularly pertinent on this point. The difficulties and dangers of subsidy competition among national governments have led the European Community to impose limits on the types and amounts of investment incentives that can be offered by its member states. Initially applied only to the "central," or industrialized, areas of the individual countries, the regulations require that the subsidies be transparent rather than hidden (which forces a shift from tax concessions to direct grants) and limits them to 20 percent of the private investment. This initial limit was set high enough to obviate the need for immediate adjustments anywhere, but the rates are to be progressively lowered. Eventually, too, the aids offered in the "peripheral" areas of the member countries are to be limited also, in the interest of fair competition. The EC is also committed to equalizing the burden of regional programs among its members through the projected common fund that will be raised from the community as a whole but expended primarily in the regions of greatest need—those in Italy, Ireland, and the United Kingdom.

The object, as seen by the advocates of regional action not only in the EC headquarters but to a considerable extent in the individual countries as well, must be to get the concept of *l'aménagement du territoire* applied on a European scale. Incentives and disincentives would be designed to "take the work to the workers" across international boundaries. Then, instead of importing Italian workers to plants in Germany, and thereby visiting hardships on the workers and their families and creating social problems in both countries, Germany would export capital to the Mezzogiorno.[19] If it were in the interest of Europe as a whole that an American- or Japanese-owned electronics plant be located in Brittany

19. In November 1973, West Germany imposed a ban on the further importation of foreign workers, who at that time numbered 2.5 million, or 10 percent of the labor force.

instead of Rotterdam, then incentives and controls would be graded so as to take it there. "The problem if the individual countries act alone," observed an EC official, "is that while the Netherlands can divert the plant from Rotterdam easily enough, it is likely to wind up in Antwerp instead of Brittany."

The Dent-Ash position runs counter to the European experience, which teaches that for a growth policy to be fully successful its areal scale must correspond to the scale of economic integration. Measures to influence the location of investment need to be applied according to plans and objectives embracing the whole of the area over which capital is free to flow. Local initiatives based on local objectives can be encouraged, but within the bounds of a common scheme predicated on the common interest of all localities.

The "Freedom of Individual Choice" Argument

The Dent-Ash report sees "the potentially serious consequences of a national policy of population redistribution" as related to "freedom of individual choice." But freedom of individual choice, except for retired people and a few self-employed persons such as artists and novelists who can make a living in any location, is largely an illusion. In the aggregate the nation's 90 million workers must distribute themselves according to where the jobs are. And workers do not decide where jobs are located; employers do.

Employers sometimes, of course, elect to locate their investments where the potential employees already live and have indicated by their behavior that they wish to stay. The process is one of mutual adjustment; jobs move to workers as well as workers to jobs. The steady decentralization of northern industry to the South has been motivated in part by the availability of an ample southern labor supply. But whether or not an employer chooses to make labor supply a major factor in his locational decision, his is at all times the decision that is controlling. If he chooses to bring the work to the workers, his decision presumably coincides with their expressed free choice. But if he locates in an area of labor shortage or of balanced supply, he will produce a net requirement for in-migrant workers, and the distribution of the labor force will adjust to that requirement through migration, regardless of whether that accords with what would have been the free choice of the workers involved.

The limitations on freedom of choice for the individual are clear enough in the case of workers whose jobs disappear, and whose skills become obsolete, in an area of economic decline. The cotton or tobacco field hand displaced by machinery has no real choice to stay where he is, if he is to avoid poverty and welfare. Nor has the coal miner similarly displaced. But it is equally true, though less visible in individual cases, of small businessmen, professional persons, and their employees who live in communities whose economic base is shrinking, or expanding slower than the natural increase of population. The community simply cannot employ as many store clerks, bankers, ministers, lawyers, service station operators, and school teachers as might wish to live there, except at the cost of reduced productivity and income for everyone. Some must leave. If South Dakota can offer satisfactory jobs to only 15 percent of the graduates of its state university, but half the graduates would prefer to live there, then 35 percent is the number who must either go or accept a job that is less than what they trained for. Those who depart are self-chosen, to a degree—though employers may have the major part in those decisions, too—but in any case, that is the extent of what is described as "freedom"; enough of each generation is compelled to leave if the living standards of those who stay are to be maintained at tolerable levels. And the choice often must be to leave not just a community and a state but an entire region and a style of life.

This proposition works both ways, of course. If the country adopted a population distribution policy that called for more dispersal than the individuals who make up the population wanted, then people would be forced to leave big cities against their will. The maximum freedom of individual choice exists when the aggregate pattern of job distribution approaches as closely as possible the way in which people would distribute themselves if they were truly free. So the objective set by Dent and Ash would require a policy directly opposite to the laissez faire doctrine they espouse; it would demand determined intervention by government to distribute employment opportunities to accord with the desires of the population. To attempt "fine tuning" of such a distribution pattern to reflect popular preferences would impose perhaps an insuperable test on the competence of government at any time. But to move now in the general direction of the public preference, based on existing survey data revealing individual preferences—and better data that could be gathered with no great difficulty—is not beyond the range of possibility. Clearly, the trend of the last few decades toward concentration has run against rather than with the public preference.[20] The notion commonly expressed that Americans have "voted with their feet" in favor of the great cities is, on the basis of every available sampling, so much nonsense.

A government dedicated to the rational planning of population distribution would, of course, have to take into account other factors than individual preferences: the relative economic efficiency, public service costs, social costs and benefits, environmental costs, and so on, of various distribution patterns.[21] Nevertheless, if the pattern formed by the aggregate of individual preferences were not conclusively outweighed by the other entries in the balance sheet, the democratic ethic suggests that what the public wants should be determinative.

What is called "freedom of choice" is, in sum, freedom of employer choice or, more precisely, freedom of choice for that segment of the corporate world that operates mobile enterprises. The real question, then, is whether freedom of corporate choice should be automatically honored by government policy at the expense of freedom of individual choice where those conflict. The United States, alone among advanced industrial democracies, has made it a matter of practice—if not, since 1970, of declared principle—to uphold the freedom of corporate choice. The others have made the deliberate decision to try to influence corporation decisions to bring them more nearly into accord with the aggregate of individual choices, as expressed occasionally in public opinion surveys and continuously through political parties and representative assemblies.

The Macroeconomic Argument

Surprisingly little attention has been paid by U.S. policymakers to the macroeconomic arguments that in Europe have been for thirty years an important part of the rationale for strong regional policies. Those arguments were usually developed well after the programs they support had been adopted by political parties and by governments, but that does not affect their theoretical validity, which appears to be virtually undisputed among European economists.

The macroeconomic reasoning holds that at any time in any country,

20. See pp. 24–30, above.
21. See pp. 16–23, above.

unemployment is bound to be unevenly distributed geographically. If the range among regions in a country is from 5 percent to the "full employment" level of, say, 1 percent, with a weighted average of 3 percent, then the economy is operating at 2 points below capacity. If the government attempts to achieve the full employment level nationally through fiscal and monetary measures, without reducing the regional differentials, it will push the demand for workers in the more prosperous regions beyond that level—in other words, create conditions of "overfull employment" and labor shortage—with inflationary consequences. Moreover, the inflationary pressures on wage levels originating in the areas of most severe shortage will spread through national processes of collective bargaining to the whole country. The only way to approach full employment without generating inflation, therefore, is to narrow the differentials.

The differentials can be reduced either through the migration of workers from areas of high unemployment or through the movement of capital in the opposite direction. Eventually, if matters are left to the free market, the adjustment is presumably made, through a combination of both kinds of moves. But a serious time lag is involved before the differentials are removed, during which individual hardship and national economic loss are suffered (and during which other differentials may develop). It is in the government's interest, therefore, to try to expedite the adjustment. As between moving the workers and moving the capital investment, the latter is the more efficient way, in strictly economic terms. "Moving workers to the work generally means pumping additional effective demand into a region that has an excess of it already; moving jobs to workers generally means moving effective demand to regions where it is deficient."[22] Since moving the workers creates a demand for additional labor in the receiving area to house and serve them, it can even be self-defeating as a means of achieving balance between workers and jobs. The typical European country began its efforts to cope with unemployment differentials by subsidizing worker relocation, as the quickest and easiest solution to what was seen as a limited and temporary problem, but shifted its emphasis to incentives for capital investment—for social and political as well as economic reasons—as soon as it came to realize that the imbalances in the economic structure were fundamental and persistent.

22. A. J. Brown, *The Framework of Regional Economics in the United Kingdom* (Cambridge, England: Cambridge University Press, 1972), p. 24.

The chain of reasoning that made regional policy an indispensable element of full employment policy began to appear in official documents as early as the wartime years in Britain and shortly after the war in Italy and elsewhere. Its most influential expression in any country perhaps was in the 1963 report of Britain's National Economic Development Council, *Conditions Favourable to Faster Growth*. Nearly a third of the booklet was devoted to regional imbalance; no other subject received so much emphasis in this broad analysis of Britain's macroeconomy. Observing that excessive unemployment had usually been thought of as "a social problem," the council argued that it was an economic problem as well, because high rates of joblessness and low rates of labor force participation were measures of "considerable labour reserves," which if drawn into employment "would make a substantial contribution to national employment and national growth." To be specific, if the difference in unemployment rates at that time between the most prosperous and least prosperous regions of Britain could be cut in half, national employment would increase by 1.3 percent.[23] In the periodic national economic reviews prepared by government agencies in every European country— counterparts of the annual or semiannual economic reports of the President and of the Council of Economic Advisers in the United States—an analysis of geographical differentials almost always accompanies any discussion of unemployment, and governmental programs for economic growth and stabilization customarily include proposals for regional action as well as measures of nationwide applicability. In each country, regional statistics are well developed and conveniently compiled to provide the basis for regional policy consideration.

In the twenty-eight years that the Council of Economic Advisers has been preparing U.S. national economic reports, no comparable emphasis has been put on the link between regional and national economic policies. Since the first report in 1947, to be sure, the problem of localized "depressed areas" has occasionally been recognized. Whenever a legislative measure such as the Area Redevelopment Act or the Appalachian Regional Development Act was included in the presidential program, the economic report included a few sentences, or a few paragraphs, of advocacy. But those paragraphs have usually appeared in the section of the report devoted to miscellaneous and incidental measures, rather than as a

23. *Conditions Favourable to Faster Growth* (HMSO, 1963), pp. 14 and 16. See also p. 56, above.

part of the central macroeconomic theme. In no report have regional economic statistics been presented and analyzed. Indeed, the council members have considered regional policy to be of such scant relevance to the statutory goals of "maximum employment, production and purchasing power" that in those years when legislation has not been offered, the whole subject of regional economic differentials has commonly been omitted altogether. This is not because American regional economists have not advanced the same arguments as their European counterparts. It is simply that their thinking has failed to register any major and continuing impact on the circle of official economic policymakers.

There have been exceptions, of course. In 1950 the council observed that "there cannot be maximum employment and production throughout the Nation so long as some areas are relatively depressed,"[24] and President Truman's final economic report in January 1953, in a section headed "Full employment requires the maintenance of economic balance," noted the "need to work toward even better economic balance in and among the different geographic regions of the country."[25] But in the next two decades the subject of geographic balance, instead of being developed and emphasized as in Europe, was all but lost. The annual economic reports of 1962, 1963, 1966, 1967, 1970, 1972, 1973, and 1974 do not find that economic problems and policies have a geographic aspect worth even a word of mention. And only twice have the reports discussed population distribution explicitly as a public policy problem—in 1968, when the council said that the questions of population distribution were "surely important" but "there does not appear to be available at the present time an adequate amount of information to answer them," and in 1971, when the council discussed the problem but announced only that the Commission on Population Growth and the American Future would study it.[26]

Perhaps all that this quarter-century of history on both continents reveals is that official economic argumentation follows political decision rather than vice versa. Once the politicians in the European countries committed themselves to righting the economic imbalance between regions, the governments' economists found that to do so served the na-

24. *Economic Report of the President, 1950; Together with the Annual Report of the Council of Economic Advisers*, p. 117.
25. Ibid, *1953*, pp. 16–17.
26. Ibid., *1968*, p. 139, and *1971*, pp. 111–14.

tional purposes of full employment and maximum production—but it is not evident that they so found before the politicians acted. As the political policies became stronger, the economic analyses deepened in their sophistication, and the whole subject became precisely as central to economics as it was to politics—no more so, and no less. So in the United States, where politicians have looked on the relief of localized distress as a social welfare problem, no more than an incidental and marginal element of any party's program, the macroeconomists have seen it as incidental and marginal to their concerns as well. By the same token, it may be that only if policymakers accept the truth of Harry Truman's commonsense observation that full employment requires the maintenance of economic balance among regions and begin to give it the emphasis he suggested it deserves can they expect to see developed the official and authoritative amplification of their own intuitive economic judgment that is needed for the refinement of their policies. And it is no doubt equally true that policy development must precede, rather than follow, the justifications that are needed from the other fields of social science, including sociology and public opinion analysis, that do not even have official status in the Executive Office of the President.

Broadening the Range of Program Measures

Since the first piece of postwar legislation enacted for the express purpose of stimulating the industrial development of lagging areas, the Area Redevelopment Act of 1961, the United States has attempted two kinds of program measures—improvement of public services and facilities in the development areas, including such infrastructure elements as highways, and loans for new enterprises. The European countries began with these two approaches also, but they concluded quickly that a broader range of measures was essential. They did not succeed in checking and reversing the forces making for concentration of investment until they had introduced such stronger measures as direct capital grants to industry, outright prohibition of industry in congested areas, and systematic dispersal of the activities of government and of government-controlled industries. There seems to be little reason to believe that a serious policy of population deconcentration in the United States would not require a similarly broad range of measures.

INFRASTRUCTURE

Expenditures in this country explicitly intended to help provide an industrial infrastructure in areas of out-migration would include most (though by no means all) of the Appalachian regional development program, which in the 1974 fiscal year amounted to an estimated $326 million, and most of the public works grants made by the Economic Development Administration, which totaled $174 million. Another $46 million was budgeted for the multistate regional commissions authorized by the Public Works and Economic Development Act. The total of direct expenditures for infrastructure in special programs for development areas, including planning, technical assistance, and administrative overhead, therefore amounted to somewhat more than $500 million. In addition, an estimated $520 million in loans to communities for public works, primarily water and waste disposal systems, were to be guaranteed by the government under the Rural Development Act of 1972, but since these involved no public subsidy they are not included in the expenditure total.

The expenditure needed to bring depressed area infrastructures up to the standard necessary for industrial development will vary among countries, of course, depending on the extent of the deficiencies. Comparisons are therefore of dubious value.[27] Nevertheless, the level of extraordinary infrastructure expenditure by the national government for regional development purposes in the United States is not high by European standards. Italy, with a gross national product about one-tenth that of the United States, spends far more than $50 million annually (which would be the equivalent of this country's $500 million) in special programs for the Mezzogiorno through the Cassa alone. Britain likewise spends considerably more, in special regional undertakings, than the $55 million that

27. It is even difficult to find comparable figures for analysis, because in most countries the extra spending in development areas financed through regular departmental budgets is not separated from normal spending and then assembled as a single figure. Indeed, the extra expenditures may be deliberately concealed to avoid arousing interregional jealousies. Moreover, the boundary between what is an extra expenditure for industrial infrastructure and what is an outlay for social welfare is indistinct. Preparation of an industrial park site, with utilities and access roads, is clearly infrastructure development, but disproportionate federal programs for human resource development—education, vocational training, health, recreation —may result from considerations of equity and have in fact only an indirect and incidental effect on industrial expansion.

would be comparable to the U.S. expenditure (its expenditures were estimated at $240 million in 1969[28]). It is likely that the other countries come close to equaling, and probably surpass, the expenditure levels that would represent an equivalent proportion of their resources—which would be $90 million in France and $20 million in the Netherlands and Sweden. So the United States, despite the publicity attending the launching of its depressed areas programs, particularly the Appalachian program, cannot be considered to be making a massive effort.

This is not to suggest, however, that an expansion of that effort should be a high priority objective in any decision to strengthen regional development policies. The experience of the European countries suggests that while a minimum level of infrastructure development is necessary to make a community basically acceptable as an industrial site, differences in levels above that minimum are of only minor importance. The British Board of Trade found that for industries that had located in development areas, direct subsidies were a far more influential factor than infrastructure improvements. Analyzing those findings, Brown concluded that "infrastructure improvement is important industrially as a permissive rather than as a sufficient condition of growth. To rely on extra good infrastructure as an attraction to growth would . . . probably be expensive in real resources in comparison with a normal standard of infrastructure plus some financial incentives."[29] Since every region of out-migration in the United States already has at least some communities adequately equipped with transportation facilities, water supplies, and other public facilities and services for any industries that might be induced to locate there, it is questionable whether additional expenditures in other communities—or the creation of wholly new communities—would do much more than change the competitive balance within the region. The competitive position of the region as a whole with other regions of the country would not be significantly enhanced; to accomplish that end the means has to be, as in Europe, the provision of direct incentives to the enterprises to make use of the infrastructure already available. The development of water and sewer systems in small communities, which has dominated discussion of rural and area development in the United States —and consequently has dominated expenditures as well—is desirable

28. See p. 59, above.
29. *Framework of Regional Economics*, pp. 314–15.

enough in itself, for equity reasons, and may warrant in terms of health and welfare consequences all of the emphasis it has been given. But water and sewer systems should not be thought of as means for the development of lagging regions, much less credited—as congressional debates over the last few years appear to credit them—with being the principal means to that objective.

FINANCIAL INCENTIVES

The only financial incentives offered to investors to locate in development areas in the United States have been loans, and this form of assistance, too, has long since been deemphasized in Europe in favor of direct subsidies. Initially in the United States the credit was offered directly by the government, which permitted an interest rate somewhat lower than the market rate, but the direct loans have now been superseded by loan guarantees, which do no more than help to get a borrower private credit at market rates. Moreover, the volume is not great. In fiscal 1974 the volume of loan guarantees for private borrowers, principally under the Rural Development Act, was estimated at $220 million. This was expected to produce fewer than 10,000 jobs a year in rural areas, which would have little impact on the country's population movements as a whole. That is only one-fifth, or so, of the number of jobs that Great Britain—with a population one-fourth that of the United States—has been creating annually in its development areas. To get comparable results, in relation to the U.S. population, would require an effort some twenty times as great.

The loan guarantee programs will help some small, local, and marginal enterprises that are located at points far from the country's major financial centers to get credit on the same terms as their competitors in the big cities, and that too is a worthy purpose in itself. But a major effort to redirect the economic growth of the United States cannot be built on small and local business. The strong, expanding companies that make most of the investment in new plant in the United States—as in Europe—do not need assistance in obtaining credit. Their investments are financed from internally generated funds or from moneys obtained in the country's capital markets without a need for government guarantees. The central objective of regional development policy in the United States should be to induce companies with ample credit, who see communities with suitable infrastructure in every region, to choose to locate in areas that under the policy have been designated for development. That obviously cannot be done by providing credit guarantees the companies do not need or by trying further to improve on infrastructure that is competitive already. Stronger inducements are necessary, as the Europeans learned long ago. In other words, subsidies.

In the United States most advocates of subsidies propose using tax concessions; the only two subsidy bills that have made progress in the Congress offered a special tax credit for investment in designated areas. The European countries, on the other hand, although they have offered tax concessions in various forms and at various times, all now rely principally on grants. One reason for the preference for grants, particularly in France and Italy, is that the amount of the grant can be varied in individual cases according to the government's resources and the company's need, and even directly negotiated by the government with the individual enterprise. The British reject variable grants as administratively difficult and repugnant to the notion of equity—even though admittedly less costly—but Britain's major parties are now agreed in preferring direct grants to tax concessions. Grants are superior for less profitable companies that have little or no tax liability to apply the credit against. They are also likely to cost the treasury less, since eligibility is determined in advance by an administrative official who can apply more restrictive standards than a tax collection agency, auditing tax returns after the fact, would be able to. Nevertheless, tax credits have so far proved more attractive to regional policy advocates in the United States, probably for two reasons: First, they appeal to the business community because they are automatic and self-administered, without red tape, delays, or any bureaucratic review beyond the normal tax audit. Second, they appeal to the political community because they are a hidden subsidy—unmeasured and unreported (although that may change under terms of the budget reform that the Congress has enacted) and exempt from the annual scrutiny of appropriations committees and annual approval in budgets passed by both houses after floor debates.

To minimize the use of subsidies, most of the European countries (Britain is the notable exception) have tried through rigorous eligibility tests to limit their subsidies to mobile industries that would otherwise not be attracted to the development areas and to exclude those that would by their nature be there anyway. Thus service enterprises serving only a local market are usually excluded. So are enterprises that exploit or process local agricultural and other resources. Investment in machinery and equipment is usually included along with buildings, but sometimes labor-saving machinery is excluded. Expansion of existing plants as well as establishment of new plants is usually covered, but with reduced benefits. The number of jobs created may be a factor in determining the amount of the subsidy. While the emphasis is on manufacturing, tertiary employment, if it serves a wide market and so adds to the development area's export base, is normally covered also.

The steady decline in the proportion of the labor force engaged in manufacturing, it has been argued, makes it unlikely that the development areas of the United States can be effectively stimulated by any policy that relies primarily on that sector of the economy. Yet the experience of Europe refutes that argument, at least in part. Though the total number of employees engaged in manufacturing has been stable or even in decline there, the construction of new factory facilities does not cease. Old plants are closed and new ones opened, and some of the new plants are mobile. These offer a substantial number of jobs that can be channeled to the development areas, while the loss of manufacturing jobs in the congested areas tends to be offset by the growth there of tertiary activities—not without adjustment problems, to be sure, for the manufacturing workers. The dispersal of the tertiary jobs themselves, the Europeans have found, is far more difficult. They are less mobile than manufacturing, and even when certain activities of tertiary enterprises—large processing operations of banks and insurance companies, for instance—can be split off from corporate headquarters and dispersed, the capital grants used as incentives may be less inducement than in the case of manufacturing since capital investment is a smaller element of cost. To disperse tertiary employment effectively might therefore require special inducements and controls of the type developed furthest in France.

GOVERNMENT OFFICE DISPERSAL

A serious population dispersal policy in the United States would also include measures to deconcentrate the federal government's own activities. While the range of state-controlled enterprises is narrow in the United States compared to Europe, government agencies do establish large laboratories and production centers which they have had the authority to locate at their discretion. The Agricultural Act of 1970 included a requirement that government agencies give preference, "insofar as practicable," to areas of "lower population density" in locating offices and other facilities, but the agencies found few such locations practicable. In the Rural Development Act of 1972, therefore, the Congress attempted to tighten the requirement by instructing the departments and agencies to develop policies and procedures for giving "first priority" to rural areas in locating their activities, and requesting the President to make an annual report on compliance with the requirement. The report transmitted to the Congress in January 1974 showed that the act had not yet had any impact: no activity employing more than fourteen persons had been moved from an urban to a rural area, and no new activities of significant size had been located in rural places except those of agencies with rural functions that would have been placed there in any case. But, at best, the rural areas to which the act is limited are not likely to be able to provide the labor market and the infrastructure for large scientific installations, like those of the Atomic Energy Commission or the National Aeronautics and Space Administration, and in that event the law contains no locational guidance as between large and small metropolitan areas. The AEC, for instance, is not discouraged from choosing to locate a major center on the outskirts of Chicago, as it did a few years ago, rather than in a smaller metropolitan community. No *rural* development policy, expressed in a *rural* development act, is ever likely to be satisfactory as a complete expression of national development policy.

Dispersal of government headquarters offices, an important part of the battery of program measures in several European countries, would be of less potential importance in the United States. Only Washington, D.C., would be affected, and while the capital area registered a greater population gain (797,000 people) in the 1960s than all but four other metropolitan agglomerations (and grew at a faster rate than any of those four), it is still a small urban complex compared to New York, Chicago, Los Angeles, or even Philadelphia or Detroit. Nevertheless, a determined decentralization policy in the United States would certainly embrace a systematic study like those carried out in Sweden, Britain, and the Netherlands of the possibilities of moving government activities from the capital.

PROCUREMENT PREFERENCE

Related to the question of government facility location is that of procurement preference, a popular and recurrent proposal in the United States. Preferences have been given by European countries to suppliers located in development areas, but it is not clear how well they have worked, and they are given little attention and emphasis when government officials and academicians discuss their countries' growth policies. Preferences were tried for a short time in the United States, during the period of the Korean hostilities, but they aroused hearty opposition from the Defense Department and other administrative agencies—who objected both to the administrative burden and the higher costs—and from low bidders who lost their contracts, and the latter's representatives in the Congress. Accordingly, though procurement preferences were initially proposed for reintroduction in the early versions of area redevelopment bills in the 1950s, they were omitted from the act that passed.

Procurement preferences are surely among the least satisfactory ways of stimulating economic growth in development areas. The agencies that administer them, preoccupied with spending their own dollars most effectively for their own purposes, inevitably resent the administrative burden and the interference with their normal and simpler ways of doing business. If the preference policy provides a price differential for the supplier in the development area, either explicitly or through a "set aside" of contracts on which only suppliers in the designated areas may bid, then it adds to the budget—and hence to the resentment—of the procuring agency; on the other hand, if it only provides the opportunity for a development area firm to match the low bid of an outside firm, the assistance is not likely to amount to much in volume and effectiveness. In either case, while procurement preferences may help to support in a development area existing enterprises that would otherwise be unable to compete, they are ordinarily too limited and speculative a form of aid, applying to too small a proportion of total sales, to serve as much of an inducement for an enterprise to choose a development area location in the first place. If subsidies are to be given, there appears to be every reason to use them in a direct and explicit way to assist firms to become established or to expand in development areas and then leave it to them to compete on even terms for government contracts.

DIRECT CONTROLS

Finally, there is the question of controls. In each of the European countries that have applied controls—whether certification systems or penalty taxes or both—they have been applied only after incentives have proved inadequate, as a kind of reluctant last resort. They are inevitably the least popular of program measures, always resisted and attacked, and the British government, at least, has felt impelled in recent years to relax them. In the United States any notion of controls imposed from Washington would appear to be outside the realm of possibility, barring some great new surge of population pressure. Conceivably the individual states could move toward prohibition of manufacturing expansion in congested areas—presumably through the application of land-use restrictions rather than through European-style licensing systems—but only a few states have so far shown a disposition to consider anything so drastic. For the foreseeable future, then, any significant expansion in the range of U.S. measures for population dispersal would appear to depend almost entirely on the introduction of direct or indirect subsidies to investors.

Planning National Growth

In terms of specificity, European national growth policies span the spectrum. At the one end are the small countries, Sweden and the Netherlands, that have tried to define precise population distribution patterns, with population targets for areas, and even for individual communities, set in quantitative terms. At the other end is Great Britain, which has couched its policy only in terms of the direction in which existing trends should be influenced, not in terms of the ultimate population distribution pattern to be achieved. In between are France and Italy, which have set some quantitative targets in terms of the allocation of new employment by regions but have not attempted to draw a population distribution map.

Any population distribution policy in the United States would no doubt be more like the British than the Swedish or Dutch, or even the French. A precise plan for the country, drawn and enacted in Washington, is hardly conceivable. The American policy would, rather, state a general objective—much as did the legislation of 1970—of developing the country's more sparsely settled areas and dispersing population. Measures would be enacted—mainly investment incentives—to reinforce the dispersal tendencies that are appearing in the economy. As the effects of these measures on investment patterns and migration flows were observed, the incentives would be raised or lowered and the areas of eligibility for particular benefits would be altered.[30]

For the more sparsely settled areas to be able to accommodate the growth that the incentives would steer their way would require a continuing emphasis on infrastructure development, no doubt assisted by federal grants-in-aid as at present. As part of its national growth policy, then, the federal government would have to concern itself with how the infrastructure planning process is organized and how the necessary public works are geographically distributed. Specifically, the argument waged in this country for more than a decade as to whether infrastructure expenditures should be concentrated in growth centers or spread more widely would need to be settled. On all these questions, too, the European experience is instructive.

All of the European countries included in this study have a growth center strategy. Their planning is based on the principle that lagging areas will be developed faster if public and private investment are concentrated in a relatively few sites that offer the greatest potential for growth, so that economies of aggregation may be realized. "Bringing work to the workers" thus has its limits. The work should be brought into the regions of labor surplus, in the European view, but to try to bring it into every village within the region would require excessive infrastructure expenditure and would be slower to produce results.

Along with acceptance of the growth center strategy, however, has come a gradual shift of emphasis from larger to smaller centers. In the initial stage in each country, when the decision was made to try to stem the internal migration flows that were producing excessive concentration, the largest city or cities in the regions of out-migration were seen as having the best chance to hold the migrants in their regions. So those cities became perforce the growth centers. France, striving to check

30. Coupled with the dispersal element of the national growth policy would probably be an element relating to the distribution of investment and population within metropolitan areas designed to assist in the revival of central cities and to channel a portion of suburban growth into planned new communities rather than into urban sprawl. The new communities, in every country, have been viewed as a means primarily for ordering growth within regions. These aspects of national growth policy have been excluded from consideration in this study.

the growth of Paris, was bound to seize upon the metropoles as the only potential rivals to the capital. Italy, confronting the problem of out-migration from the South, turned to the largest city in the Mezzogiorno, Naples, as a growth center, just as Britain, concerned with the north-south drift, sought to stimulate growth in the largest Scottish city, Glasgow (and still seeks it, since Glasgow continues to be a city of out-migration and population decline). Sweden, similarly, recognized the largest cities of Norrland—tiny as they might be compared to the other countries' growth centers—as the most likely candidates for holding in place that region's potential migrants. Indeed, Sweden set out to discourage the growth of Stockholm at the same time that other countries were trying to spur the growth of provincial metropolitan complexes already several times as large because they were potential rivals to even larger capitals.

But that was during the first stage. The second stage was a more refined examination of the problems and prospects of development within the regions of out-migration, and the development of individualized regional plans. At this stage it might turn out that the large growth centers had drawbacks and the smaller ones might, after all, offer better prospects. Or it might be clear that within a large region of out-migration, like the Mezzogiorno, there might be a subregion of heavy in-migration, like the metropolitan area of Naples, that was a fair candidate not for stimulation but restraint. Thus Italy, concerned with overcrowding in Naples and the neighboring Campanian plain, shifted its emphasis to a ring of towns beyond the edges of the plain, and then introduced a new scale of investment incentives that gives the highest benefits to mountain towns in even more remote locations. And France has moved from the metropoles to the *villes moyennes* as the focus of its current efforts.

The impulse for these shifts has been partly political—the protest from smaller communities excluded from assistance could not be withstood—and as such was to some extent resisted by the planning technicians. But to some extent the motivation for the shift came from the planners themselves, who perceived that while building Lyon and Marseille and Naples might in the short run take some of the pressure off Paris and Milan, it would in the long run create or intensify other problems, for the largest provincial cities were by no means free of the evils of congestion themselves. The logic that led initially to some dispersal now led to more dispersal, not only out of the capitals but out of the larger metropoles; indeed, the smaller the growth center the better—so long as dispersal was not pushed to the point where significant loss of economic efficiency was felt.

There is no consensus as to where that point may be. The Swedish Labor Market Board is virtually alone in offering a specific figure— the minimum of 30,000 population that it defined as necessary for a community to offer an adequate range of business services. Government agencies in other countries, judging by the programs of those countries, would probably select a higher figure if they were forced to choose. But in practice, they do not have to select an arbitrary number, because the selection of growth centers and the allocation of public investment have now become matters for determination through the regional planning process.

The regional plan in Europe, as in the United States, has been primarily a guide for infrastructure expenditure, with the objective of ensuring that a region achieve a maximum of economic stimulus with a minimum of expenditure of infrastructure funds. It governs the location of industrial sites and accompanying transportation, housing, and utility development, and speculative factory buildings where those are erected with public money. It may provide for new residential-industrial communities. To assure that the infrastructure expenditures would not be wasted, France and Italy went so far as to make their original industrial incentives conditional on an enterprise's locating in a growth center. The northern European countries have seen no need for such restriction, relying instead on controls exercised through the land-use planning process to assure that industrial development takes place in appropriate growth centers.

The outstanding weakness in this planning process in Europe has been the absence of suitable organization at the regional level. Only the Netherlands had regional governments of adequate authority in being; it could use its provinces, and in any case the country is small enough to permit treating its whole territory essentially as one region for planning purposes. Sweden could use its counties also, even though they were too many and too small, but it had to organize new planning machinery at that level. Italy is preparing to rely on its new regional governments, but they are still far from proven instruments. France and Britain have improvised; the former now has a somewhat makeshift but uniform structure for regional planning throughout the country while the latter still attempts to do the job through temporary, ad hoc committees.

The United States, being a federal nation, was born with the inter-mediate level the European countries are struggling to create. Beyond that, institutions have been created in the past decade at two other inter-mediate levels to undertake comprehensive development planning. One is the substate district, intermediate between the states and their munici-palities, which is now taking form in almost every state. The other is the multistate regional commission, jointly sponsored by federal and state governments. Eight of these exist, but only one—the Appalachian Regional Commission—has had the funds and authority to firmly estab-lish itself.[31] With all this apparatus the United States has little to learn from Europe about the organization of planning mechanisms; indeed, the teaching could go the other way. But the substance and processes of developmental planning are other matters. This country is far behind the more advanced European countries in developing a coherent plan-ning process. Indeed, the concept hardly exists in the United States, and the procedures that were introduced when the notion, and the agencies, of developmental planning were young are to a large measure now dis-integrating.

This was perhaps predictable. A nation that has not yet decided that it ought to have a growth policy is not likely to sustain for long the agencies and processes that were devised to design and implement growth policies. Only a purpose gives meaning to a process. So the Nixon ad-ministration was reasonable enough, when it renounced any ambition to adopt a growth policy, to propose as well to dismantle the Economic Development Administration—the principal instrument of such a policy at the federal level—and eliminate direct support to both the multistate and substate planning bodies. The Congress thwarted the aims of the administration in this regard (and the administration reversed itself, under pressure, and supported continuance of the Appalachian Regional Commission and creation of two new multistate commissions), but the agencies and programs have enjoyed only the toleration of the White House, not its warm support.

Even when it had strong presidential backing, however, the develop-mental process in the United States was more chaotic than orderly and more fragmented than comprehensive. The substate planning bodies

31. The multistate regional development commissions are appraised in Martha Derthick, *Between State and Nation: Regional Organizations in the United States* (Brookings Institution, 1974), chaps. 4 and 5. The fullest treatment of the Appa-lachian program is Monroe Newman, *The Political Economy of Appalachia: A Case Study in Regional Integration* (Lexington Books, 1972).

sponsored by EDA—economic development districts (EDDs)—competed with rival substate planning mechanisms sponsored by other federal agencies or by the states, and no one had authority to force their merger into a single system of substate bodies.[32] Yet where the EDDs were well organized, they did take a comprehensive approach to developmental planning. Under the statute, each district was required to prepare an overall economic development program and to designate one or more growth centers. The trouble was, and is, that no federal or state agency, or even EDA itself, was required to pay any attention to the comprehensive plan. In fact, the EDA in authorizing public works expenditures adopted a "worst first" policy that was the very antithesis of a growth center strategy; it gave top priority not to the communities with greatest potential but to those suffering the deepest distress.[33] The Dent-Ash report specifically criticized EDA (an agency responsible to Dent) for not having "attempted to focus funding on areas with the greatest potential for self-sustained growth," and noted that more than half its funds had gone to towns under 5,000 population and one-third to communities under 2,500.[34] The EDDs were given no general "envelope of credits," in the French term, to enable each district to build the infrastructure visualized in its development program according to its own priorities, when the program won EDA approval—or even to proceed with the highest priority projects listed in the plan. The growth center concept thus lost its meaning. And since the plan turned out to have no force, the planning process itself became a ritual. The districts have been going through the necessary motions in order to meet the statutory requirements, but little more than that.

This accounting of weaknesses suggests the steps that would be necessary to introduce in the United States a developmental planning process

32. The competing structures in the development areas are described in James L. Sundquist (with the collaboration of David W. Davis), *Making Federalism Work* (Brookings Institution, 1969), chap. 5. Some progress has been made since 1969 in encouraging the consolidation of planning bodies, under the leadership of the Advisory Commission on Intergovernmental Relations (ACIR) and the Office of Management and Budget, but the problem has not been fundamentally resolved. See the ACIR's encyclopedic *Substate Regionalism and the Federal System* (Government Printing Office, 1973), especially vol. 1, chap. 6, which recommends that the state governments, or local governments acting together, create umbrella multi-jurisdictional organizations (UMJOs) covering all areas of their states and that the federal government rely on the UMJOs for planning related to federal grant-in-aid programs rather than sponsor rival substate bodies.

33. For a critique of the "worst first" policy, see Niles M. Hansen, *Rural Poverty and the Urban Crisis* (Indiana University Press, 1970), pp. 147–50.

34. "Report to the Congress," p. 25.

on the European model—an idealized European model, to be sure, for European practices still fall short of the concept of comprehensive regional planning that each of the countries has officially embraced. In each substate district designated for development, a single planning body with functions even broader than those of the present economic development districts would have to be created by the state—if such a body does not exist already—and given clear responsibility, along with the necessary funds, to conceive a developmental strategy and to prepare and maintain a comprehensive developmental plan.[35] As in Europe, the purpose would be to make the most of infrastructure funds; insofar as those funds were supplied by state and federal governments, the plan would need to be reviewed and approved at state and federal levels—perhaps, where multistate regional commissions exist, through the mechanism of those commissions. It would also have to be examined for consistency with such state or national growth policies as might have been adopted. Once the plan was approved, however, it would become binding on all agencies of government at all levels—federal and state as well as local. Then, in order to assure that high priority projects as designated in the plan were in fact given high priority in execution, federal funds available for infrastructure development—and, ideally, state funds as well—would be consolidated into a block grant on the pattern of the French envelope of credits. It goes without saying, of course, that such a process would be far more difficult to establish and sustain in a large federal country such as the United States than in the smaller unitary states of Europe.

The number of planning districts would, as in Europe, set a minimum on the number of growth centers the federal government would underwrite. Some of the centers would inevitably be small, much smaller than the population minimums that many leading regional economists have considered necessary for a community to achieve self-sustaining growth. Niles M. Hansen, for instance, has long argued that any population distribution policy should be based on channeling migration to cities in the 50,000–1,000,000 range, and more particularly in the 250,000–750,000 bracket.[36] Yet the acceptance of smaller places as growth centers would be quite consistent with what other students of regional policy believe that the 1970 census figures—and, even more strongly, the provisional

35. This would be consistent with the ACIR recommendation in *Substate Regionalism and the Federal System* for creation of the UMJOs.
36. Hansen, *Rural Poverty*, pp. 249–53.

census estimates for 1973—tell about the viability of smaller cities. Glenn V. Fuguitt notes that two-thirds of the cities in the United States over 10,000 population outside metropolitan areas (all of them, by definition, under 50,000) grew between 1960 and 1970, and 145 of them grew by 20 percent or more—well above the growth rate of the country as a whole. While the smaller cities of the Northeast and the West were more likely to grow if they were located near a metropolitan area, this was not the case in the South, and the difference was not great in the North Central region. "Larger nonmetropolitan cities," concludes Fuguitt, "should not be dismissed as potential growth centers."[37] The fact that in the early 1970s the nonmetropolitan part of the United States taken as a whole, including the most rural areas, grew at a faster rate than the metropolitan part suggests a capacity for growth in smaller places beyond what has usually been acknowledged.[38] In any case, however, the regional plans would embody a growth center strategy, whatever the size of the centers, and from the standpoint of any advocate of growth centers that would be an improvement over present policies that disperse infrastructure funds without regard to growth center strategy at all, and often with a prohibition—as in the Rural Development Act—against their expenditure in cities above a specified population size.

Organizing the Government for Leadership and Coordination

To define and carry out a policy of balanced growth, or population dispersal, as called for by the two statutes enacted in 1970, would impose

37. "Population Trends of Nonmetropolitan Cities and Villages in the United States," in Mazie, ed., *Population Distribution and Policy*, pp. 124–25.

38. A study of population trends in the predominantly rural state of Arkansas, which was converted from a net loser of population in the 1940s and the 1950s to a net gainer in the 1960s, attributes the turnaround to the ability of counties of all sizes—even the most rural—to attract industry and in-migration. Counties with no town of more than 5,000 (constituting 56 percent of all counties) showed a gain in manufacturing employment of more than 90 percent between 1958 and 1966, compared to 58 percent for the state as a whole. In the 1950s every one of the state's twenty-four most rural counties had net out-migration but in the period 1960–66 only four continued to lose population and seventeen experienced net in-migration. E. S. Lee and others, *An Introduction to Urban Decentralization Research* (Oak Ridge, Tenn.: Oak Ridge National Laboratory, 1971), pp. 39–42. Similarly, the Nebraska Department of Economic Affairs reported in 1972 that only three of sixty new factories located in the state that year were built in metropolitan areas and two-thirds were in communities under 10,000 population. *Interchange* (National Area Development Institute, Lexington, Ky.), vol. 3, no. 8 (April 15, 1973), p. 4.

on the U.S. government tasks of leadership and coordination far more complex than those encountered by the governments of Europe.

Even in those countries, however, administrative responsibility is divided. In Britain, for instance, one department administers the investment incentives for the assisted areas and the controls on industrial expansion in the London region, while another is responsible for land-use planning nationwide and for administration of office building controls in the South East. Various other departments are responsible for infrastructure programs, and all are coordinated to only a limited degree through the regional planning process. Britain has no real equivalent of the Executive Office of the President in the United States, but a small cabinet office concerned primarily with long-range planning exercises a degree of surveillance over regional policy as a whole.

Administrative responsibilities are similarly divided in the other countries, but the larger ones—France and Italy—have introduced stronger formal devices for governmentwide coordination. France has above the departmental level not only its national planning commission, which produces the national plan and reconciles the regional developmental plans with it, but its office for territorial planning and regional action (DATAR) that plays a broad role of coordination and leadership in the execution of national growth policies.[39] In Italy the cabinet committee responsible for the economic plan, served by its own specialized staff, has a mandate to strengthen and unify the effort of the many participating agencies to develop the Mezzogiorno.

The national programs necessary for a policy of population dispersal would inevitably be scattered among many departments in the United States as well. Indeed, even the present limited activities are widely scattered. If present jurisdictional lines are followed, industrial incentives would be assigned to the Department of Commerce, supervision of land-use planning (and hence growth center planning) to the Department of Housing and Urban Development or the Department of the Interior, or both, and rural development to the Department of Agriculture, with housing and public works responsibilities and grant-in-aid programs lodged in many places. Cutting across these would be the multi-

---

39. Though moved recently from the direct control of the premier to one of the regular ministries, DATAR still operates with a de facto supradepartmental status. See p. 122, n. 62, above.

state regional commissions with their territorial planning responsibilities and, in the case of Appalachia, substantial program funds as well.

While reorganization of government departments, as President Nixon advocated, might combine some functions related to population distribution that have been divided, no reorganization could come close to placing all the pertinent activities in any one department. In any event, there are few policies that do not have an impact on population distribution—antipollution regulations, for instance, are beginning to have important, unanticipated effects—so once a national growth policy were established, policies throughout the government would have to be mutually reconciled with it. Perhaps primary responsibility for monitoring the execution of the policy and analyzing the consistency of agency activities could be entrusted to one department, such as the Department of Housing and Urban Development. Yet experience in the United States government, and the European governments as well, indicates that one department can rarely become the effective coordinator of any program that requires the disciplined participation of other departments of equal rank; and if a coordinated regional planning process were introduced, that would surely rank high among national governmental enterprises requiring the tightest of interdepartmental discipline.

The conclusion seems inescapable that a point of strong leadership and coordination would have to be created in the Executive Office of the President. This was the conclusion reached by the Commission on Population Growth and the American Future in its recommendation for an office of population growth and distribution in the Executive Office. Similarly, Senator Humphrey has introduced a bill to create an office of national growth and development in the Executive Office. Those proposals parallel the recommendations of innumerable commissions, task forces, and congressional committees for units in the Executive Office to concern themselves with a wide range of other problems. By common consent, where governmentwide leadership and coordination are required, interdepartmental committees are dismissed as ineffectual and staff entities are demanded. Advocates of some functions—poverty, drug abuse, telecommunications, environmental quality—have been able to win their point, and units have been created in the Executive Office.

There is obviously a limit to the number of coordination units that can be housed in the Executive Office, all reporting directly to the

President, without creating an insuperable problem of coordination and leadership within the Executive Office itself. Yet no satisfactory substitute has been devised for the Executive Office staff agency if coordination is to be provided, and that fact must be confronted. If and when a national growth policy is adopted in this country, therefore, the kind of office proposed by the Population Commission, or some mechanism likely to be equally effective, needs to be established in the Executive Office to oversee the execution of the policy and guide its evolution. It could, of course, be placed under the direction of a general-purpose interdepartmental committee such as the present Domestic Council, or a special committee created for the purpose.

The same problem of coordination confronts the Congress. Responsibilities for various aspects of national growth policy are scattered among committees there, with a division of labor paralleling that found within the executive branch. Legislation bearing on population distribution passes through four main committees in each house—agriculture, banking (urban affairs), interior, and public works—and if new programs were adopted, other committees might be involved. And in the legislative branch there is no coordinating machinery at all. If the development of national growth policy were effectively coordinated within the executive branch, and if the individual congressional committees accepted the President's recommendations, then a consistent and comprehensive national growth policy could become possible—if only through a kind of abdication on the part of the Congress. But that would be a state of affairs unlikely to be satisfactory, for long, to the Congress. Eventually, if the nation is to have a consistent and effective population dispersal policy, a device for comprehensive consideration of the policy has to be established in the legislative branch too. The only device for such purpose that the Congress appears to have available, although one that is used rarely and with great reluctance, is the special committee, such as proposed by Congressman Ashley and Senators Humphrey and Hartke.

Dispersal: An Attainable Goal

The ultimate implication of the European experience can perhaps be stated in a sentence: If the people of a democratic country want a pattern of population distribution less concentrated than that which results from the natural play of economic forces, there is no reason that they cannot have it. Through governmental action the influences at work within the economy that make for concentration can be neutralized and those that make for deconcentration can be reinforced.

Whether the United States should adopt a policy of dispersal is a separate question. The decline in the birth rate and the spontaneous decentralization trends that have appeared in the early 1970s certainly reduce in some measure whatever degree of urgency may have attached to the question a few years ago. But if a slow rate of natural dispersal is good, a faster rate stimulated by governmental measures might be better. That is the issue for public policy.

To render a judgment on the issue requires that the apparent public preference for such a policy (and some will question whether public opinion surveys are yet sufficiently conclusive on that point) be weighed against the costs, less the benefits—economic, social, psychological—of such a policy. So many of the latter factors are so resistant to attempts at measurement, and so many of the measures—when they exist—are subject to the assignment of so wide a range of values, that in the end the policymakers have to reach their conclusion on the basis of essentially subjective judgment. That, indeed, is what the policymakers in the European countries have done.

The Europeans cannot teach America that its values should be the same as theirs. But if, in the end, the values do accord, America can learn from Europe these things: A population dispersal policy and the programs to execute it can be conceived simply enough. They are likely to be popular. They are not unduly costly. And they work.

Index